The Finest Road in the World

The Story of Travel and Transport in the Scottish Highlands

James Miller

BIRLINN

This edition first published in 2019 by
Birlinn Limited
West Newington House
10 Newington Road
Edinburgh
EH9 1QS

www.birlinn.co.uk

ISBN: 978 1 78027 573 4

British Library Cataloguing-in-Publication Data
A catalogue record for this book is available from the British Library

Typeset by Sabon LT by Hewer Text UK Ltd, Edinburgh
Printed and bound by Clays Ltd, Elcograf S.p.A.

Contents

List of Plates and Maps

List of Plates

List of Maps

'The Ord of Caithness had been represented to me by many in so frightful a Shape, that I longed much to see it, and when I came to it, my Imagination had far outshot reality; for I rode up every Inch of it, a thing rarely done by any Persons, and all along looked down ye dreadful precipice to the Sea . . . My fellow-Travellers, both Gentlemen and Servts, took to the Foot, and walked it from the Bottom to the Top, a full long Mile. Its Steepness, and being all along on the very Brink of a Precipice, are the only Difficulties; for otherwise it is one of the finest Roads in the World, being so broad, yt in most places two Coaches might pass one another . . . But then so very steep it is, particularly at entering upon it, that no Machine can be drawn up it by any Cattle whatsoever, unless it be empty; and even then there must be some Sturdy Fellows at the back of it, pushing it forward to assist the Horses . . .'

> – From *Journals of the Episcopal Visitations of the Right Rev Robert Forbes* on his first visit to Caithness in 1762 (Craven, 1886)

'The new Glasgow–Inverness road was one of the finest roads in the world and fitted in with the most delightful Highland scenery one could see anywhere.'

> – *Sir Murdoch Macdonald MP in tribute to the engineer Major Robert Bruce after the construction of the A82 in the early 1930s*

Introduction

'*Yin muckle hill at islands Caithness*' – so reads the first line in a poem I wrote a few years ago in my mother dialect about the Ord, the ridge of moor that forms the boundary between my native county and Sutherland, our neighbour to the south.[1] It is not especially high, rising to a mere 650 feet or so above sea level at the viewpoint beside the A9, but it makes up for this deficiency by its windy bareness and the precipitate drop to the sea below. In my boyhood, it still carried a reputation for being, if not dangerous, as Bishop Robert Forbes had found out in 1762 and had dismissed with amused irony, a place that required respect. In a real sense, it did make an island of the county to the north, as there was only the single railway line and one other road across the county boundary, and in winter blizzards all three routes could be blocked.

Until the recent past for the Caithnessian, as I have written elsewhere, crossing the Ord for the first time was something to remember, a rite of passage.[2] At the layby on the summit stands a stone with an inscription commemorating a traveller, a vagrant called William Welch, who perished here in a snowstorm in 1878. 'Be ye also ready' warns the crudely carved wording. The grandeur of the hills, the distant horizon of the sea, the inherent danger – the Ord just about summarises the story of land travel in the Highlands, travel in a country with a relatively sparse population clustered in widely scattered settlements, and a climate with winters that can be brutal. In the past, many parts of the Highlands could have been viewed as islands, so far separated were they from each other by long miles of mountain and moorland. Travellers have had to contend with and overcome these difficulties, as have the engineers, surveyors and labourers who have sought to ease their lot.

But, no matter the obstacles, where there are people, there will be roads. We are a travelling species and everywhere we have marked places with our paths. When we run out of land we make trade routes – 'roads' – on the sea, and in the twentieth century our technology allowed us to establish 'roads' in the air. The modern term for the links between one place and another is connectivity. High connectivity is essential for healthy economic life and, in the north of Scotland, in the Highlands and Islands, the infrastructure that allows it is especially of concern. We are deemed to comprise a remote society. Our connectivity within the region and to the rest of the world is crucial to our economic well-being.

A glance at a relief map of the Highlands shows the pattern imposed on travel and makes it obvious why, after crossing the Forth in Scotland's egg-timer waist, there were only a few routes that seemed natural ones for travellers from the south to follow. The most obvious one bears to the east, along the corridor of Strathmore and the Howe o' the Mearns, to squeeze over or around the eastern slopes of the Cairngorm massif to reach the fertile lowlands of the Moray Firth. This is the way the Romans came, and the invading armies of Edward Longshanks, and centuries later the first railway lines and the A90. There is no comparable route to the west through the crumpled mountains and glens, and here in the distant past sea travel was more the norm. For the daring and those who had local knowledge, however, there were other routes north through the Highland wall, from Perth via Dunkeld and the braes of Atholl, from the Clyde via Loch Lomond to the natural corridor of the Great Glen. These of course are the routes now graced by the A9 and the A82, the Highland Main Line and the West Highland Line.

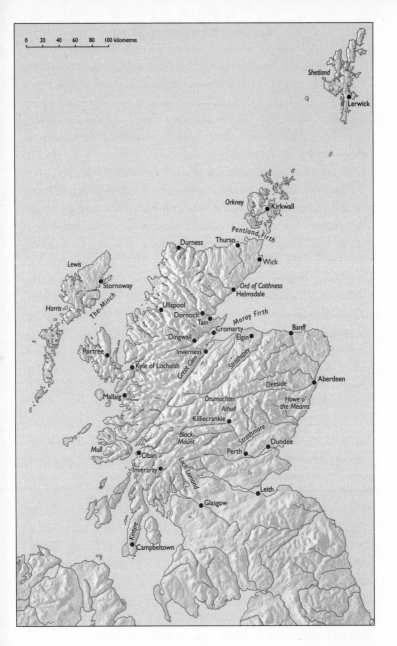

Map 1. *The rugged physical landscape of the north of Scotland – with mountains, rivers, sea lochs and many islands – presents challenges to transport infrastructure.*

The network is mainly of indigenous origin, the response of the people to the need to connect with each other and with the world beyond the horizon. Elements of it, however, have been imposed: Wade's soldiers laid their roads across the hills to occupy and pacify the country, and the railway surveyors cut their tracks in response to gradients and the demands and constraints of steam technology.

The network of routes for travellers to follow, the choices as to which way to go and which mode of transport to adopt, developed as technology improved, opening new possibilities while making older solutions redundant or obsolete. This can be seen with striking effect in the pass of Killiecrankie, where the Garry threads through a narrow, steep-sided glen. The old drove road called the Bealach follows the bank of the river. Above it passes the railway viaduct built in 1863 to a design by Joseph Mitchell; above that, following the route of an old track, passes the military road cut by General Wade's men in 1728, more familiar as the old A9 and now the B8079; and above that again, as the uppermost stratum in an archaeology of transport, the modern A9, a dual carriageway.

The older forms of transport were built and serviced by local people, by the horse breeders, saddlers, wheelwrights, blacksmiths, boat-builders and seamen of the Highlands, and were usually well adapted to the environment. This is not so with modern transport. Since the appearance of the steam engine, but more so since the introduction of its internal combustion successor, fuelled by petrol or diesel, there has been a loss of control over local transport to outside bodies. Although almost every village has a garage where a car can be fixed, the machines themselves are inevitably manufactured elsewhere and are not always suitable for local conditions. For example, the less sturdy stretches of the Highland roads take a destructive pounding from juggernauts.

In this book I hope to take the reader on a journey through the last few centuries and describe how the present network of

connectivity evolved. Along the way we meet some colourful char-
acters and spend a little time with each mode of transport – travelling by foot, horse, coach, schooner, steamer, locomotive, motor
car and aircraft – in a way that I hope the reader finds entertaining
and informative. In my own lifetime the transport infrastructure in
the north has improved in great measure. I can recall train journeys
south from Wick in winter in which we joked about conditions in
the carriages being reminiscent of the train journey across Russia
in *Doctor Zhivago*, the David Lean movie current at the time, with
music and drams and an occasional glance through the frosted
windows to see how far we had yet to travel.

*

As with all works of this kind, I owe an unlimited debt to those
who have trod the road before me, and to those who have
helped me on my way. Written sources are detailed in the Notes
and References section; and for help with research, comments
and illustrations I would also like to thank the staff of the
library and archive services of High Life Highland in Inverness,
Dr Cait McCullagh and Lesley Junor at Inverness Museum and
Art Gallery, Rachel Chisholm at Highland Folk Museum, Dr
Juliet Gayton, Jamie Gaukroger of Am Baile, Heike Gehringer
at Ullapool Museum, Sinclair and Kathleen Dunnett, Allan
Cameron and Maureen Kenyon of Inverness Local History
Forum, Alasdair Cameron, Kathryn Logan of Moray Firth
Partnership, Willie Morrison, Roy Pedersen, Dr Andrew Rae,
Mairi Stewart, and Pauline Ward – worthy fellow travellers all.
A special thank you goes to my agent, Duncan McAra, to Hugh
Andrew and his colleagues at Birlinn, and particularly to editor
Deborah Warner, for their seemingly inexhaustible patience.
Mistakes en route are, of course, my own doing.

Currency

Before 1971 and decimalisation, readers should remember that
prices in Britain were expressed in pounds (£), shillings (s) and

pence (d). There were 12d in each shilling, and 20s in each £1. The Scots pound was used in accounting and rentals, among other things, and was valued by the eighteenth century at one-twelfth of the pound Sterling.

PART I

The old ways on land and sea

CHAPTER 1

Foot and saddle

'we sett upon our way and journay, and cam forward . . .'

In 1804, Donald Sage, the 15-year-old son of the parish minister in Kildonan in Sutherland, left home to begin his studies at Aberdeen University. In his autobiography, he recalled the journey:

> ... on Monday morning early, my father, Muckle Donald, and I set out for Aberdeen. My father accompanied me as far as Tain, where we arrived on Tuesday morning. The night previous we spent at Dornoch. At Tain we breakfasted at Turnbull's Inn ... After breakfast [Mrs Turnbull] stuffed my pockets with fine large apples; and my father parted with me to return home. Muckle Donald and I then tramped it on foot from thence all the way to Aberdeen. The day we left Tain, crossing the Invergordon ferry, we slept and supped at the Inn of Balblair ... the length of the journey proved too much for me. Within two miles of Inverurie I fairly broke down and fell prostrate upon the roadside ...

After a much-needed rest, the youth and his companion reached Aberdeen the following day. Sage does not tell us for how many days they walked after leaving Balblair on the Black Isle or where they stayed at night, but it must have taken them at least three days to get as far as Inverurie. This is assuming they kept up a pace of 25 miles daily.[1]

Sage's story is a vivid reminder that up until the relatively recent past most people, even on substantial journeys, walked. It is a curious though understandable feature of Scots dialects, although one that survives in the speech of only a few localities, that 'traivel' specifically means making a journey on foot, while its equivalent 'travel' co-existed with the conventional English meaning. This could give rise to such exchanges as:

'I went til the toun.'

'Did ye traivel?'

'No, I took the bus.'

In his account of his boyhood in the early 1800s, Hugh Miller recalls walking with his mother the 30 miles from Cromarty to Lairg to visit a relative and arriving 'early on the evening of the second day'; later, as a young apprentice stonemason, he walked from the banks of the Conon via Contin and Loch Maree to a job in Wester Ross, staying in two inns en route.[2] A family tradition in my boyhood was that the women of Dunnet in Caithness, including my great-grandmother, wove herring nets during the winter and in the summer walked with them to Wick on the other side of the county to sell. Only the better-off could afford to own or hire a horse or a carriage and, in any case, the state of the roads before 1800 was such that venturing any distance in a vehicle was a highly risky business. The north of Scotland was covered by a well-trodden network of routes, but these were often little better than tracks – dry enough in the summer but in the winter often impassable with mud, snow or ice – and it was wise and often quicker to rely on Shanks's pony.

Roads were poor throughout the country, including the Lowlands. William Cunningham of Craigend in Renfrewshire recorded in his diary in the 1670s how he always went by horse to Edinburgh – trips he called 'voyages' – as that was the only feasible means of transport outside the immediate environs of any urban centre. It was normal for a lady to ride on a pillion or pad behind her husband in the saddle, and luggage was carried strapped on pack horses. Cunningham kept in his account book details of his expenditure on 'voyaging': perhaps 5s for a night's accommodation for his horse with an extra shilling or two for the stable lad; £3 12s for the freight of his wife's coffer (chest) from Glasgow to Edinburgh; a cost of between £500 and £700 to keep a horse for a year.[3]

James Brodie described a difficult journey in December 1680, from Edinburgh north to his home at Brodie near Forres, a trip that normally could be accomplished in five days. The problems began when the riders approached the ferry to cross the Firth of Tay to Dundee – 'The frost hinderd our passage many hours.' The party continued north. 'We cam nixt forenoon to Brichen, and on this Saturday at evening we cam to Fettercairn, wher we purposd to stay the nixt day, being the Sabbath.' The threat of approaching bad weather forced a change of mind on the Sabbath:

> ... fearing a storm in the Kairn [Cairn o'Mount] and the waters, we considered on it as fitt to croce the water of Die [Dye]. After we had worshipd God ... we sett upon our way and journay, and cam forward ... We cam to Lumfannan finding no good lodging elswher ... The nixt morning [it was now 20 December] we cam to Putachie [near Alford]; had verie ill way, and ill crossing of the water of Dolie ... I staid there al night.

On the 21st, Brodie struggled north from Putachie to Mulbenn, and on the 22nd, as he wrote, 'I was in a most immanent and apparent danger beyond what ever I was al my lyff tym.' The Spey had swollen with the winter rain.

> The [ferry] boat and al in it was caried doun by the force of the speat ... more than half a myl ... We wer, in the opinion and estimation of onlookers, past al hop and expectation of coming to land, and ther was nothing but a present looking

for death. It pleasd God at last that we wer brought to land to the sam syd of the water which we entred in ... I cam back to Mulbenn ... We crocd the Spey in the evening and cam lait to Elgin.

Brodie eventually won home on the 23rd after another challenging river crossing at the Findhorn, eight long days after leaving the capital.[4]

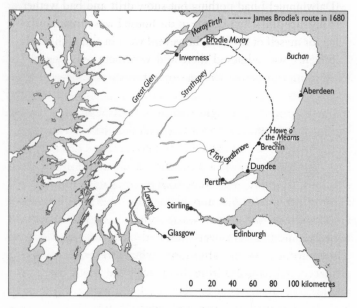

Map 2. James Brodie's route in 1680.

For all the problems, people did travel – and often quite widely. That long journeys required time, preparation and endurance had to be accepted as an unfortunate but inescapable fact of life, perhaps much as we expect today to be held up in city traffic. As long as people relied on their own feet or their horses, and the elements remained reasonable, a journey was usually more time-consuming than dangerous. Eight days was regarded as normal for an overland journey from Caithness to

Edinburgh. John Sinclair of Barrock made this trip in February
1734 and wrote to a friend afterwards:

> I had good traveling wether and good ludging untill I came
> to Reven [Ruthven in Strathspey] which was on a Saturday
> night. Sunday's morning was frosty, windy and cold. I took
> my horse in the morning and road [rode] five or six miles
> without seeing any snow but after that to Delquhiny
> [Dalwhinnie] I had nothing but snow drift and bad wether
> in my face and when I came to the house I was refused ludg-
> ing for myself or my hors, however I went in and with much
> difficulty was admitted there and was there only one bed
> free from snow and there was six officers possessed of it ...

Sinclair put up that night with snow drifting in through the
walls and roof, melting to form a great puddle on the floor, the
company of a crowd of soldiers and no food 'but drink enugh'.
He managed to share a bed with a customs officer from
Dornoch. The two men kept their clothes on and spent the
night under a big coat and plaid 'with abundance of snow
above all'. On the next day, warm enough in Sinclair's view, his
horse laboured through deep snow and came to 'Dalnachurdich'
(Dalnacardoch) in the afternoon 'where we were exceeding
well accommodate and from that place I had very good wether
and ludging'. By the time Sinclair reached Dysart the snow had
been left behind but horse and rider fell twice on the ice –
'However I got no harm.'[5]

The rough accommodation was not unusual. In 1769,
Thomas Pennant had to lodge in a whisky house that passed for
an inn at the east end of Loch Maree: 'Mr Mackenzie compli-
mented Mr Lightfoot and me with the bedstead, well covered
with a warm litter of heath: we lay in our clothes, wrapped
ourselves in plaids; and enjoyed a good repose.' Pennant was
surprised some locals chose even less comfortable arrangements, forming a bed from wet hay and flinging a plaid over it.[6]

A particular example of a route with a special purpose was the 'coffin road', the path along which men bore the remains of the dead to their last resting place. In Wester Ross, the coastal route between Ullapool and Achiltibuie has won a measure of fame as the Postie's Path, after a postal service opened in the 1860s and the postmen began to use it on a regular basis. The postman Kenneth Maclennan of Blairbuie followed it to Ullapool twice a week for the mail, 15 miles each way at 2s 3d a time. The route, however, had probably already enjoyed centuries of use by the local people; it appears on Aaron Arrowsmith's map of Scotland in 1807.[7] In the Middle Ages, some routes became associated with pilgrimage, the most notable example in the north being the route to Tain, to the shrine of Saint Duthac, a pilgrimage made every year after his first visit in 1493 by James IV (1488–1513).

In general, only a few of the old routes are recorded on early maps or mentioned in charters.[8] Timothy Pont includes hardly any roads on his maps drawn around the turn of the 1600s, but his scattering of settlements, more or less foreshadowing the present distribution of population, implies an infrastructure of connections. The *Blaeu Atlas of Scotland*, published in Amsterdam in 1654 and based on information supplied by Robert Gordon of Straloch, and in turn drawing on Pont's work, indicates the existence of the Causewaymire route across the Caithness moors.[9] One route that Pont does show is the Causey Mounth, an important and ancient way south from Deeside; and in his surviving notes Pont mentions a *rad na pheny*, a road for wheels from Ruthven to Blair Atholl.[10] This may be the same as one of the two routes called Comyn's Road and Minigaig Pass respectively.[11] Both of these are more direct than the route eventually chosen by General Wade through the central mountains via Dalnaspidal but climb to higher altitudes.

When Joseph Mitchell took part in a survey in 1837 of alternatives to the military road then followed by the stagecoaches through Drumochter Pass, he proposed a practicable route between Glen Feshie and Glen Bruar that was ten miles shorter than the current one but rose to an altitude 660 feet higher.[12] Mitchell had, as it were, rediscovered Pont's *rad na pheny*, although it had probably remained a customary way for shepherds and drovers. In 1806 the surveyor Alexander Nimmo mentioned that a track led from Blair Athol via the Bruar Water to the glen of the Feshie, and also that the post to Ruthven barracks used to come this way from Perth, 'descending by the Frommie'.[13]

Some of the old ways have names that are evocative of a bygone age. D.G. Moir recorded many in two small booklets he compiled under the name of *Scottish Hill Tracks: Old Highways and Drove Roads* first published in 1947 and re-issued several times.[14] Moir aimed his work at the hillwalkers and hostellers who were frequenting the countryside in increasing numbers, emulating earlier generations who had laid down the ways through necessity rather than for recreation. Thus we have a series of named routes, passes through the hills of the Mounth, connecting the low country of the Mearns with Deeside and further north. Similar networks existed in other parts of the Highlands. There is evidence now for an ancient continuous route from the Beauly to the Dornoch firths, fragments of which survive as double embankments, paths and field boundaries.[15] Indeed, the network of paths in the central Highlands, as mapped by Moir, suggests the country was better served in the old days than it is now by paved roads, and conjures the image of a countryside with a continual, albeit low, level of traffic. In his study of old roads, the Inverness architect Alexander Ross mentioned the tradition of routes and tracks called Picts' roads in the Mearns area.[16] Parts at least of the network are incorporated into the better known distribution of drove roads.

Before the eighteenth century, accounts of travel survive in the context of military campaigning and there are few records of journeys for peaceful or quotidian reasons, but one is a summary of the route followed by the messengers sent north to greet the Princess Margaret, Alexander III's grand-daughter, on her voyage from Norway in 1290, admittedly a very special errand. The men stayed on three successive nights at Skelbo, Helmsdale and a place on the Caithness coast referred to as the Hospital, probably near Latheron, an itinerary that means up to 20 miles per day.[17] Hospital or spital, in variant forms, is found in several place names, all of which mark where in medieval times a hospice provided travellers with refuge and shelter. In the summer of 1654, General Monck marched troops through the Highlands as far as Inverness and Kintail in pursuit of rebels against the regime of Oliver Cromwell. Leaving Perth – or S. Johnstons, as Monck has it – on 9 June, the soldiers reached Loch Tay on the 12th, covering a distance of some 30 miles, suggesting that the going must have been relatively straightforward. Speed of travel slowed when the troops moved further into the mountain fastnesses:

> The 30th the army march't from Glenteugh to Browling the way for neere 5 miles soe boggie that about 100 baggage horses were left behinde, and many other horses begg'd [bogged?] or tired. Never any Horse men (much lesse an armie) were observ'd to march that way.[18]

The construction and maintenance of roads, at least outside settlements, was haphazard. There are some early statutes, from the reign of William the Lion (1143–1214) onward through the centuries, that refer to highways and rights of passage but it is doubtful if any of these had impact in the Highlands. In 1610, the justices of the peace in each shire were charged with 'the upholding and repairing of the briggis that ar not utterlie ruined'. They were also 'to provide for helping of the kingis heiche wayis alsweill for the benefite of careagis as ease of passingeris' and 'to consult eftir what forme the cuntray may be best provydit of goode innes and luidgeings for the ease of passingeris of all sortis'.[19] Such legislation had little permanent effect and it was to be a very long time before 'passingeris of all sortis' were well lodged. These pronouncements from the Privy Council were repeated by an Act of Parliament in 1617 which also laid down that all the common highways leading to market towns should be at least 20 feet wide.[20] A new Act in 1669, during the reign of Charles II, reiterated these demands and gave power to lairds to call out their tenants to perform six days' statute labour on road-making – the roads were to be fit to take horses and carts in summer and winter – and while this no doubt had beneficial effects in some localities, it was never enough to bring about large improvement over long distances. Occasionally, we come across a local solution to an infrastructure problem, such as in 1649 when the Presbytery of Dingwall deployed the stipend funds for a vacant kirk to fix old bridges in its vicinity.[21] Patrick Graham in his account of Aberfoyle for the Statistical Account of Scotland also noted that 'several bridges have been thrown over the torrents, by the judicious application of the vacant stipend'.[22]

Robert Greene's map of Scotland of 1679 is the earliest to show several roads. It includes a route north from Perth through Dunkeld, Blair, Ruffen (Ruthven), Dundaf (Dava?) and Taruway (Darnaway) to Forres. A fork west from Dundaf leads to Nairn and on to Inverness, while another road runs from Nairn to the coast at Ardersier to connect across the firth to Chanonrie (Fortrose) and overland to Cromartie. The map also indicates a ferry from Inverness to the Black Isle and a route proceeding to Dungwell (Dingwall). A road also runs all the way up the east coast to Duncansby. Another road cuts east from Perth to Brenchun (Brechin), Monros (Montrose), Aberdeen and so on up to Fraserburgh, before turning west along the Moray Firth to Elgin and Forres. What is surprising about the map is that it shows no roads at all running beyond Dumbarton or Stirling into the western Highlands. There was, however, a west coast route that passed by Loch Lomond over what was later to be dubbed the Rest and Be Thankful to Inveraray and Dalmally, and northward by the Black Mount to Glencoe and the Great Glen.

A Dutch or German mapmaker with an inventive frame of mind, Herman Moll settled in London in 1678 (he died in 1732). His 'A pocket companion of ye roads of ye North part of Great Britain called Scotland', published in London in 1718, shows not only many roads – with double lines for major routes and single lines for the secondary ones – but also the mileages between key points.[23]

Few, if any, of the references to roads and travel before the eighteenth century relate to the northern Highlands. This is hardly a surprise, as documents from this time in general concern mainly the low country to the south and east. In the north-east, the road network was basic but comprehensive, much as in the Lowlands. In the descriptions of Aberdeenshire parishes gathered by Walter Macfarlane, clan chief and devoted collector of manuscripts, there is mention of many bridges of stone or wood as well as fords and ferries. For Caithness, it was noted that the river in Wick was bridged by timber laid over 11 pillars of loose stone. There was 'a good timber bridge' on the Orrin in Easter Ross, but the difficulty of travel where there was none was evident in part of Strathnaver, where 'the river Bagasty' – the Vagastie, draining into Loch Naver and forming a natural routeway from the eastern lowland of Sutherland into the Mackay country to the north – 'is very troublesome when high, the passengers that ride being obliged to cross it upwards of four and twenty times in the distance of three or four miles, and all the adjacent ground is boggy and full of stanks [pools]'. What is called the 'highway' between Perth and Inverness passed through the parish of Strathdon and a bridge was erected over the Don at the 'Pot of Pool d'oylie' in about 1720.[24] This reference to 'highway' is clearly to the same route followed by James Brodie in 1680, and the standard way around the Cairngorm massif for travellers between Angus and the Moray Firth. This eastern route was facilitated by the construction of a wooden bridge over the Dee in about 1230 at Kincardine O'Neil and the establishment there of a spital for travellers.[25] In the far north of the mainland, however, in the parish of Canisbay, washed by the Pentland Firth, the contributor to Walter Macfarlane's collection wrote that the district

> has no highways except what leads from all quarters to the church, and the roads everywhere so bad, that there is scarce any travelling betwixt any two towns in the parish by horse except by bridges made of turff and heath, which must be changed once in the two or three years when the soft mossy ground being cutt by the feet of cattell becomes impassable; such bridges we have in store, frequently 30, 40 or 50 of them in less than half a mile of way and some good large ones too. One particularly that is ¼ mile long and called the Long Bridge.

These 'bridges' were probably thick carpets of turf laid to provide a relatively dry, although short-lived, path over boggy ground.

In the Highlands we can accept that many modern roads follow roughly the routes people have always taken for their daily purposes. There are, on the other hand, instances of once customary routes being relegated to some minor purpose or abandoned altogether. One notable case occurs in the parish of Kintail. In 1792 the minister, the Revd Roderick Morison, noted that the shortest route from his district to the main towns – Inverness and Dingwall – on the east coast lay through Glen Affric, a distance of 13 miles, he reckoned, between Kilduich and Strathglass. This path was in daily use at the time, even by people 'with heavy loads'. From the head of Loch Duich the route lay through Strath Croe before climbing steeply – in its higher part 'truly steep and vexatious' – up Gleann Chòinneachain to the narrow Bealach na Sgàirne. Once through this rocky gap that Morison called the 'Belloch', which was wide enough for three people to proceed abreast, the path falls gently eastward through Glen Affric. There was no inn on the way and the only shelter in bad weather was provided by crude shepherd 'booths' which from time to time were burnt by benighted travellers for fuel. 'Of all the roads, none calls for more attention,' wrote Morison. The Belloch was, however, fated never to have any attention from road builders: they preferred to approach Loch Duich through the easier Glen Shiel to the south and it has been left to enjoy a modern popularity among hillwalkers.[26]

Other traditional routes that did not become roads include one that lay from the Glutt in the upper reaches of the Thurso river to Dunbeath in Caithness; another led through Glenfeshie from Strathspey to Deeside. One ancient route from the west through the Great Glen towards Inverness passed by Bunloit down to the low swampy ground at the mouth of the Enrick and then up a steep climb to Achpopuli and Blackfold.[27]

In his now classic work *The Old Deeside Road*, which tells the stories of old routes associated with the River Dee, G.M. Fraser has left us an almost unique example of research into the subject. The Causey Mounth was the most celebrated road south from Aberdeen – it had a toll on it in 1634 – but it was just the foremost in a list Fraser compiled of 15 passes or routes leading out of Deeside mainly to the low country of Strathmore but also south-west to central Perthshire and to Strathspey. The traveller who wished to cross the Dee also seems to have been spoilt for choice; Fraser counted 27 ferries in the early eighteenth century between the river mouth in Aberdeen harbour and Braemar, and 36 fords, where there are now some 16 bridges. Fraser argued that the Causey Mounth road was probably an established route when William the Lion (1143–1214) granted a charter to the burgesses of Aberdeen in around 1175. The first documented source for it occurs in 1384 in a contract in which the Aberdeen burgess John Crab provides to his son Paul money to maintain the Causey Mounth and the bridge of Dee.[28] Professor Geoffrey Barrow summarised the evidence in medieval Scotland for the wide existence of a road network, albeit only fit for foot or horse, and pointed to the existence at that time of a bridge over the Spey a few miles below Rothes, where later there was the ferry called Boat o'Brig, and to the earliest record of a ferry on the same waterway being in the thirteenth century with a ferryman called Dougal at Fochabers.[29]

CHAPTER 2

The drovers

'the Horse is the surest Judge of his own safety . . .'

A.R.B. Haldane's seminal study *The Drove Roads of Scotland*,
first published in 1952, firmly cemented in the public mind the
existence of the network of routes associated with the droving
of cattle from the Highlands to the southern markets.[1]

Droving began in the seventeenth century and increased
greatly in scale after the Treaty of Union in 1707, but the routes
used by the drovers almost certainly have a much older pedigree. As Haldane points out, in the more distant days of inter-
clan strife at least some of the routes would have been the ways
by which cattle thieves drove home their booty. The Gaelic term
bealach, meaning a pass between hills, and the obvious way to
drive cattle, occurs in many places throughout the Highlands.
And no doubt the same routes would have been used by other
travellers with no nefarious purpose in mind. A glance at the
map of drove roads as compiled by Haldane reveals that by and
large they follow the paths logically suggested to the traveller
by the Highland landscape, and it is no surprise to find that
Thomas Telford and his engineers also followed drove routes in
places when they were building a new road network for the
Commissioners for Highland Roads and Bridges in the early
1800s. The drovers had in mind the needs of their beasts, such
as access to grazing and water, and soft ground that was kind to

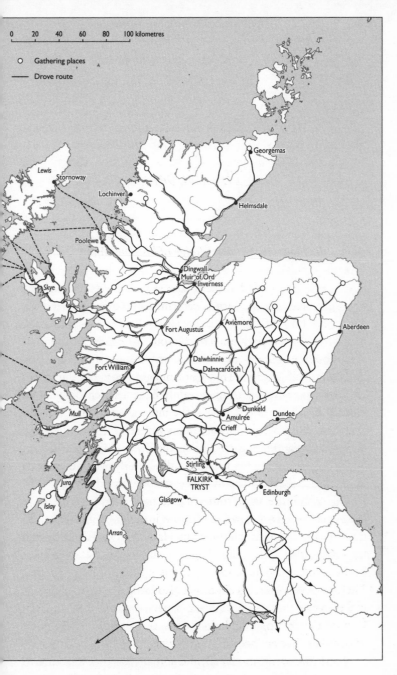

Map 3. The main drove roads in Scotland.

hooves, but other desirables – convenience and the shortest possible distance – were as for any traveller.

The drovers enjoy a romantic reputation and even Haldane, for all his sober scholarship, succumbs and imagines drovers in old age by their home fires recalling the adventure and comradeship of the open trail. It is easy to understand how the concept of droving, with its image of a herd of shaggy, wide-horned cattle moving over a great distance through the glens, fosters such a response. A similar evocation springs from the cattle drives of the American prairie, as portrayed in countless westerns, and it is historical fact that cattle ranching in the United States owes much to the enterprise of Highland emigrants already steeped in the tradition of shifting beasts over long distances.[2] The Scottish drovers acquired a reputation as a tough, honest breed of men, worthy successors to their clan-warrior forebears. They often slept out beside the animals in their charge, wrapped in their plaids against frost and rain, sustained by oatmeal and whisky and, during the time of the Jacobite risings when Highlanders were forbidden to carry weapons, they were among the selected groups who enjoyed the licence to bear arms. In his report to the government on 31 January 1725, General Wade stated that he had issued 230 licences to the 'Forresters, Drovers and Dealers in Cattle, and other merchandize, belonging to the several clans who have surrendered their arms'.[3]

The romantic aura of course obscures the hard-headed business that was the real driving force. This is exemplified by John Cameron from Lochaber, better known as Corriechoillie. Joseph Mitchell wrote:

He was the son of a crofter, who died early in very poor circumstances, his only stock being a few goats. When quite a lad he [Corriechoillie] was employed by the principal dealers to drive their sheep and cattle to market. He was so poor that his first journeys south were made without shoes, he wearing only a pair of footless stockings ... He soon acquired a character for acuteness in the buying and selling of stock as well as being the largest sheep-farmer in the Highlands. At one time he was tenant of 11 farms and reputed possessor of 60,000 sheep.

Mitchell also says he was 'a badly dressed little man, about five feet six inches in height, of thin make, with a sharp hooked nose and lynx eyes', but he was tough and kept his word. 'A man of great energy,' wrote Mitchell admiringly, 'he frequently rode night and day on a wiry pony from Falkirk to the Muir of Ord, 120 miles, carrying for himself some bread and cheese in his pocket and giving his pony now and then a bottle of porter.'[4] Corriechoillie, who died at Spean Bridge in 1856, is commemorated in the name of a lively bagpipe march tune.

The drove routes led from all the corners of the north and west to a few gathering points dictated by geography. Thus, from Ross, Caithness and Sutherland, they focused on Muir of Ord on the neck of the Black Isle, between the eastern firths and the hills, the departure point for the main routes south through the Cairngorms. A series of gathering points for droves marked the northern fringe of the eastern Grampians – at Grantown, Craigellachie, Cabrach, Huntly, Turriff and Aikey. Some major sea crossings were swum by cattle, most notably the half-mile between Kylerhea on Skye and Glenelg but also the Dornoch Firth between Creich and Easter Fearn. The longer sea crossings between the Outer Hebrides and the mainland were done by boat to Poolewe in Wester Ross or to Skye, and boats also took the cattle from Coll and Tiree (the two islands exported 400 and 500 head per year in the 1780s) to Mull, and from the southern islands such as Islay to the drove heads in Lorn and Argyll. In 1622, Sir John MacDougall, the laird of Dunolly, was punished for levying heavy tolls on cattle shipped from Mull by having property and the ferry removed from his hands.[5]

The scale of droving thrills the imagination now. In 1723,

more than 30,000 cattle were being sold in Crieff, mostly to English drovers, who paid down 30,000 guineas in cash to the Highlanders.[6] By the end of the eighteenth century more than 60,000 head of cattle were being handled at the Falkirk Tryst every year. At Dalwhinnie in 1762, Bishop Robert Forbes encountered a party of drovers en route from Skye to Crieff:

> On the dusky Muir of Drumochtir we had a full view of all the Cattle, from Rear to Front, which would take up about a Mile in length, and were greatly entertained in driving along through the midst of them, some of them skipping it away before us, like so many Deer. They were sleek and in good Order ... [at] Lochgarry ... we saw another Drove of Cattle, about 300, resting, on their way to Crief-Fair, some of them, through the Heat of the Day, wading into the Loch.[7]

The railways were to bring an end to large-scale droving but some continued in a small way into the late nineteenth century. A few drovers, strengthened by the ordeals of their job, survived to old age to find themselves the symbols of a long-gone era. Such a one was Alexander Gordon of the Gauch, Cabrach, who died early in 1922 at the age of 85 and who, in his boyhood, had driven cattle with his father from Aberdeenshire to the Falkirk Tryst via Braemar and the Spittal of Glenshee; on the return journey he recalled walking 40 miles a day and sleeping wherever they found shelter.[8]

Rivers had either to be forded or swum by human travellers, horses and herds alike, a nerve-wracking undertaking whenever the rainfall had raised the water level. 'I have always found, as the Rivers while they are passable, are pretty clear, the Horse is the surest Judge of his own safety,' advised Edmund Burt in one of his letters from the Highlands, continuing:

> There is a certain Giddiness attends the violent Passage of the Water when one is in it, and therefore I always at

entering resolved to keep my Eye steadily fixed on some remarkable Stone on the Shore of the further Side, and my Horse's Ears, as near as I could, in a Line with it, leaving him to choose his Steps ... I still retain the Custom of my own Country [England] in not sending my Servant before me through these dangerous Waters, as is the constant Practice of all the Natives of Scotland.[9]

Burt admired the way in which a herd of cattle took to a river crossing: 'The cows were about fifty in number and took the water like spaniels, and when they were in, their drivers made a hideous cry to urge them forwards: this, they told me, they did to keep the foremost of them from turning about.'[10] The technique did not always guarantee safety and there were times when cattle were plucked from the throng by the current and carried off to be drowned before they could be rescued.[11]

On the occasion described by Burt, the drovers themselves had crossed the spate by boat. Ferries of this simple sort were maintained on many river crossings, often by the local laird or a tenant. As usual, Burt deployed a critical eye for his English readership. Referring to a crossing of an unnamed river but probably the Beauly, he wrote: 'We ... passed a pretty wide River, into the County of Ross, by a Boat that we feared would fall to Pieces in the Passage.'[12] Several places along the Spey and other larger rivers are named after the ferries that used to operate at them: among these we find Boat of Garten, Boat of Insch, Boat of Cromdale and Boat o'Brig. On some of these crossings the vessel was a coracle, and it must have taken some courage or faith on the part of a stranger to step into such an apparently frail cup of wood and hide.

Seagoing crossings to the islands for a long time were probably organised on an ad hoc basis, a boatman or shipmaster taking to the water when required and travellers finding a passage or hiring a boat where they could. We do have scant records of one regular crossing: John o' Groats famously derived its name from Jan de Groot, either Dutch or of Dutch extraction, who was charged in the late fifteenth century with running a ferry between Caithness and Orkney, then recently having become part of the Scottish realm. Many tall stories have accrued around Jan de Groot but a charter from the Earl of Caithness to John Grot in March 1496 of a pennyland of ground at Duncansby would seem to confirm the essence of the matter.[13]

CHAPTER 3

Coastal seas

'a small barke once in a yeere from Leith . . .'

While livestock could be driven to market, bulk commodities such as grain, meal, bolts of cloth and peats were usually transported by horse in baskets or packs slung on wooden saddles. The state of the roads precluded much wagon haulage, but a type of sledge, sometimes called a slipe, could be dragged along by a horse, the rear end of the long shafts or poles trailing on the ground. A platform fixed between the poles allowed the use of a basket, box or wicker container.[1] Thomas Pennant saw strings of pack ponies bringing in peat to Tayside in 1769. Joseph Taylor, the parish minister of Watten in 1792, when road building had barely begun in his area, recorded that everything was carried in small loads on horseback.[2] William Sutherland, the minister in the neighbouring parish of Wick, noted the technique, how goods were placed in straw creels, called cassies in the dialect of Caithness, which were slung over a wooden pack saddle (clubber), tied with straw ropes (simmans), with a straw cushion (flet) between the wood and the horse's back. Variants of this apparatus existed across the country. 'When a call comes to ship the master's victual [grain],' wrote Sutherland, 'some scores of the garrons or small horses . . . are sent out by the tenants, tied to one another by the tail, with a cassie of meal or bear [a form of barley] on either side of every horse. A boll of meal or half a boll of bear is all the load each can carry in this miserable mode of conveyance.'[3] The boll is a measure of volume and the weight varies according to the commodity, but a boll of oatmeal would have tipped the scale at around nine stone (roughly 60 kilos). Smaller quantities of goods could be borne by men and women in baskets on their backs. In Strathspey and other valleys where river transportation was feasible it was customary to float timber from the forests to where it was needed, the workers often waiting for a spring spate to bring down large quantities of felled trees.[4]

Osgood MacKenzie described in his memoirs how in the days of his grandfather, around 1800, a team of men and ponies would come from Gairloch to bring the laird and his family across the county from the east side to their home on the west coast. A day would be spent in packing. 'Everything had to go west – flour, groceries, linen, plate, boys and babies, and I have heard that my father was carried to Gairloch on pony-back in a kind of cradle when he was only a few weeks old.' The pack train went as far as Scatwell on the first day where there was an inn 'and as there was a road of a kind thus far and no farther, the old yellow family coach carried "the quality" (i.e. the gentry) there before dark'. The second day of the journey ended at Kinlochewe, 12 hours or more of slog across the high country, and the third day was spent sailing or rowing the goods and chattels down Loch Maree to the west end, and another short distance of road to the destination. Such travelling was open only to those who had command of considerable resources in manpower and money.[5]

The sea offered the best opportunities for transporting both people and goods. On his journey up the west coast from Oban to Durness in 1786, John Knox frequently took to the water among the islands and sea lochs rather than travel overland.[6]

Just as for land travel, much of what we know about coastal shipping before the eighteenth century is anecdotal. We can be sure, nevertheless, that both the sea and fresh water have supported a steady traffic from the earliest times. Several examples of prehistoric logboats have been found in Scotland. One was uncovered at Carpow on the Tay: dated to 1000 BC, this slim vessel, 30 feet long, fashioned from a single oak log, was probably typical of the craft used on inland and inshore waters for fishing, fowling and transport in the Bronze Age. The substantial, sturdy hull, with a few shaped features in the interior such as ridges capable of supporting seats, and evidence of maintenance – plant material soaked in oil and fat and stuffed into a split – point to craftsmanship and a long working life.[7] An older logboat, albeit incomplete, was found at Locharbriggs in Nithsdale in the 1970s; it dates to 1900 BC. But this is much younger than the oldest vessel of this type uncovered in western Europe, in the Netherlands at Pesse: this hull carved from Scots pine has been dated to 7900–6500 BC.[8]

The Carpow logboat is unlikely to have ventured safely far from the seashore; some other design of craft must have been used to travel among the islands. Boats made from planks lashed together have been found in Britain – for example, the Ferriby boat, discovered on the Humber. This technology could have allowed the construction of a more robust seagoing vessel. The lashing together of two or more logboats to support a floating platform or a raft-like boat is another possible solution. Plank-built seagoing boats were also in use on the Atlantic coast by the first century BC, when Julius Caesar described the seaworthy boats used by the Veneti people on the coast of Brittany. In the Hebrides and the Northern Isles, where timber is scarce, it is more likely that the skin boat became the customary craft. Hide boats were widespread along the Atlantic seaboard in Roman times and were used, for example, for shipping tin from Cornwall to the continent. The Irish curragh is a well-known variant, and the *Brendan*, a replica sailed by Tim Severin and his crew from Ireland to Iceland and Newfoundland, showed the seagoing capabilities of the craft.[9] Our knowledge of prehistoric boats is set to increase as more discoveries are made, but it is clear enough that travel by sea is a long-established practice. The technologies are likely to have been common along the Atlantic coast, contributing over time to a North Sea/Atlantic seaboard design tradition, incorporating such innovations as clinker planking and rectangular sails. Variants of the basic boat design adapted to local conditions evolved among the coastal communities, hence we can be sure that yoles and scaffies appeared early on the east coast, and we have a rare written reference in 1608 to 'gallayis, lumfaddis and birlingis' – galleys, lymphads and birlinns – being used in the Western Isles.[10]

The oldest surviving written records of trade around the northern coasts of Scotland date from the fourteenth century and relate to the customs duties levied on the export of a few raw products such as wool, fleeces and hides.[11] The bulk of this recorded trade took place through a handful of ports between the Firth of Forth and Banff but Inverness also features for 1337 and from 1359 onwards.[12] Occasionally we are afforded a glimpse of trade through legal records: for example, in 1304 four Saint Omer merchants raised a complaint about goods – wool, skins and hides – that they had bought in Moray that, they claimed, had been sequestrated by the bishop.[13] Such scant and intriguing records reveal only one aspect of the commerce that must have gone on. The boats that carried goods around the North Sea in the medieval period are typified by the Bremen cog, a cargo vessel that survived in the mud of the Weser estuary and is now preserved in the Maritime Museum in Bremerhaven. The Bremen cog was a single-masted, square-rigged vessel, slightly over 76 feet long overall, with a beam of 25 feet and cargo capacity of 80 tonnes. Other examples of cogs have been found in Denmark and, in 2012, in the silty bed of the river IJssel in the Netherlands.

Thomas Tucker listed northern ports in 1656 as part of a Cromwellian investigation into customs revenues. He noted that Aberdeen had a flourishing inward trade from Norway, 'Eastland' (by which he means the Baltic), Holland and France, a commerce that had spin-off benefits to Stonehaven, Newburgh, Peterhead, Fraserburgh and Banff. Tucker called Inverness the last port to the north, where there was 'only a coast trade, there being noe more than one single merchant in all the towne, who brings home sometimes a little timber, salt or wine'.[14] The Highland capital may well have been experiencing a depressed phase brought on by the civil wars or other misfortune, as it appears to have enjoyed a larger trade at other periods. Tucker went on to report that in Inverness 'there is a collector, a checque and one wayter' – customs officials – who also visited Garmouth and Findhorn. The latter exported some 60 lasts of salmon per year. Inverness imported salt from France and occasionally received a small vessel from Holland or Norway. Tucker found only two ports worthy of mention in Ross – Cromarty and Tain – and in Sutherland only Dunrobin 'and some two small creekes more' where grain was exported. A customs wayter in Caithness made sure that the export of beef, hides and tallow from Wick and Thurso did not go to 'forraigne parts' but to Scottish ports; and Kirkwall also had a wayter to look after the northern isles with the same remit. The mouth of the Wick river, where boats could have beached for the handling of cargo, was exposed to south-easterly gales and swells and, until an enclosed harbour was built there under the aegis of the British Fisheries Society in the early 1800s, seafarers preferred to use the creek of Staxigoe as a haven. Inverness had one 'barke' of 10 tons, Garmouth one of 12, Cromarty one of 16, Thurso two of 30, and Orkney three with a cargo capacity of 15, 13 and 13 chalders. The chalder, the largest volume measure for grain, comprised 16 bolls, an amount equivalent to almost 1,000 kilos. Of the west coast, Tucker had nothing to say beyond describing 'Stranaverne, Assinshire and the Western Isles' as 'places mangled with many arms of the Westerne Sea'.

The burgh records of several towns around the north survive from the sixteenth century and include some information about local and international trade. Inverness merchants in the mid-1500s were dealing with Hamburg, Dieppe and ports in the Low Countries.[15] Direct trade between Shetland and the north of Germany, the heartland of the powerful trading empire of the Hanseatic League, is known from the early 1400s.[16] In November 1633 John Forbes wrote from Dieppe to his father in Inverness to say that he had failed to sell the barrels of salted salmon they had brought to the continent, that the market for hides was oversupplied, that they had not as yet sold any plaiding, that the price was good for tallow and that there would be good profit in bringing home a consignment of tobacco.[17] To boost trade, the burgh council of Inverness decided in April 1648 to build a proper harbour at the mouth of the river and laid down the dues to be paid by different classes of trader.[18] In 1650 the Inverness traders suffered a severe setback when a ship bound from Holland went down 'with fyftie thousand markes and upwardes, quhilk hes ruined many honest merchants most part of the said loading being taken upon trust'.[19] Tucker himself says of Cromarty 'with one of the delicatest harbours reputed in all Europe' and Tain that the former imported only a little salt and the latter received 'a small barke once in a yeere from Leith' to collect timber from the hinterland.[20] A Dutch ship was captured by a Commonwealth frigate as she left Staxigoe in 1651, the incident illustrative both of the trade and the dangers it faced.[21]

Before the surveying and printing of charts became widespread, navigational instructions were presumably passed from one generation of seafarers to the next by word of mouth. Written sailing directions are known to have existed in different places from very early times but in the sixteenth century they began to be recorded in documents called rutters. The word derives from the French *routier* and appears first in English in 1528. One rutter for Scottish coastal waters survives from 1540, when it was compiled by Alexander Lindsay for James V's voyage around the coast that year.[22] It contains brief details of tides and currents, distances, compass headings and other crucial information, including the names of safe anchorages. 'A longe the cost of Murray are manie good ryding places for shippes at x, xij or xvj fadomes,' it assures the navigator, before continuing: 'Above all hauens in the yle of Britane for saifftie of shippis both great and small is the Fyrth of Crumberte [Cromarty] for all kynd of windis and strome, in which hauen schippis may enter at all tyme of flood.' Lindsay warns of the dangerous sandbanks at the mouth of the Dornoch Firth, the risks from sailing with south and south-east winds along the Caithness coast (a lee shore in such conditions), and the perils of the Pentland Firth. Kirkwall and St Margaret's Hope are good anchorages in Orkney, and along the northern and western coasts he lists similar safe places at, for example, Scrabster, the Kyle of Tongue, Loch Eriboll, Loch Broom, Loch Ewe, Kyleakin, Kyle Rhea (but beware of 'a dangerous stream') and so on down the rugged west coast through the labyrinth of islands and seaways.

Trade connections with the south-west Highlands are not well recorded for the Middle Ages, but there was traffic in live-stock, cheese and meal.[23] A ship and cargo belonging to Alexander of Lorn, head of the MacDougall clan, was seized on suspicion of piracy when it put into Bristol in 1275; the men were later released.[24] The same man, Alexander of Lorn, was given permission by Edward I in 1292 to buy and sell in Ireland. From Southend at the tip of Kintyre, there were ferry connections to Ulster. Edward Lhuyd, the Welsh travel writer, crossed from Ballycastle in 1699, and a legal case in 1710 in Argyll recorded a connection with Cushendun.[25] Inveraray is described in around 1630 as 'one frie litle burgh in Argyll having libertie and full power to buy and sell all kynd of Merchandize and wares ... both of the countrie stuff and other wares which they may bring with them out of other countries'.[26] The names of many merchants are included in the bonds, receipts and other legal documents registered in the sheriff court books at Inveraray from December 1689 onwards.[27] These show that, as well as a pocket of mercantile enterprise based in Inveraray itself, a range of places along the south-west Highland littoral from Campbeltown, Loch Linnhe and out to Islay and Jura had their resident merchants who together would have kept afloat a network of seagoing trading craft. In his study of trade on the eve of the Union in 1707, T.C. Smout describes how trade between the western Highlands and the Clyde grew out of the fishing, as the Highlanders followed the herring shoals and ended up at Greenock, where they bartered their catch for the 'Glasgow wares' they needed.[28] The trade was limited by the small size of the boats and the poverty of the fishermen. One wonders whether commerce on the west coast was as limited as the surviving evidence suggests. The coastal movement of goods and people in various kinds of boat, to and from markets and settlements, must have been a normal feature of daily life, passing for the most part unrecorded.

CHAPTER 4

The early post service

'once a fortnight for the mail . . .'

It is safe to assume that letters were carried where feasible by
seafarers already outward bound on trade. On land other
arrangements had to be made. News – about trading conditions, political developments, outbreaks of plague and war, religious ideas, anything – has always been important. Then, as
now, success in trade relied on good communications, and all
the ancient empires, royal houses, governments and international institutions, such as the Catholic Church, had their postal
and courier services. In contrast, the formation of the public
postal service familiar today was a relatively late development.
The Union of the Crowns in 1603 led to the establishment of
posting stages where couriers could change horses between
Berwick and Edinburgh.[1] England acquired its first postmaster
general in 1635, in the person of Thomas Witherings; all letters
were routed through London and postal rates were fixed – a
letter to Scotland cost 8d. Edinburgh, Glasgow and some other
burghs organised their own local delivery systems over the
following decades, and these gradually expanded to bring in
more of the country, reaching Aberdeen in around 1650. The
Privy Council granted warrants in 1669 for a foot post between
Edinburgh and Aberdeen, to go twice a week to the granite city
and once a week onward to Inverness 'wind and weather

serving'. Later a public announcement was made in Edinburgh
that a wagon would leave the Grassmarket for Inverness every
Tuesday, God willing, but if not on the Tuesday the Wednesday
'whether or no'.[2] The Post Office took over private services and,
in its contract with postmaster general John Blair in 1689, the
Privy Council in Edinburgh set out the charges: 2s for a single
letter to towns as far north as Perth, 3s for the longer distances
to Aberdeen, Dunkeld, Portpatrick and Carlisle, and 4s for the
marathon to Inverness.

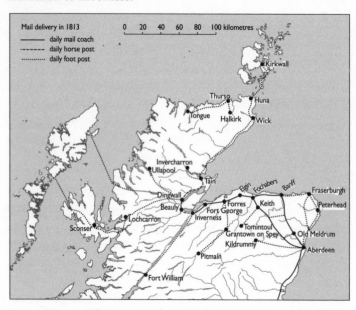

*Map 4. The extent of mail delivery in 1813 in the
far north, by coach, horse or runner.*

For a long time the mail was carried by men on foot, called
runners. These carriers on the thrice-weekly service between
Edinburgh and Glasgow took two days to cover the 46 miles
between the cities, calling at Linlithgow and Falkirk on the way.
A horse post began in 1715, and very soon afterwards the army
established its own mail service, with riders carrying letters

between Perth and Inverness via Blair Atholl and Kingussie. Despite the earnest pleadings of the Inverness burgh council this service was withdrawn after two years, and the mail delivery reverted to the former, longer route via Aberdeen. Riders also began to deliver mail from Glasgow to Inveraray in 1717. The postmaster in the Argyll burgh, the innkeeper Archibald Campbell, kept details of this connection in a notebook that has survived to give us a rare glimpse into the postal service at this time. Between April and December 1734, he handled more than 2,450 letters in a weekly service provided by a foot runner to Dumbarton. Although some letters were paid in advance, it was normal for the recipient to pay on delivery. Slowly the provision of a mail service spread and improved so that by the mid-1700s most if not all of the main burghs and settlements in the north – Fort William, Wick, Thurso, Kirkwall, Loch Carron, Portree – had been drawn into regular contact with the south. Stornoway got its first post office in 1756, and in 1759 a packet boat was established 'which for some years went to the opposite coast once a fortnight for the mail, by-letters and passengers, and on occasions carried cattle and horses'. Twenty years later the increase in business led to the packet sailing weekly, funded partly by the government and partly by the Earl of Seaforth.[3]

The post runners who provided the backbone of the service do not figure often in the surviving annals, an unfortunate lapse for such a group of dedicated men; one was drowned trying to cross the burn at Loth on the east coast of Sutherland in 1755.[4] Whether in the employ of the Post Office or of individuals, they must have been a hardy breed, connecting remote places with the outside world across miles of countryside in all weathers. Macleod of Dunvegan had a man who carried letters to Edinburgh, receiving the sum of 15s for each trip; he made three in 1711.[5] Alexander Mackenzie, factor of Ardloch, paid Finlay Macra 30s for 12 trips from Assynt to destinations in the 'low country', the east coast of Sutherland or Ross, in 1767. Another runner, John Macleod, received 15s for six journeys from Assynt and the post office at Tain. A new post was formed in 1773 and paid the runner a fee of £2, probably for one year although this is not specified.[6]

In his comprehensive book on the history and lore of the Gairloch area, J.H. Dixon devoted some space to the post runners.[7] During the first half of the eighteenth century, it seems a runner operated only when the laird was in residence in the summer and autumn, usually walking or riding – despite the sobriquet, it seems doubtful that any of them ever actually ran – west from Dingwall via Strath Bran, Glen Docherty and the east side of Loch Maree. Dixon quoted a description by a Dr Mackenzie of the runner who went on horseback in the early 1800s:

> our only letter-carrier was one of my father's (Sir Hector's) attachés, little Duncan, a bit of kilted india-rubber, who, with a sheepskin knapsack on his back to keep his dispatches dry ... left the west on Monday, got the sixty miles (to Dingwall) done on Wednesday, and returning on Thursday delivered up his mail to my father on the Saturday ... and so all the five months of our western stay ... I never heard of his being a day off work in many a year ... When we retired to the east the natives left behind us got their postal delivery the best way they could.

The constant travel was too much for some runners, as would appear to have been the case with a young man called M'Leay from Poolewe, who was found dead about a mile from the inn at Achnasheen, still with bread and mutton in his hand that his sister had given him shortly before he had left it. Dixon says that the last runner to Gairloch was John Mackenzie, the son of the man referred to above as little Duncan, who was more properly called Donald Charles. John was known as Iain Mor am Post – Big John the post – and, when the construction of the road to Gairloch enabled the mail to be brought in by horse and trap three times a week, he emigrated to Australia.

As the postal service improved, so expectations surrounding it began to swell, and grumbling when it appeared not to be functioning properly: in 1781 the Commissioners of Supply in Inverness noted in their annual general meeting that 'many Complaints are made from all the Countys to the northward of Banff that the Post at Banff is detained for many hours unecessary by which the Lieges suffer'. A few weeks later the Commissioners learned, presumably with some contentment, that the Postmaster General was taking action over the Banff problem.[8] In January 1796, the provost of Aberdeen circulated a memo around the other neighbouring counties to petition the Postmaster General in the name of all the magistrates and traders in towns north of the Forth to change the hour of despatch of the north mail from Edinburgh and for conveyance as far as Aberdeen by a coach or diligence 'instead of the present tardy manner on Horseback'. The Cullen magistrates thought the diligence should carry on to Inverness.[9]

The expense of the postal service did not stop certain lairds and lawyers from extensive, frequent letter-writing. A surviving account in the Dunbar Papers in Caithness tells how in 1744 Sir William Dunbar and two merchants together owed a third trader 8s 4d for the postage of some items between Wick and Edinburgh.[10] This was not a problem for gentlemen with a cavalier attitude to debt but bothered some such as the minister of Inveraray who, in 1792, wrote: 'The postage of a letter from London to Inveraray, which is 491 miles, is 1s and of one from Oban, which is about 35 miles, is 3d.'[11] The daily wage for a labourer was 1s at this time. The minister thought it would be 'more conformable to equity' to charge in proportion to weight and distance. 'Letter carriers deliver letters to the inhabitants of all the other post towns in Scotland,' he continued, 'ought not the same to be done here?' Despite the complaint the service had improved slowly over the decades. Before 1745 a runner had carried mail between Dumbarton and the Argyll town only once a week, and postmasters had become insolvent, but there was now a despatch and delivery every weekday and the receipts at the post office had become sufficient to return a profit of £319 17s 6d. That there were now ten post offices in Argyllshire was proof, wrote the minister, 'of the increase of trade and correspondence'. Similar progress was occurring throughout the Highlands. In Stornoway, Post Office business almost doubled in the five years between 1791 and 1796 from £50 to £90, measured by the amount charged by the General Post Office in Edinburgh.[12] The postmaster in Thurso had an allowance – £47 4s a year in the 1790s – to pay for runners between the town and Dunbeath. Business was brisk – for one thing, litigation-minded Caithness lairds kept up a steady correspondence with Edinburgh solicitors – and in 1796 the Post Office had £220 19s 'of clear revenue, exclusive of the postages of letters sent in bye-bags'.[13] Thurso had three deliveries a week at that time but the local gentry wanted a daily service, as Dornoch had. The lairds and gentlemen in Kilmorack employed a runner to carry mail to Inverness three times a week until Colonel Fraser of Belladrum managed to persuade the authorities to open a post office in Beauly.[14]

Once a week a boat made the crossing between Huna, west of John o' Groats, and Burwick, on South Ronaldsay; this comprised the mail service between Orkney and the northern mainland in the 1790s.[15] The Pentland Firth ferry also carried passengers, at the fare of 1s on the trip with the mail or 7s if the traveller at other times hired the boat for himself.

PART 2

The military roads

CHAPTER 5

Wade's work

'Had you seen these roads before they were made,
You would lift up your hands and bless General Wade ...'

This famous couplet celebrates the one name that everyone links with roads in the Highlands.[1] It is a slightly unjust association insofar as George Wade himself was responsible for the construction of fewer miles than his successors, but he deserves to be remembered as an innovator. It is a tribute to the impact he made that his name was to be often repeated in relation to developments in transport long after he had died. He was born in Ireland in 1673, the grandson of a Cromwellian officer who had been granted lands near Dublin, and was commissioned at the age of 17 as an ensign in the 10th Foot. He smelt battle smoke in Flanders before he was 20 and rose steadily through the officer ranks until he was promoted to major general and given command in Ireland in 1714. In his military experience and in his parallel career as an MP (for Hindon in Wiltshire, and after 1722 until his death for the constituency of Bath), he was typical of his class; he would probably have been forgotten today but for his work on a civil engineering project unique in the political circumstances of his time. (Wade was also responsible for building a stretch of military road in England, now part of the B6318 in Northumberland, in 1746.)

The union of Scotland and England, begun in 1603 with the single monarchy and completed in 1707 by the formation of the British parliament from its Scottish and English predecessors, did not immediately bring about the vaunted promise of economic progress north of the border. Grumbling became open discontent in 1714 after the death of Queen Anne, the last Stuart monarch, and the succession of George I of Hanover, contemptuously labelled 'German Geordie' in Scotland. Jacobites toasted the exiled Stuart King James and planned rebellion. Armed risings in 1715 and 1719 were defeated, but the threat to take again to the field remained strong among the disaffected pro-Stuart Highland clans.

Political unrest was accompanied by a general disregard for the laws of the government. Outside the burghs, where the merchants and the Presbyterian clergy maintained a degree of civil order, much of the Highlands was divided into clan territories where local chiefs acted as petty warlords and implemented their own justice. One of the more powerful, Simon Fraser, Lord Lovat, appealed to the government to do something to suppress the feuding and tit-for-tat cattle stealing, and helpfully suggested what that something could be – that he be appointed lord-lieutenant of Inverness-shire and put in charge of armed independent companies of militia to police the north. Lovat's concern was fuelled by the fact that the 'two deputies of the shyre of Inverness' had both been out in the 1715 Rising and had been Lovat's prisoners, and he now had, as he put it, 'the mortification to see and feel them triumphant over him, loading him with marks of their displeasure'.[2]

In 1724, Major-General Wade was ordered to travel north to learn what might be afoot in the near-foreign environment beyond the Highland Line. He set off in July and submitted his report before the end of the year. This included the important conclusion that 'the great Disadvantages Regular Troops are under when they engage with those who Inhabit Mountainous Situations' could be reduced by tackling the want of roads and bridges. In 1708, during the capture of Minorca, Wade had experienced the need for road-making to move field guns; he would also certainly have been aware of the time it had taken men and guns to move to meet the Spanish when they landed in Wester Ross in 1719: more than four days to go from Inverness by Invermoriston to within striking distance of Glen Shiel. 'The Sevennes in France and Catalans in Spain have in all times been Instances,' continued the general. 'The Highlands of Scotland are still more impracticable, from the want of Roads, Bridges, and from excessive Rains that almost continually fall in these parts, which by Nature and constant use become habitual to the Natives, but very difficultly supported by the Regular Troops.'[3]

Wade also recommended the improvement of the existing military bases at Kilchumein (shortly to be renamed Fort Augustus), Fort William, Bernera in Glenelg, and Ruthven near Kingussie, the establishment of an additional fort at Inverness (this was erected on Castle Hill in the centre of the town and named Fort George), and a boat able to carry up to 80 soldiers to ply on Loch Ness. Almost immediately in the wake of this submission he was appointed to command the armed forces in Scotland and was given the opportunity to put his ideas into practice. In 1667, the Earl of Atholl had first been given a royal commission to raise a peacekeeping force of local men and over the succeeding years a series of these independent companies had existed. Lovat's plan had precedent, but the problem in his case was that he was seen by the government as the wrong man for the job. Wade recruited six new companies in the spring of 1725, three of 114 men and three of 71. Four more were raised in 1729. During 1739–40, all ten were amalgamated into a single regiment listed as the 43rd. They acquired the nickname in Gaelic Am Freacadain Dubh, from the dark colour of the government-issue tartan, and thus became the forerunner of the Black Watch. Commenting on the birth of this famous regiment almost a century later, Colonel David

Stewart of Garth noted how the men who came forward to join the Companies 'were of a higher station in society than that from which soldiers in general are raised'. Enlistment restored the privilege to bear arms, esteemed as a sign of social rank, and was welcomed as a way around the Disarming Acts. As Stewart of Garth noted, 'In such a range of country, without commerce, or any profession for young men but that of arms, no difficulty was found in persuading individuals to engage in a corps which was to be stationery [*sic*] within the mountains, and of which the duties were such as to afford them merely an agreeable pastime ... Hence it became an object of ambition with all the young men of spirit to be admitted, even as privates, into a service which procured them the privilege of wearing arms.' Colonel Stewart has nothing to say about how well his Highlanders took to the plying of pick and shovel but the roads were built.[4]

Wade himself arrived in Inverness in August 1725. Three companies were posted to guard key routes in the Highlands and the others placed in barracks. The campaign of pacification began to have an effect by the end of 1726. In September that year the Lord Advocate, Duncan Forbes, wrote in a letter from his home at Culloden near Inverness, 'last year's madness is altogether cooled and ... the spirit of disaffection ... has to my observation very much lost its edge. The Highlands are at present in full rest.'[5] At the same time as he was deploying his forces, Wade launched his road-building programme, working first on the stretch between Fort William and Kilchumein. In September he wrote to Lord Townshend, secretary of state for the Northern Department in the government, to say that he had inspected the new road and now wished to have it 'enlarged and carried on for wheel-carriages over the mountains on the south side of Loch Ness as far as the town of Inverness, so that before midsummer next there will be a good coach road from that place to Fort William, which before was not passable on horseback in many places'.[6] The story survives that Lord Townshend did indeed bring a coach to Inverness by the coast road from Aberdeen, that local people were so taken with the unusual sight that they saluted the coachman and ignored the toffs inside, and that Townshend did drive the length of the Great Glen to Fort William just as Wade had promised he could.[7] The Companies had proved to be better at the work than he had foreseen and, said Wade, 'the Highlanders, from the ease and conveniency of transporting their merchandise, begin to approve and applaud what they at first repined and submitted to with reluctance'.

There is some doubt over a part of the route that Wade's men first carved through the rugged country on the south-east side of Loch Ness.[8] The first few miles pioneered what is now, with some later deviations, the B862 from Fort Augustus via Glen Doe and Loch Tarff, as far as the viewpoint on the summit of Carn an t-Suidhe, with its fine prospect of the country falling away to the north-east. It is likely that Wade and his designers tapped into local knowledge in planning where to go through the convoluted landscape they now had to penetrate. Between 1725 and 1730, Joseph Avery made a map of the first Fort Augustus to Inverness road but both it and William Roy's military survey of 1747–55 do not make clear exactly where the road ran. It is possible that it went through Glenlia, skirting Foyers and following the route of the present single-track side road to the Pass of Inverfarigaig and then north past Aultnagoire to ford the Farigaig river and continue along the west side of Loch Ceo-Ghlais. Four years after this route was pioneered it fell out of much use when Wade's engineers laid out a new way to Foyers that ran closer to the Loch Ness shore, now the B852. The Inverfarigaig bridge was built in 1732, at a cost of £150.

Wade's men worked to construct a road to a standard breadth of 16 feet, making it wider on occasion and, in constricted lengths, as narrow as 10 feet. The surveyors marked out the route as straight as the gradients would allow and behind them the men toiled with pick, spade, lever and jack-screw to heave aside boulders and clear the ground down to a level where they could start building up a roadbed, laying large stones and then topping them with three or more feet of finer stones and gravel to 'form a smooth and binding Surface'.[9] To cross the frequent stretches of bog, the soldiers dug down until they reached bedrock, strewing the excavated moss along the roadsides beyond the necessary drainage ditches. On deep bog, the roadbed had to be laid on a raft of timber and fascines, which hardened into a durable foundation in the anaerobic conditions. Rather than raise embankments, the men cut a shelf to direct the road along a hillside, and to save time in the initial phase of road-making they chose to lay causeways as fords rather than pause to build bridges. The causeway would need to be reset after a spate but as a temporary measure until timber and later stone bridges could be erected the method was acceptable.

'The private Men were allowed Sixpence a Day over and above their Pay as Soldiers,' recorded Edmund Burt. 'A Corporal had Eight-pence, and a Serjeant a Shilling; but this Extra Pay was only for working-Days, which were often interrupted by violent Storms of Wind and Rain, from the Heights and Hollows of the Mountains. These Parties of Men were under the Command and Direction of proper Officers who were all Subalterns and received two Shillings and Sixpence per Diem to defray their extraordinary Expense.'[10] Those with special skills, collectively known as artificers and including smiths and carpenters, also received one shilling a day. The double pay for the road-builders was undoubtedly a welcome incentive in work that must at times have been arduous toil in remote, inhospitable terrain. On one stretch north of Foyers the men had to hang in ropes on a precipice to bore holes into the rock and then blast the obstruction aside with gunpowder. At the Slochd, Burt tells how an old woman laughed at the fools of soldiers when they set about moving a fallen mass of rock that had been in situ 'for ever', but she screamed and ran away when 'she saw that vast Bulk begin to rise, though by slow degrees . . . I make no doubt she thought it was Magic, and the Workmen Warlocks.'

More than 60 years later, the intrepid traveller Lady Sarah Murray, of whom more anon, came in her carriage past the Black Rock 'and it seemed as if it were impossible to pass by it; in truth it does require courage and steady horses to venture upon a very narrow shelf blown out of the rocks; and to get upon it you ascend a road almost as steep as the ridge of a house, winding round a huge projecting mass'. Lady Murray found that the scene revealed before her made amends for the 'little palpitation' induced by the height of the road above Loch Ness.[11]

Wade's strategy of garrisoning the Highlands and building roads had the pacifying effect he desired, but he had to remind his superiors of the benefits of spending public money on the work. After the death of German Geordie in June 1727, Wade had to present a case to the government of the new king, George II, for the allowance to be continued, explaining that 'with some Addition for erecting Stone Bridges, where they are wanting, a Military Way may be made through the Mountains from Inverness Southwards as far as Perth, which will open a short and speedy Communication with the Troops Quarter'd in the Low Country, Contribute to civilize the Highlanders and in my humble opinion will prove the most effectual Means to continue them in a due Obedience to Yur Maty's Government'.[12]

Work on the all-important Inverness to Perth route – then, as now, the spine of communication through the central Highlands – began in 1728. 'I am now with all possible diligence carrying on the new road for wheel-carriages between Dunkeld and Inverness, of about 80 English measured miles in length,' wrote the major-general in Blair Atholl in July, 'and, that no time may be lost in a work so essential for His Majesty's service, I have employed 300 men on different parts of this road that the work may be done during the favourable season of the year.'[13]

According to Lady Sarah Murray, the 'old road' was 'tremendous' but now that the soldiers had placed it higher up the mountainside 'it has lost all its horrors'.

By the autumn of the following year, considerable progress had been made and in early October, at the end of the working season, Wade joined his 'Highwaymen', as he called them, to celebrate with a feast of four roast oxen at Dalnacardoch, near Dalnaspidal. The lieutenant-general – Wade had been promoted in 1727 – and his guests travelled in a coach 'with great ease and pleasure', as he later told the Lord Advocate, to where the soldiers had set up their fires and spits. 'We dined in a tent pitched for that purpose,' he wrote, 'the Beef was excellent; and we had plenty of Bumpers, not forgetting your Lord and Colloden; and after three hours stay took leave of our Benefactors'. Wade stayed for five days in the vicinity in a temporary dwelling he called his hut, clearly enjoying the experience – '[it] set me upon my leggs again' – and thinking about next year's project, the road between Dalnacardoch and Crieff.[14]

Duncan Forbes, the Lord Advocate, wrote from Perth in August 1730: 'I have visited Mr Wade at his new Roads which go on with all the Dispatch and Success imaginable. The Highlanders begin to turn their Heads to Labour which in little time must produce a Great Change upon the face as well as on the Politicks of this Country.'[15]

In 1731 work started on the road from Dalwhinnie to Fort Augustus. More effort was now being put into the project. More than 500 men laboured at various times between April and the end of October to lay a metalled way for 28 miles over the broad ridge of the Corrieyairack. This route rises to 2,526 feet, a thread of roadway now much eroded but famous among hikers and mountain bikers. A series of buttressed hairpin bends, 17 in all, overcame the steep gradients of the Yairack-Tarff watershed, 'by which', recorded a commentator in the *Scots Magazine*, 'the ascent is easier for wheel-carriages than that of Highgate'.[16]

Edmund Burt was also moved to compare the new roads to the streets of London, commenting:

> The Roads on these Moors are now as smooth as Constitution Hill, and I have galloped on some of them for Miles together in great Tranquility; which was heightened by Reflection on my former Fatigue when for a great Part of the Way I had been obliged to quit my Horse, it being too dangerous or impracticable to ride, and even hazardous to pass on Foot.[17]

A traveller called N. Macleod recorded an encounter with a working party in the Corrieyairack. In a letter, he wrote:

> Upon entering into a little glen among the hills, I heard the noise of many people and saw six great fires, about each of which a number of soldiers were busy. During my wonder at the cause of this, an officer invited me to drink their majesties' healths. I attended him to each fire, and found that these were the six working parties of Tatton's, Montague's, Mark Ker's, Harrison's, and Handyside's regiments, and the party from the Highland Companies, making in all about five hundred men, who had this summer with indefatigable pains completed the great road for wheeled carriages between Fort Augustus and Ruthven. It being the 30th of October, his majesty's birthday, General Wade had given to each detachment an ox-feast and liquor; six oxen were roasted whole, one at the head of each party. The joy was great, both upon the occasion of the day, and the work's being completed, which is really a wonderful undertaking.[18]

The Corrieyairack remained a daunting road to follow. Lady Murray met at Fort Augustus a young Oxonian who had just ridden over it: 'He thought it almost a miracle to escape unhurt from such horrid wastes, roaring torrents, unwholesome vapour, and frightful fogs; drenched from top to toe, frozen with cold, and half dead with fatigue.' It was August and the fellow had clearly been exaggerating his brush with doom, and was astonished to be told that Lady Murray was about to go over the Pass in a chaise the next day. 'I wished to see it,' wrote Lady Murray, 'and I had come back from Fort William on purpose.' Needless to say, the indefatigable widow with proper care and good horses felt not a tremor of fear but, drinking in the view from the highest point, rather 'My mind was raised to a state of awe and seriousness, that led to the great Creator of all; and I almost forgot I belonged to this world, till the postillion reminded me it was time to re-enter the carriage.'[19]

In the summer of 1732, Wade's men returned to familiar ground to construct a new road between Fort Augustus and Inverness along the line more or less of the present B862. Plans were also made for a new bridge over the Tay at Aberfeldy, a handsome structure of five arches spanning 370 feet, designed by William Adam, the leading Scottish architect of the period. Its cost of over £3,500 soaked up around three-quarters of the road-building budget for 1733. In October that year Wade informed the Lord Advocate that bad weather had interrupted the work – '. . . floods so violent that little could be done'– and now a press was on to complete as much as possible before the winter closed in: 'I am labouring to get it as high as the Pavement and leave the Parapet Wall for another year.'[20] The general came to consider the Tay Bridge his highest achievement. Its opening was attended by a review of the troops in August 1735, and Alexander Robertson, the laird of Struan, celebrated the event with a poem published in the *Edinburgh Evening Courant*.

The supervision of the work on the Aberfeldy bridge fell to Wade's subordinate, William Caulfeild, another Irish officer who was appointed inspector of roads in 1732. Caulfeild took on a more important role as the years passed until in July 1739, after Wade was promoted to full general and was succeeded as commander in Scotland by Lieutenant-General Jasper Clayton, he was given full command of the continuing programme of road-building. During Clayton's time (1741–42), Caulfeild oversaw the laying of the Stirling–Crieff road (now the A823) and, in 1744–45, he turned his attention to the west coast, to the road between Dumbarton and Inveraray (now the A82 – A83). He planned and executed the route north from Inveraray to the head of Loch Awe. From this location, he oversaw a branch to the east to Tyndrum and the onward connection via Glen Orchy (now the B8074) to the military road across the wastes of Rannoch Moor to Glencoe; and the road west through the Pass of Brander, which passage was completed in 1754, to Bonawe. The extension further west to Connel and Oban was not finished until after the building of the Bridge of Awe crossing in 1779.[21]

William Caulfeild's contribution to the road network has tended, at least outside the Highlands, to be overshadowed by that of his commander. In the event, he oversaw the construction of more road miles than Wade, some 700 to his predecessor's 250, and made more impact at least in Inverness, where he is remembered in the name of Caulfeild Road. When Sir John Cope took over as commander in Scotland after Lieutenant-General Clayton was killed at the battle of Dettingen in 1743, Caulfeild served as the army's quartermaster. Reputed to have been a good-natured and generous host, there is a story, probably apocryphal, that his house on the outskirts of Inverness acquired its name of Cradlehall from a device that was used to hoist inebriated guests upstairs to bed. He held the post of inspector of roads until 1767, when he died or retired, to be succeeded by Lieutenant-Colonel Skene.

Road-building resumed after the defeat of the Jacobites in 1746.[22] The army was particularly busy at this time; as well as roads and fortifications at Fort Augustus, Fort George was being constructed at Ardersier, east of Inverness (the original Fort George on Castlehill in Inverness having been destroyed by the Jacobites). Men from five regiments were assigned to road-building in 1749: 300 from Guise's regiment to work on the Braemar–Spittal of Glenshee road; 300 Welsh Fusiliers on the Blairgowrie–Spittal of Glenshee section; 300 respectively from Pulteney's Regiment and Sackville's Regiment on the road from the head of Loch Earn to the Pass of Leny; and 150 from Ancrum's regiment on the road from Dumbarton to Inverary. Further contingents worked on repairs to existing military roads. This immense effort was part of a larger project to occupy and pacify the Highlands, continuing on a more expansive scale what Wade had set out to do 20 years earlier. Now, considerable sums of money were being spent: £3,933 between June and mid September 1749, more than Wade's whole budget for 1729. Caulfeild reckoned in 1749 that for three years' work, needed to complete the Dumbarton–Inverary, Stirling–Fort William and Fort Augustus–Bernera roads, a sum of £14,301 would be required.

In the next decade the soldiers completed the link between Dumbarton and Inveraray; the Stirling–Fort William road via the Devil's Staircase and Kinlochleven (A84, A85, A82); the route between Tyndrum and Inveraray (A85, A819); and the Lecht road, linking Blairgowrie via Braemar to Grantown-on-Spey and the new Fort George on its peninsula commanding the northern end of the Great Glen (A93, B976, A939). Work began in 1748 on the road from Luss via the west shore of Loch Lomond to Inveraray. 'This way was carried on by 50 or 100 men at a time and before Winter they brought it to Loch Skeen [Loch Fyne?],' noted Sir John Clerk of Penicuik. 'However, there were several beginnings made to it, even in 1745, when the Rebels carried away some of the men prisoners.'[23] Sir John says that he intended to have an inscription made in Latin to be erected at the Bridge of Luss to commemo-rate the endeavour but changed his mind when he found how much it would cost to have it cut in stone. The effects of some of this road-building were recorded some years later in the pages of the *Statistical Account of Scotland*. For example, it was noted that in former times the ferry at Dunoon had been the principal 'inlet' from the low country to Argyll but that the 'great road ... carried by Lochlomond round the head of Lochlong and through Glencroe to Inverary' had led to a fall in population in Dunoon.[24]

During this period the first military road to be laid north of Inverness was the 52 miles constructed between Contin and Poolewe, in 1762–63, by 70 men of the 8th Foot. Wade himself had conceived the road over the Devil's Staircase linking Fort William to Glencoe, but one other route for which Wade foresaw a use remained on paper; this was a road from Ruthven via Glen Feshie to Braemar to link Strathspey to Deeside. On a bend on the A939, where it drops northward from the Lecht towards Tomintoul, the soldiers left a small memorial to their passing. Somewhat eroded and spattered with lichen, the inscription on the stone by the well records the work of five companies of the 33rd Regiment who made the road in 1753–54. In 1748, Lord Ancrum's Regiment, the 24th, made the road through Glen Croe and put up the stone on the ridge between it and Glen Kinglass with the inscription that has bequeathed its text to the spot. Lady Sarah Murray noted this event as follows:

In the year 1746 [*sic*], the 24th regiment, Lord Ancram Colonel ... being employed in making that road to Inveraray, as I have been informed by a good friend of mine, who was then a young Lieutenant in that regiment; when they had completed the zig-zag to the top of the hill, they set up a stone like a tombstone, under a black rock, and engraved thereon the words, 'Rest, and be thankful'.

Lady Murray also says that the stone was broken not long after its erection but was repaired by the 23rd Regiment in 1768; here she is mistaken, as the repairs were done by the 93rd.[25]

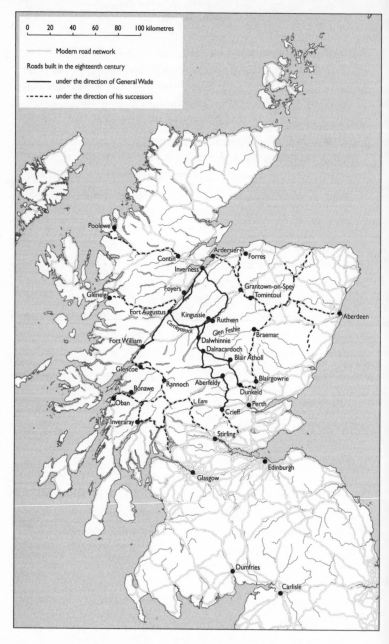

Poolewe

Ardersier

Contin

Forres

Inverness

Foyers

Grantown-on-Spey
Tomintoul

Glenelg

Fort Augustus

Kingussie

Ruthven

Aberdeen

Corrieyairack

Glen Feshie

Braemar

Fort William

Dalwhinnie

Dalnacardoch

Glencoe

Blair Atholl

Bonawe

Rannoch

Aberfeldy

Blairgowrie

Oban

L. Earn

Dunkeld

Inveraray

Crieff

Perth

Stirling

Edinburgh

Glasgow

Dumfries

Carlisle

*Map 5. The military roads built under the direction
of General George Wade and his successors.*

The military road-building programme continued for another 20 years or so after William Caulfeild's death in 1767. On the last day of August 1773, Samuel Johnson and James Boswell reached Glenmoriston on their way to Skye and came upon 'a party of soldiers, under a serjeant's command, at work upon the road. We gave them two shillings to drink. They came to our inn and made merry in the barn.'[26]

CHAPTER 6

Hard travelling

'it was dark night ... and we were all much fatigued ...'

The estates of the lairds and chieftains who had chosen the Jacobite side in the 1745 Rising were forfeited and taken over by the government – in effect, nationalised – and put under the charge of a commission dedicated to their management. The commission's surveyors were soon commenting on the infrastructure. 'The Roads in the East part of this Barony [i.e. close to Inverness] are pretty good tho' not made,' wrote one about the Lovat country. 'But the Communication with Glenstrathfarrer (the West part) is very difficult, the making of a road to that part of the Country, and building a Bridge near the Water of Bewley [Beauly] would be very useful.'[1] Work was in progress on the road between Beauly and Inverness in June 1762, and at around the same time another road was being laid between Castle Leod and the Conon. 'The Key of all improvements in the Highlands is by first making the country accessible,' declared Sir Alexander Mackenzie of Coul in a letter on 12 February 1760.[2]

The list of improvements to be implemented on the Struan and Lochgarry estates in the summer of 1773 included the small sum of £8 for roads out of a total of £444; the largest item, £300, was earmarked for building a new inn at Dalnacardoch. The benefit of a route running east–west across the central

Highlands was recognised in 1754 by a Colonel Watson; such a thoroughfare would cross the three north–south roads already built or in progress. Watson named Alyth as his starting point in the east and, with a dozen men and a sergeant, completed the section from Tummel Bridge west along the north side of Loch Rannoch (now the B846). The country people, it was reported, were so fond of these 16 miles of metalled way that they worked cheerfully on it and wore out the allocated spades and shovels in four years.[3]

That Alexander Robertson of Struan, along whose lands Rannoch lay, had saluted the Tay Bridge in verse was no indicator of a generally favourable attitude to the new roads. He had died at the age of 81 in 1749 but, because of the Jacobite sympathies of the family, his heirs had lost the estate in 1754; when it was restored to them 30 years later, it was noted that 'Till last year there could be no country worse of access or with fewer conveniencies for communication than Rannoch, as there was no road to it but was extremely bad and even dangerous for Riders. It was a saying of the late Strowan's that be the roads never so bad, his friends would see him, and he wanted no visits from his enemies.'[4] Despite the efforts of Colonel Watson the road across Rannoch was never completed and the western part of Rannoch Moor stretching from the railway station to where the A82 plunges into the throat of Glen Coe remains untarnished by tarmac. Caulfeild's verse calling for a blessing on General Wade expressed a sentiment most travellers would endorse but this feeling was not universal throughout the Highlands. Burt recorded different reactions from the three classes he saw in Highland society. The chiefs and other gentlemen feared that incoming strangers would, with their 'suggestions of liberty', erode their local power, lay them open to invasion, and make their followers effeminate once they no longer had to wade through rivers. 'And there is a pecuniary Reason concealed, relating to some foreign Courts, which to you I need not explain,' wrote Burt, probably alluding to Jacobites receiving money from the exiled Pretender, or rents being collected to be sent overseas to absent chieftains. 'The middling Order' protested that the new roads meant they had to shoe their horses – well, why not, argued Burt, before giving the reply himself: 'But where is the Iron, the Forge, the Farrier, the People within a reasonable Distance to maintain him? And lastly, where is the principal requisite – Money?' The 'lowest Class' who walked without shoes were said to complain that the gravel hurt their feet whether naked or enclosed in thin brogues. Burt dismissed this opinion as the contemptuous thoughts of strangers and added that ever since he had known the Highlands, 'I never doubted but the Natives had their Share of natural Understanding with the rest of Mankind.'[5]

Cattle drovers also complained, and with more justification, that the gravel harmed the hooves of the beasts, and it became customary to shoe cattle.[6] In his history of the Mackintosh clan, published in 1880, Alexander Mackintosh Shaw wrote that Wade's roads were 'resented by all classes from a dislike of innovation, and by the chiefs particularly because such an opening of the country would diminish the strength of their fastnesses in time of war, and expose their clansmen to the tampering of strangers in time of peace'.[7] Thomas Pennant discovered as much on his journey to the north in 1769, that the military roads had been 'at first very disagreeable to the old Chieftains, and lessened their influence greatly; for by admitting strangers among them, their clans were taught that the Lairds were not the first of men'.[8] Shaw also noted how in 1729 Wade had to ask Lachlan Mackintosh, chief of the clan that occupied the territory to the south of Inverness through which the new road was being driven to Strathspey, to desire his people not to molest the workmen. Shaw's view was written long after the events but that this was the reality in the 1720s is given credence by the comment of the Revd Roderick Morison who, in his account of the parish of Kintail in 1792, noted: 'Till of late, the people of Kintail, as well as other Highlanders, had a strong aversion to roads. The more inaccessible, the more secure, was their maxim.'⁹ The benefits to commerce were unquestionable and the ease with which troops could now move through the central Highlands played a part in suppressing lawlessness. No one, however, missed the irony in 1745 when, as government troops under Sir John Cope hurried north to Inverness, the Jacobite forces raised by Prince Charles at Glenfinnan adroitly avoided confrontation and gained untrammelled access to Perth by nipping over the Corrieyairack Pass along the road Wade's men had made there 14 years earlier.

Sir John Clerk of Penicuik ventured north on the new military road in 1739: 'We lay a night at Perth and from thence by way of Dunkel came to General Wade's high road, which I pursued to Ruthven in Badenoch, where it ended . . . I traveled it in a chaise, and found all the parts of this useful way exceedingly good.'¹⁰ Simon Fraser, Lord Lovat, who was brave enough to run a carriage, a four-wheeled vehicle he called his chariot, and to travel in it between his home near Beauly and Edinburgh, had a less 'happy' experience. This was in 1740, only 15 years after the first private carriage had been seen on the streets of Glasgow.¹¹ Lovat recorded his travail in a letter written after he had reached the capital. Two days before they set off, one of his coach mares suddenly dropped dead. It could have been an omen. On the day before departure, a hind wheel broke, delaying them by two days. Finally on the road on 30 July with his two daughters, Lovat passed through Inverness and 'came all night to Corribrough [near Tomatin] with Evan Baillie and Duncan Fraser, and my chariot did very well. I brought my wheelwright with me the length of Aviemore in case of accidents, and there I parted with him . . .' Despite the assurances of the wright, the hind axletree broke eight miles south of Aviemore. 'My girles were forced to go on bare horses behind footmen, and I was obliged to ride myself, tho' I was very tender, and the day very cold.' A gang of men pulled the carriage to Ruthven, where another wheelwright and a smith could make repairs.

This cost another two days of time, not to mention the costs of the work and accommodation. The Highland road, however, was not yet done with Lovat's chariot as less than four miles south of Ruthven the axle broke again. The disconsolate Lovat carried on to Dalnacardoch, where the innkeeper tried to cheer him by telling him that wrights at Blair Atholl were as good as any in the kingdom. The carriage fixed and once more on the road, the party made it as far as Castle Drummond before bad weather forced them to halt for another two days. Three miles from the castle on their resumed journey, the front axletree broke and they had to wait on a stormy hillside until help could be summoned and a new axletree fashioned – 'it was dark night before we came to Dunblaine, which is but eight miles from Castle Drummond, and we were all much fatigued'. Better progress next day brought them to Linlithgow and at last, on the following day, to Edinburgh, a total journey time of 12 days 'which was seven days more than the ordinary'.[12]

Travel became a little easier as the decades passed. From 1770 we have the bills incurred by Frances Cochrane for driving a coach from Novar in Ross-shire to Edinburgh, a five-day journey. The first item on the account is 3d, the cost of crossing the Conon on the ferry at 'scuddel' [now Conon Bridge]. Cochrane had a companion, not named but always referred to as 'the boyie', for whom he bought several items en route: a pair of gloves, a handkerchief, half a pound of soap, two pairs of shoes. These were all charged to the account, along with feed for the horses, accommodation, meals, tolls, and so on. The travellers stopped overnight at Inverness, 'Dalmagerrie' near Moy, Dalwhinnie and Perth.[13] (See Table 1.)

We owe gratitude to several travellers who left us their impressions of travel in the north during this time. One such was the Right Revd Robert Forbes, whom I have already quoted. Aberdeenshire-born, Forbes as an episcopal clergyman was arrested for his Jacobite sympathies and imprisoned until the middle of 1746. Elected Bishop of Ross and Caithness in 1762, he set out that year with his wife to travel from his home in Leith to see his new diocese. The road from Perth to Dunkeld was 'most charming', he wrote. 'Strath-Tay is one of the most amiable Countries Eye can behold.' A little later he was noting the 'huge mountains, beautifully spangled with woods and adorned with large flocks of sheep' in the vicinity of Blair Atholl. Forbes and his wife overnighted at Perth, Dalnacardoch and Aviemore on their way to Inverness. Mrs Forbes grew frightened in the pass of Killiecrankie by the proximity of their wheels to the edge of the precipice, declined the bishop's offer to divert her mind by kissing, and insisted on getting out to follow the equipage on foot. The Slochd was wilder still, 'a very low and narrow Pass ... when you see nothing but ye Heavens above, and an Hill on each hand', where the wild goats seemed to hang on with their beards and feet, although even in such a bleak spot there were plenty of 'large, juicy, wild Strawberries of a Flavour peculiarly fine'.[14]

Fearing that the roads in Ross-shire and beyond would be bad, the bishop left his wife in Inverness and crossed in the ferry from Ardersier to Fortrose. To his chagrin he found the roads 'tho only natural, extremely good' and travelled by chaise as far as Tain. Here he and his companions had to abandon wheels in favour of the saddle, 'as there is no Chaise-Road through Caithness, but through Sutherland a Machine may drive very well'. Here, the bishop is probably talking of roads that lay over pasture on gravelly and sandy links, of which there are long stretches along this coast. On 4 August the party rose very early and set off from Clyne (Brora). They forded the Helmsdale at half past six to begin the ascent over the Ord. They breakfasted at the inn at Ousdale, where they were astonished by the choice of teas and coffee in what they had been advised to be a 'poor and despicable Country'. Crossing the Causewaymire proved a trial – one of the riders and his horse sank in a slough, and had to be hauled to safety – but at last they won to Thurso before 11 o'clock at night – '36 long Scots miles', in the bishop's words.

The Flintshire-born naturalist and travel writer Thomas Pennant had an easier time of it during his first journey to the north in 1769. He took a month to ride from his home in Chester via Berwick and Edinburgh to the edge of the Highlands and, after a night in a good inn at Inver, near Dunkeld, crossed the Tay on the ferry to find 'a most excellent road' on the north bank that had been made 'at the sole expence of the present Lord Breadalbane who . . . also erected thirty-two stone bridges over the torrents that rush from the mountains'.[15] Pennant noted the 'very fine' military road through Killiecrankie before riding east to Glen Tilt. Here he recorded that the road he followed above the Tilt was the 'most dangerous and the most horrible I have ever travelled', and this from a man who had travelled widely on the continent of Europe. On the narrow, rugged path, the horses 'often were obliged to cross their legs in order to pick a secure place for their feet'. The intrepid horseman carried on via Braemar and Ballater, over the hills to the east of the main Cairngorm massif, and crossed the Spey on a ferry to reach Fochabers. As he progressed up the east coast of Ross and Sutherland, he commented on the 'great ferry' (Meikle Ferry) and the 'little ferry' (Littleferry, or Portbeg, at the mouth of the Fleet), where 'the boat [was] as dangerous as the last'. While fording the river at Helmsdale, he dismounted to look for lampreys and then tackled the Ord 'ascending that vast promontory on a good road winding up its steep sides, and impending in many parts over the sea, infinitely more high and horrible than our Penmaen Mawr'. On his southward journey, Pennant followed the east shore of Loch Ness, where he thought the road sometimes 'resembled a fine and regular avenue' but elsewhere 'wound about the sides of the hills . . . frequently cut thro' the rock which on one side formed a solid wall; on the other a steep precipice.' South of Fort William the road climbed to an 'awfull height' above Loch Leven. The route over the mountain south of Kinlochleven, he thought the 'highest publick road in Great Britain'. His view of the military roads in general was that they were 'excellent' but in places 'injudiciously planned, often carried far about, and often so steep as to be scarce surmountable; whereas had the engineer followed the track used by the inhabitants, those inconveniencies would have been avoided'.

Pennant's published account of his journey to the far north proved very popular, encouraging him to make a second visit to the Highlands in 1772, this time focusing on the west coast and, with some companions, hiring a cutter from Greenock to explore the islands. Landing on the mainland from Skye after some weeks exploring the Hebrides, the travellers rode through Strathcanaird and past Suilven, where 'the blackness of the moors by no means assisted to cheer our ideas'. The naturalist had now gone well beyond the reach of the military roads. In Assynt they were told that the way further on was impassable for horses and, giving up on their plan to reach 'the extremity of the island', the party turned south again, 'the same road through a variety of bog, and hazardous rock, that nothing but our shoeless little steeds could have carried us over'. Loch Broom was busy with herring fishers but they secured a boat and made a stormy passage to Dundonell. The rest of their journey south was done by a combination of riding and sailing, but mostly the latter, clearly the easier way to cover long distances on the west coast, until the voyage ended in the bay of Ardmaddie. Travelling south, Pennant rode along the Tay in the direction of Killin. 'The military road through this country is planned with a distinguished want of judgement,' he complained, 'a series of undulations, quite unnecessary, distress the traveller for a considerable part of the way.' At Kenmore, he crossed the Tay on a temporary bridge close to which 'a most elegant bridge is now constructing ... under the direction of captain Archibald Campbel [*sic*] at the expense of Lord Breadalbane, consisting of three arches; and a smaller one on each side in case of floods.'

Among the travellers, Lady Sarah Murray stands out as the most engaging. Her book begins with 'Advice for the Traveller':

'Provide yourself with a strong roomy carriage, and have the springs well corded; have also a stop-pole and strong chain to the chaise. Take with you linch-pins, and four shackles ... a turn-screw, fit for fastening the nuts belonging to the shackles; a hammer, and some straps.' Thus equipped with tools and spares, and a strong, handy postillion to manage the driving and the equipage, Lady Murray, aged 52 and the widow of a naval officer, set off in 1796 to travel through Scotland for some 2,000 miles. In the Trossachs near Loch Katrine, she thrilled to the wildness of the scenery: 'My heart was raised to heaven in awful silence; whilst that of my poor man was depressed to the dread of hell. He was walking somewhat before the horses, who were step by step thumping the carriage over rocks.'[16] She does not record any need for the spare 'linch-pins' and shackles.

The works of Ossian, James Macpherson's recreation of ancient Gaelic poetry, and the influence of the Romantic movement in the arts, were encouraging more people to travel in the Highlands by this time. Accommodation standards were inevitably and, many would say, none too soon being driven upwards in the competition to attract guests. 'Nowhere in the Highlands has more attention been paid to the accommodation of the traveller than on the property of Lord Breadalbane,' wrote the minister of Glenorchy and Inisshail. 'In a line of public road, of above 90 miles in length, extending from Inveraray to Perth, good inns, with suitable offices, are built, at proper stages, and kept in repair at considerable expence by his lordship' and the innkeepers were carefully chosen and 'of civil and obliging deportment.'[17]

In September 1784, Lieutenant-General Mackay, commander-in-chief in Scotland, wrote that the military roads under his command amounted to around 1,100 miles. 'The first observation I would therefore make is that however proper and necessary the making of these roads may originally have been, a line should be drawn where the country is capable of keeping them in repair by the Statute Labour, and where, from the wildness and barrenness of the country and the small number of inhabitants, the expense must unavoidably be defrayed by the public.'[18] The general said more investigation would be needed but he thought the military roads in the south and south-west (from Dumfries around to Ballintrae in Ayrshire, to quicken the movement of troops to Ireland) and the roads in the north-east (from Stonehaven via Aberdeen to Portsoy and via Huntly to Fochabers and Portsoy) could go onto the purses of the county gentry; that is, be left to the care of the Commissioners of Supply in the various counties.

'The rebuilding and repairing of bridges that suffer by sudden torrents from the mountains is a large annual expense,' he noted. Also: 'I think it proper to inform your Lordships that at present all the Highland roads are in general in very bad repair ... it has not been in [my] power to remedy this, from want of troops to work upon them ...' The remedy, from the point of view of the military, was to recruit civilian help. This, however, was not always forthcoming. When the Duke of Argyll, as commander-in-chief in Scotland, and Colonel Robert Skeen, inspector of roads, wrote to the Commissioners of Supply in Inverness in 1774 to ask for some statute labour to be assigned to work on the military roads, as was now the practice in other counties, the Commissioners decided that as all their statute labour would be needed to complete their own roads 'for several years to come', it would be 'improper at this time to order out the inhabitants to work on the military roads'. They also pointed out a problem in that in many places the military roads lay a great distance from the settlements.[19] The surveyor Alexander Nimmo, when he came to map the bounds of Inverness-shire in 1806, thought that Wade had been 'no engineer', possibly an unjust judgement coloured by hindsight, and observed that the military road that came down the hill from Achindown by Kilravock had been 'quite abandoned' in favour of the county road to the east of Cawdor.[20] The army authorities continued to express a wish to get rid of responsibility for roads that they probably no longer saw as fulfilling a military need. In 1798 the commander-in-chief in Scotland, Sir Ralph Abercromby, told the Treasury that the roads no longer needed government support and should be passed to the care of the county authorities, although the maintenance of bridges would still need government funds that could be paid through the civil power. The military roads were being gradually abandoned by this time, until only some 500 miles remained on their budget.[21] The responsibility for all roads was soon to pass from the hands of the military to the civilian power.

PART 3

The public roads and new ways of travel

CHAPTER 7

County roads

'very troublesome to all passengers going that way . . .'

The army took care of the construction and maintenance of only a number of key strategic routes. Most of the road network in the eighteenth century fell under the jurisdiction of the civil authorities. The Commissioners of Supply, the committees of landowners and heritors originally formed in 1667 to assess properties for the land tax, came to acquire additional duties that included responsibility for roads and bridges. Their powers were renewed by two Acts in 1718 that gave them and the Justices of the Peace in each shire (there was often considerable overlap between the membership of these two bodies) the right to call out the workers for three days' labour before the end of June and another three after the harvest-time. Throughout Scotland during the later eighteenth century it must have been common to see gangs of locals toiling with pick, shovel and wheelbarrow on the roads. However well-intentioned, the Commissioners were severely constrained by the resources at their disposal and by the likelihood or not of their fellow land-owners cooperating in releasing tenants to carry out statute labour. Some roads were constructed privately at this time. The Duke of Gordon considered having a carriage road, four feet wide, built between Badenoch and Lochaber in 1784, as he mentioned in a letter written to his factor, but we cannot be certain this project was ever realised.[1] Sir John Sinclair of Ulbster, in Caithness, is reputed to have called out statute labour to form the road called the Causewaymire across the great boggy moor in the centre of the county between Latheronwheel and Halkirk in a short space of time but, as the existence of this route was indicated on the maps in Blaeu's Atlas in 1654, it is more likely the case that Sir John's effort at road-building was directed at repairing or improving an existing track.[2]

Among the oldest surviving sets of minutes for Commissioners of Supply in the Highlands are those for the county of Sutherland, which start in June 1736, when a meeting was called by the sheriff to appoint a collector for the land tax. It is not until 1763 that the county's roads find a mention in the proceedings.[3] At around the same time the condition of the roads appears in the records for other counties. The minutes of the Inverness-shire Commissioners for 2 June 1762, for example, note that they 'took under their Consideration the Representations now as then made of the loss and Disadvantage sustained by the County and travellers in generall thorrow the neglect of not repairing publick high roads leading from this town'.[4] The state of the road from Inverness to the ferry over the Beauly river, the single land route to everywhere to the north, was especially troubling because it was 'of constant resort as much so as any road in Scotland by Wheel carriages as well as Horses'. To keep it in order and to erect bridges over burns was beyond the capacity of the statute labour gangs without 'a considerable outlay' on tools, materials and the employment of skilled 'artificers', concluded the commissioners, who applied their right to levy a duty for roads on the heritors of 10s Scots for each £100 Scots of rental value of their properties, to be collected along with the annual land tax or cess. The money thus ingathered allowed a sum of £30 sterling to be earmarked for roads, funding that was to be committed each year for the next few decades for the same purpose. It was an amount that proved to be hardly enough and it was regularly augmented by sums from the so-called contingency fund also raised by the Commissioners. Inverness-shire is the largest of the old counties in Scotland at nearly 3,000 square kilometres and it probably had as many miles of road, even although many may have been little better than tracks, in 1760 as it has now.

Captain John Forbes, as factor on the Lovat estate in charge of the Beauly road work, presented a receipt in April 1762 for the £30 he had been granted in the previous year. At the same time the Commissioners received a petition from James Grant of Grant and his fellow heritors in the parishes of Urquhart and Glenmoriston to have the Inverness–Fort Augustus road along the north side of Loch Ness repaired. Other petitions followed – what one parish received, neighbouring parishes tended to seek – and the repair of roads soon became a standard item on the agenda of the Commissioners. Between 1762 and 1784, they were asked for aid for roads in Strathnairn, on Skye on the lands of Alexander MacDonald of MacDonald and the laird of Macleod (they were granted £20 each), in the parish of Durris [Dores], and in Glenurquhart, Glenmoriston, Stratherrick, Alvie, the Lochiel country in Lochaber, and Badenoch. In some years, petitioners were awarded very small slices from a small cake, as the Commissioners strove to help as many as they could – in 1775 only £2 was committed to the Aird and Strathglass roads, and £5 to each of Glenurquhart, Strathnairn and Stratherrick. Duncan McDonell of Glengarry let the Commissioners know in 1774 that 'for several years past, he has been at great expence and trouble in making and repairing the high roads in the Country of Sleismeen & Sleishgarve which leads to Knoidart Morar and Glenelg', that he had not asked before for help from the Commissioners but that now they had come on some pieces of 'Rockish' ground and that it was 'absolutely necessary to build a few arches over waters and Burns'. He was granted £30.[5]

One high road features in the Inverness Commissioners' deliberations year on year – the one to Nairn. Despite running over fairly level ground and being only some 12 miles in length before it crossed the county boundary and became the problem of the Nairnshire Commissioners, it seemed to be a continual headache. Its very proximity to the town where the Commissioners met and its being the busiest road in the county, used by the citizens with the most influential voices, kept it foremost among their concerns. In 1765 attention was drawn to it being 'in great Disrepair and has been now for severall years neglected notwithstanding of repeated Complaints from Passengers and particularly from the Lords of Justiciary as often as they come here on Circuit'. Robert Walsh or Welsh, presumably a surveyor of some kind, was appointed to line out the Nairn road, taking care to do as little 'dammage' as possible to the cornfields, and 'Call out the People residing in these Bounds to work the Statute labour thereon.' The call was not always answered: in 1766 the Commissioners learned that one estate factor had prevented his tenants from 'going to work any more than for one day'. The naming of constables and overseers to 'punish those that shall be refractory in terms of the Statute' may not always have been very effective. In 1768 the tenants on the Earl of Moray's lands protested that the improvement of the road through Petty to Nairn would have damaged their cornfields, and the factor had been instructed to let the Commissioners know that he would put a stop to the work. To advance the roadworks 'with all possible despatch', as the delay was not only 'attended with some loss' but also reflected on the gentlemen's 'want of attention' to the policy on roads, the Commissioners called on all the inhabitants of the burgh to the east of the river Ness and all the tenants on the estates in the district to turn to, but in recognition of the Moray tenants' complaint, they had 'a skilful person' re-examine the line of the road to cause less damage to the fields. In 1772 a sub-committee was formed to deal with the Nairn road and given a £10 budget; it met on 23 June under a sense of urgency, 'as now the season is so far past', and called on tenants to turn out for work a week later from all the districts on the east side of the Ness. The labourers were to be supplied with 12 wheelbarrows, 13 picks and 21 spades. The committee felt that a constable need only be employed for one day in each week while the people were at work; it was his duty to warn the inhabitants at their homes and provide the overseer with a list of their names. The 'refractory' were to be prosecuted. Decades later, in June 1811, we find the Commissioners of Supply for Nairnshire fining 'as usual . . . the absentees from the roads during the last season in the sum of 9s each' before adjourning to consider appeals and 'otherways', which unfortunately appear not to have survived.[6] The Inverness–Nairn road remained unfinished in 1776 and the funds allotted for bridging some burns had not been sufficient. There was also a difficulty arising from the fact that the Nairnshire Commissioners of Supply had drawn the line of the road to pass to the north of the Muir of the Clans, '[which] is at times Impassable and very Dangerous'. The Inverness-shire Commissioners felt that the road should go by the south side. There was already to the north the post road, 'much frequented by strangers and passengers', running via Fort George. At last, in April 1778, the clerk of the Commissioners could record that the Nairn road could possibly be finished that season.

Unfortunately, the minutes of the Nairnshire Commissioners survive only from 1790, too late to leave for us any response they may have made to their neighbours' moans a decade earlier. As it was, in Nairn at that time the main problem was 'the wretched state of the Bridge', which had been built in 1632 by William Rose of Clava and damaged by a flood in 1782.[7] In July 1786 the burgh council approved a plan to repair it to permit carts and carriages to pass in time of flood, but no progress was made and in 1789 it was again a matter for discussion. The county, however, appears to have been in financial difficulty:

> That the Bridge is necessary will admit of no doubt, and if
> the funds of the Community were sufficient to make a

proper and permanent repair they could not be better laid out – But the situation of the Bridge at present is evidently such that the whole funds of the Borough if sold by rowp would not be near sufficient to repair it.

It would be throwing money away, concluded the councillors, to continue to make temporary repairs. Government aid would have to be sought and all should unite in claiming it, they argued, 'as it is well known that a passage Boat cannot be plyed in any part of the River near to the town, and that neither the Judges on the Circuit or the Kings Troops can do their duty ... unless the Bridge is either repaired or rebuilt.' In 1799 when the river flooded and all communication with the surrounding country was cut off for a time, the town leaders were moved to open a subscription fund for a new bridge. The provost, Alexander Penrose Cumming Gordon of Altyre, gave £100 from his own pocket and 'with the approbation of several Gentlemen of the County & respectable inhabitants of the town & neighbourhood, subscribed another Hundred pounds from the Community's, in order to assist in completing the said necessary Erection'. By March 1800 the fund was nearly equal to the work, and an architect, George Burn, had agreed to undertake the contract for not less than £1,000, and more if the subscriptions allowed. George Burn would later build the new bridge at Wick for the British Fisheries Society but in the meantime he and his elder brother James tackled the Nairn project. The work was fairly well advanced when in November 1803 another flood 'impaired' the centre pillar of the great arch 'and a considerable part of the foundation and superstructure carried away so as to endanger the whole fabric'. Major repair could not be effected until the later summer of 1804. The Burn brothers, however, could not afford the expense for the repairs and the burgh had to borrow another £100 before the work could proceed to completion.

The Inverness Commissioners devoted much attention to other routes leading from Inverness. 'Frequent complaints' led the president of the Commissioners to call a special meeting in July 1768 to consider 'the most effectual & speedy manner of makeing and repairing the high roads' to the west, to Lochend and Bunchrew, as well as to Nairn. In the summer of 1767 two burns – 'very troublesome to all passengers going that way' – had to be bridged on the Inverness–Beauly ferry route, and Captain Forbes was given £10 to cover the costs. Forbes came back in 1771 to ask for a further £12 to rebuild the bridge over the Bunchrew burn, a significant obstacle only three miles west of the town. It was brought to the Commissioners' attention in 1780 that the Beauly road had become encroached upon at the Green of Muirtown on the western fringe of Inverness and was no longer the legal breadth of 24 feet.[8]

For the Lochend road, the president of the Commissioners, William McIntosh, who happened also to be the provost of the burgh at the time, ordered all the inhabitants on the west side of the Ness to turn out to do statutory labour on the problem. But it was not enough. The lairds in that area agreed that what had been done had been 'well execute' but those who had done their three days' worth of toil had left at least four-fifths of the job unfinished. As is often the case with infrastructure projects, some locals objected. The several committees of Commissioners in the northern shires cooperated at least once on a large project. In December 1771, the Inverness-shire minutes note that an application on behalf of all was to be made to the Treasury for bridges over three major rivers – the Beauly, the Conon and the 'Auldgrand' (the lower stretch of the River Glas at Evanton, now called the Allt Graad on the A9 road sign): 'Such Bridges will be of great benefit in trade improvement and other accomodation which all the northern parts of Scotland would reap great benefite by and more particularly his majesty's tenants on the annexed estates of Lovat and Cromarty.' A Mr Smyton (Smeaton?) had prepared a report and estimates for this from the rents of the annexed estates; the 'preses' (president) of the Commissioners, John Forbes of Culloden, was to write to Simon

Fraser, MP for Inverness-shire, on the subject. This initiative failed and at least two of the bridges – over the Beauly and the Conon – were not to be built until 1809–10 under the auspices of the Commission for Roads and Bridges.

CHAPTER 8

Patchy improvements

'*the want of good roads . . .*'

By the end of the eighteenth century the road network varied widely in extent and quality. In a few far-flung parishes, there were no roads at all. The reader can almost feel the resignation in the statement of the author who described the Shetland parish of Nesting for the *Statistical Account* in 1793: 'The roads, bridges, etc are in the same state here as in every other part of Shetland; that is to say, there are none.'[1] Durness was without any, as was neighbouring Edderachilis save for such roads 'as the feet of men and cattle have made'.[2] Elsewhere they were described, for example, as 'quite neglected' (Craignish)[3], 'exceeding bad' (Kilfinan)[4], and 'exceedingly deep in winter (Dingwall)[5]. The minister in Watten in Caithness summarised the onslaught wrought by the elements on an unmade route:

> We have a more plain and direct tract, during the dry season of the year, to the ports of Wick and Thurso, for travellers as well as riders and carts: But . . . they become so soft after rain, and so blown by frost that in many places, during winter and spring, the best horses are not fit to drag a cart with safety.[6]

'The want of good roads,' wrote the same man, the Revd Joseph Taylor, was one of several things that were retarding the improvement of the place. Around Inverness, however, by this time the roads appear to have been much more satisfactory: 'properly attended' and 'annually repaired' in Dores[7], 'in excellent repair' in Petty[8], and 'in good repair' in Avoch on the Black Isle, where signposts stood at crossroads to direct the traveller[9]. The great north road through the parish of Urray at the root of the Black Isle was also 'kept in tolerable repair'.[10]

The variation in standard owed as much to local geology as to the use made by the Commissioners of Supply of statute labour or the income they could raise from assessment. With regard to Dornoch and the sandy, well-drained glacial soils in its vicinity, the Revd John Bethune had no doubt that 'Nature has made the public roads here passable; they owe little to industry . . .'.[11] The situation was similar in Golspie to the north: the public road was 'in tolerable repair' but was 'for the greatest part made by nature.'[12] Far to the south, in Argyllshire, the roads in Ardchattan and Muckairn were in good repair and had 'greatly improved within these last few years', although 'the bye roads especially such as lead to the glens are rugged, slippery and dangerous, lying in some parts along the brink of precipices, and so narrow that two men can hardly pass each other.'[13] A few lairds and gentlemen made good use of statute labour. This seems to have been the case in Cromdale: 'statute work goes on very punctually, without the smallest murmur. Stone bridges are erected over almost every rivulet, either by the proprietor or the county; and of course the roads are in the highest order.'[14] A compliant tenantry may have been rare; more often the locals found the demands of statute labour a nuisance. The Watten minister described his parishioners as being reluctant in this regard,[15] and in Rogart labour was 'not popular'.[16] By the end of the century, the statute labour requirement was being commuted either fully or partly into payment of a local tax. Apparently this may have become customary before Acts to allow it were passed for Ross and Cromarty in 1807 and for Inverness-shire in 1808.[17] These Acts brought in a graduated scale of tax depending on the rental value of the tenant's property. In Inverness and the parish of Urquhart and Glenmoriston, each man over the age of 15 paid 2s a year instead of turning out with spade and pick at times when he probably had already more than enough urgent work on his own land.[18] These contributions of a florin were supplemented by an assessment of 1d in the Scots pound of the valued rental and, in all, the commutation brought in road money amounting annually to £9 4s 11d in the 1790s to be used to hire labourers to do work. The anonymous contributor to the *Statistical Account* admitted the fund was small but, 'being managed with great care and economy', did 'wonders' in upholding the 50 or so miles of public road in the parish. The commutation rate varied – it was, for example, 1s 6d a year in Avoch from each 'liable' man, and 2s 6d from tenants 'for the strength of each plough'. This may have seemed hard for the poor without ready money, acknowledged the Revd James Smith, but every 'judicious farmer or well employed mechanic' could see it was 'more expedient' than spending summer days on road work.[19]

Reluctant or not, squads of men continued to tackle road improvements across the land. In Glassary in Argyll, where statute labour had not succeeded in keeping up the roads, the heritors had come together to secure an Act of Parliament to allow them to impose a road stent, a tax, at the rate of 1s to the pound sterling. Fired with enthusiasm, most of them advanced at once 15 years' stent, even in some cases borrowing hundreds of pounds on their own security, according to the minister, the Revd Dugald Campbell, a show of public spirit that resulted in a few years in some 12 miles of good highway, 24 feet wide, making six miles of the way from Inveraray to Campbeltown, and six miles from Lochgilphead 'up the country' in the direction of Lorne.[20] A similar scheme was started in Saddel and Skipness, where the roads were 'kept in good repair'.[21]

Road-making began on Lewis in 1791. After five years, some four miles had been laid across the deep bogs in the centre of the island in the direction of the west coast, and work had started on another road north towards Barvas.[22] On Mull, however, road-making was proceeding slowly and it was acknowledged that the available funds were 'disproportionate' to the natural 'impediments' that the engineers had to over-come.[23] 'It was not many years since roads began to be made in this parish,' wrote the ministers in Tongue on the north Sutherland coast. 'They are now carried on with great spirit and rendered as convenient as the nature of the ground will admit.[24] An 'excellent' road was started in 1792 to link Dingwall to Ullapool, site of one of the planned fishing settlements of the British Fisheries Society (see page 133).[25] Improvement to the road through the parish of Kiltearn on the north side of the Cromarty Firth was made with statute labour in 1790–91.[26] A road from Inverness to Glenelg along the west side of Loch Ness had been surveyed on the order of Lord Adam Gordon, the military commander in Scotland, but in 1796 it still awaited construction.[27]

A network of road connections, still skeletal in 1792, when the Revd Patrick M'Donald described them, spread out from the Oban–Connel axis. These had all been made in the last 33 years and were graced with four 'main inns', although, in the minister's opinion, 'rather too much whisky [was] drunk in all of them'.[28] Argyllshire seems to have been well served with roads – 'in no county has more been done during the last 20 years', wrote the minister of Glenorchy and Inishail in 1792, thanks to statute labour and an annual road assessment of more than £600. Two military roads passed through his parish and he felt moved to criticise them, saying the original line taken by the surveyors had been neither obvious nor proper: 'the road was brought to the gravel, and not the gravel to the road,' he states, before acknowledging that 'a more enlightened and liberal system of road-making is now adopted', which, he hoped, would smooth out some of the 'incommodious' gradients.[29] The recent 'very judicious' alteration of the road line from the 'excellent' inn at Dalmally to the Bridge of Awe had cost over £400 and 'presented such varied and agreeable views of water, of islands, of towering mountains, and sloping hills, as give an uncommon grandeur and sublimity to the landscape'.

The Duke of Argyll contributed a memorial to the government that was later published as an appendix to the first report of the Commissioners for Roads and Bridges: he protested that his lands in Argyll-shire and Inverness-shire, and those of his neighbours, suffered from a want of roads, and he had in mind one from Loch Moidart to the Corran of Ardgour to connect with the ferry across the narrows on Loch Linnhe to the Fort William road, a distance of nearly 35 miles that would cost up to £3,500. (The duke's road became in time the A861.)

The geography of the country, the east–west orientation of major glens, and a natural desire to establish connections between main centres and outlying districts led to the road network taking the form of radiating axes. This was true of Wester Ross, where all roads tended to lead towards Dingwall, and in the western regions of Inverness-shire, where the Great Glen was the focus. Even today to travel, say, from Shiel Bridge to Mallaig, some 20 miles as the eagle flies, involves a long drive and a ferry crossing via Skye, or an even longer drive via Fort William. The need to establish what was called cross-roads was recognised at the end of the eighteenth century. 'Perhaps a few cross roads would be also proper,' thought Roderick Macrae in Applecross, having in mind one between Ullapool and Poolewe, adding that, if that could be extended to Lochcarron 'it would be of vast service to the West Highlands in general'.[30]

It was mentioned earlier how in 1762 Sir James Grant sought support from the Commissioners of Supply in constructing a road from Inverness along the west bank of Loch Ness. This became very slow work, both from the 'extreme difficulty' of the terrain and 'the narrowness of the funds', but perseverance and donations of funds by some gentlemen kept the project alive, with the result that in 30 years there existed what was described as 'an excellent road ... through the woods and rock of Abriachan'. In some places the labourers had been forced to cut and blast rock with iron tools. Sir James had also built 'an exceeding good inn' in Glenurquhart. The more southern section of this route, between Drumnadrochit and Fort Augustus, was by 1796 still too narrow for carriages but these could be driven west from Drum to Corriemonie.[31]

Bridges were obvious key components of the road network. The military built a considerable number during the eighteenth century but several were the result of local initiatives and were already quite old by the time Wade and Caulfeild's men hove into view. One such was the single-span arch over the stream at Latheronwheel in Caithness built in about 1726.[32] The old bridge at Brora dates from 1758 [33] but the name of the place – in Norse, 'bridge river' – is a reminder that a crossing over the gorge here has existed since at least the Middle Ages. The old bridge at Invermoriston is of eighteenth-century vintage, and the long pedigree of the place-name Drumnadrochit – the ridge of the bridge, in Gaelic – would suggest an old crossing of the Enrick at that settlement. The high arch of the packhorse bridge at Carrbridge is deservedly famous, its battered state a reminder of how it has survived several destructive floods. The Grant lairds had it built with funds from the stipend for Duthil parish and the work was done in the summer of 1717 by a stonemason called John Niccolsone. A fine bridge, built in 1731 by John Sinclair of Ulbster, the grandfather of the famous Sir John, spanned the Thurso river at Halkirk, 70 years before Thurso itself could boast of such a structure.[34] In the Kintyre peninsula the Commissioners of Supply were in the habit of laying large planks across burns 'for the security of foot travellers ... yet ... speats or floods are so high and rapid that the strongest horse cannot cross them'.[35] A similar though possibly more lasting form of construction was to be found in Orkney at the mouth of the Loch of Stenness, where logs of wood were laid across stone piers.[36] A bridge over the Ness at Inverness, a crucial link in the route across the Great Glen, was constructed in the mid-fourteenth century, a wooden structure that had a chequered existence; in 1411, it was set alight by the marauding followers of the Lord of the Isles. This bridge collapsed in 1664, reportedly when a carpenter at work on repairs inadvertently cut a supporting beam, taking some 200 pedestrians with it, a catastrophe described by James Fraser, minister of Wardlaw: 'Four of the townsmen broke legs and thighs, some sixteen had their heads, arms and thighs bruised; all the children safe, without a scart; and, by Providence, not one perished.'[37] Such was the poverty-stricken state of the town's finances that it was not replaced until a stone bridge, funded to the tune of £1,300 by subscriptions ordered by the Privy Council in March 1680 to be taken up throughout the country, was completed in 1684. Parliament granted the rights to the town to charge tolls to maintain it.[38]

The funding of bridge construction was commonly supported by local tolls. In September 1681, parliament in Edinburgh passed an act in response to a petition from Andrew Fraser, the laird of Kinmundy, empowering him to uplift a toll on the stone bridge he had constructed over the Dye 'upon one of the most impetuous waters within the kingdom' on the Cairn o'Mount road between Fettercairn and Banchory. The initial funding for the construction had come from a mortification of 2,000 merks but that was not enough to cover maintenance; parliament set the tolls at 8d Scots for each saddled horse and his rider, or each horse with a burden, and 4d for each man, woman, horse, ox, cow or other small beast, the charges to run for the ensuing 19 years.[39]

In the absence of bridges, travellers had frequent recourse to the more dangerous option of fords, where a safe crossing depended on a degree of fitness as well as the state of the water. In 1791, Daniel Rose recorded how the ford across the head of the Cromarty Firth between Ferintosh and Dingwall would be attempted by some at the wrong time of the tide with 'frequently fatal' consequence, and argued that a bridge over the Conon would save many lives.[40]

The income to the government from the forfeited estates began to be ploughed back into infrastructure. This was the largest single source of funds for the new bridge over the Tay at Perth, which Thomas Pennant thought the 'most beautiful . . . of the kind in North Britain' when he rode across it barely two years after it had been completed in 1771. Built by John Smeaton, 40 per cent of its cost of £26,000 had come from the Commissioners for the Forfeited Estates, and the remainder from the burgh of Perth, private subscribers and the Earl of Kinnoull, who received the security of the tolls.[41] The Perth bridge was a crucial strategic link in the transport network extending into the north and its earlier incarnations, presumably wooden, had been destroyed by rampaging floods on several occasions – in 1210, 1573, 1582, 1589 and 1621. Smeaton's structure survived a similar assault in 1774.

At the end of the eighteenth century, local ferries also played a large part in the transport network. The Findhorn river in the 1790s in the parish of Ardclach had only one bridge across it, at Dulsie Bridge on the military road, and was otherwise 'rapid and frequently impassable everywhere'.[42] There were three ferries, 'but owing either to the mismanagement of the boatmen, or temerity of the people, many lives are lost', wrote the minister. On the other hand, the minister in Rosemarkie could boast that the ferry between neighbouring Chanonry (Fortrose) and Fort George was 'so safe . . . that there is not an instance of any being lost on it in memory of man'.[43] There were frequent calls for bridges to be thrown across the Spey, a more significant obstacle than the Findhorn, especially in the vicinity of Fochabers.

Throughout the eighteenth and nineteenth centuries a series of parliamentary acts relating to roads and bridges were passed, producing an array of arrangements that varied from county to county. The first Scottish turnpike roads, routes where travellers paid a toll to be spent on upkeep, were approved in 1713, but only in Midlothian, then known as the county of Edinburgh. Over the succeeding decades other counties applied for and acquired turnpike acts and by 1800 they were quite general throughout Scotland. Some of them were approved for a limited duration, perhaps 20 or 31 years, but these terms could be renewed.[44]

CHAPTER 9

The Commission

'rendering our roads as complete as possible . . .'

The passing of the parliamentary act on 4 July 1803 to establish a Commission dedicated to the making of roads and bridges in the Highlands, followed on 27 July by an act to authorise the construction of a canal through the Great Glen, were landmark events. Over the ensuing 60 years the Commission for Roads and Bridges, building on the existing pattern of roads, laid down the network that still channels road travel through the region today. That the Commission came about when it did was due to a social crisis. By the end of the eighteenth century, revolution and the rise of democratic ideals in France, along with reports of civil unrest beyond the Highland line, quickened fears in the British government that trouble could come from the north unless steps were taken to boost the economy and provide gainful work for a growing population.

The engineer Thomas Telford was despatched to visit the Highlands to see what might be done not only to improve communications but also to promote sea fishing. Telford made his long tour of inspection to the far northern mainland, and recommended the development of the road network, the construction of the canal through the Great Glen and the development of a fishing port at Wick. The latter was to be the responsibility of the British Fisheries Society; established in

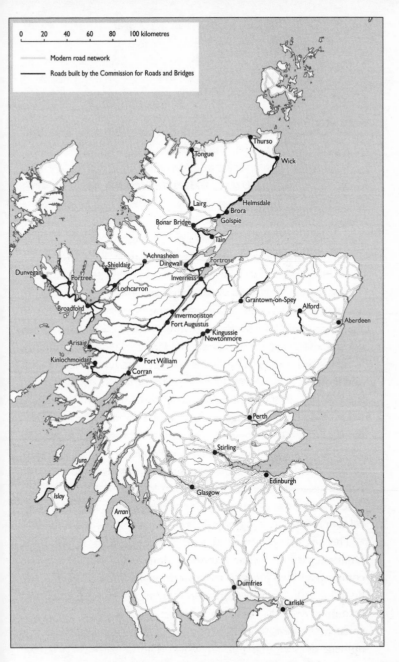

Map 6. Roads built under the Commission for Highland Roads and Bridges by 1821.

1786, the society had already founded fishing stations at Tobermory, Lochbay and Ullapool to exploit a resource considered to have great potential, and it was hoped that more could be achieved in this way (see page 133).

The Commission for Roads and Bridges met for the first time on 7 July 1803. The chairman was Charles Abbot, the Speaker of the House of Commons, and the other members were William Dundas, MP for Sutherland; William Pulteney, a wealthy advocate, baronet, landowner and erstwhile MP who had long been a supporter of Telford and his ideas; Isaac Hawkins Browne, a Tory politician and mine owner; Nicholas Vansittart, the Chancellor of the Exchequer; Charles Grant, MP for Inverness-shire; and William Smith, the dissenting MP for Norwich. Some of these men were also prominent members of the British Fisheries Society.

They wasted little time in tackling their task, and began by sending letters to the conveners of all the Highland counties 'lying North of the Line of Lakes and Forts', the Great Glen, to spread the good news of their intentions and placing advertisements in the Edinburgh and Glasgow newspapers. Several roads had already been surveyed by George Brown of Elgin – Telford had made use of this work – but the rise in the price of labour since these had first been done, from 1790 onwards, led the Commission to ask Brown to revise his figures. In all, the Commission listed in its first report a total of 31 road lines already surveyed; plotting their distribution results in an impressively comprehensive network. Telford was appointed to be the engineer in charge of the road-building. The whole endeavour was financed from a government grant of £20,000 to be supplemented with match-funding from the districts that would benefit, and priority would be given to those roads where the earliest contributions were paid.[1]

The Commission's expenditure in its first year was of necessity modest: £278 16s 11d on surveys in various areas, and £115 2s 11d to Telford for his travelling expenses. The pace of development soon picked up. By the time the second report was published in the summer of 1805, contractors had sent in tenders and offers for work, and the lairds had responded well. Unsurprisingly, the assessments necessary to determine local contributions caused some bother. No landowner was willing to stump up more than he absolutely had to; and as the assessments were based on the rental value of property, surveying to determine the precise location of boundaries became suddenly crucial. When it came to recording things on maps and paying taxes, a laird could no longer rely on a gentleman's agreement for acceptance of where his land ended and his neighbour's began. County authorities were no less anxious about their boundaries. All in all, it was a good time to be a surveyor.

Alexander Nimmo, the rector of Inverness Academy, was appointed by the Commissioners at Telford's request to survey the boundaries of Inverness-shire, a task he undertook during May and June 1806. Nimmo used existing maps drawn by estates and farmers, where he could find them, and elsewhere rode along the boundary, mapping it in consultation with local gentry. This was no easy jaunt. Boundaries could be uncertain or controversial, snaking hither and yon across the land without obvious logic, as Nimmo recorded in his journal with regard to Cantray to the east of Inverness: 'The farms seem alternately in Inverness and Nairn, but without any kind of order or connection.'[2]

With construction projects under way in many parts of the country, Telford must have seemed at times to be constantly on the move by gig or boat or in the saddle, visiting, advising, solving problems. Born in Eskdale in Dumfries-shire in 1757, the son of a shepherd, he had started work as a stonemason at the age of 14 and had gone on to make his name as a designer of bridges, roads, aqueducts and canals. He remained single and made his home after 1800 in rooms at a coffee house in Charing Cross in London, although in later life he had a large residence in Abingdon Street where he also housed his apprentices. John

Rickman, the editor of his autobiography, compared his life-style to that of a soldier – and his immense achievement as an engineer lay partly on his ability to find able assistants to work under his long-distance direction. His first general inspector of the road works was an engineer called Duncombe but, when this man fell ill, Telford appointed a mason from Forres, John Mitchell, a skilled, modest man, scarcely literate, described by Telford's friend the poet Robert Southey as 'incorruptible'. Under Mitchell, six mason-engineers ran the various districts: Robert Garrow in Argyll, Alexander Martin in Lochaber, George Macfarlane in Badenoch, John Findlay in Ross, James Smith in Skye, and Peter Lawson in Caithness and Sutherland.[3] In 1806 Mitchell moved to live in Fort Augustus, as central a spot as any for the work he now had to direct. His son, Joseph, who was later to succeed his father and become a noted engineer in his own right, was three at the time and could recall seeing the soldiers, still in garrison there, drilling in the square of the fort.[4] During the 18 years in which he worked on the roads, John Mitchell travelled constantly, enduring the lack of roads, 'crossing dangerous rivers and streams, travelling in wet clothes, and for shelter living in smoky and wretched huts where oat cakes, milk and whisky were the chief or only refreshments', racking up a total of some 10,000 miles, his son reckoned, a labour that tried his health and possibly brought on his death at the age of only 45.

Telford began the Commission's programme in 1803 with bridges over some of the main rivers – on the Tay at Dunkeld, the Spey at Fochabers and the Findhorn near Forres. As work progressed on the roads, requests came in for more projects – from Arran, from Deeside where the bridge at Ballater built with forfeited estates money in 1783 had been swept away by an 'uncommon flood' on the Dee in 1799, from the Cairn o'Mount area to build a road from Clattering Brigs to Whitestone Bridge over the Feugh and on to join the turnpike between Aboyne and Aberdeen, and from Argyll for the Leckan road from Cladich at the north end of Loch Awe towards Lochgilphead.[5] The Commissioners were soon handling considerable sums of money: in August 1807, they reported that they had income over £52,000 and had spent over £23,000 on surveying, construction and management. Parliament passed an act in July 1806 to grant them the funds left over from the forfeited estates, a tidy sum of £12,931. They were also expecting, although not soon, payment of a debt of £25,000 from the city of Edinburgh and a similar sum from the Crinan Canal Society.[6]

Requests for assistance from the Commission diversified. Islay and Colonsay wanted quays, several ports wanted new harbours, Dingwall sought help with a small canal to improve its landing facility at the mouth of the Peffer where boats had hitherto beached to handle cargo. The latter request resulted in 1815–17 in the construction of a canal and two wharves for a cost of £4,365, of which £600 was a grant from the Convention of Royal Burghs. The improvements did not greatly increase the use of the landing, and the canal revenue in 1828 was noted as only about £100, scarcely enough to pay for the upkeep.[7] Perhaps most unusually, in 1824, the Commission was asked to build new churches and manses in those parts of the country where the population had increased and lived far from the existing parish kirks; the result was Telford's so-called parliamentary churches. In such an ambitious array of tasks, delays inevitably cropped up, and plans began to alter. The original route for a road on Mull was changed in 1808. Sir John Sinclair of Ulbster in Caithness caused a flutter by raising the matter of compensation. Perhaps the last landowner who might have been expected to quibble over progress – he had, after all, done much to promote improvement in agriculture and fisheries, had edited the monumental *Statistical Account of Scotland*, and had been involved in countless schemes of his own – he sought recompense for the land he would lose to the new road over the Ord and for the removal of the fences that it would intersect.

The Commissioners, anxious to avoid a costly precedent and fearful of becoming ensnared in the litigation so beloved of some lairds, responded indignantly that the first of these claims was entirely new and unexpected and the second had only occurred 'in a trifling instance'. The Act, they opined, had intended an equality of expense between the Public and the Contributors, and so far only they and the government had spent anything, and 'on this consideration we had not expected any claim ... for land occupied by new Roads, to the Especial benefit' of the property through which they passed. The Commissioners told Sir John that, apart from the 'not unreasonable' claim for fences which could be added to the road estimates, his compensation claim for land could not be admitted, and advised the Caithness county authorities that 'no step could be taken until the [claim for] payment for land was withdrawn'. Nothing more seems to have been said on the matter, and the contract for the road over the Ord was advertised.

The new bridge over the Conon, built in 1807–08, withstood a battering from river ice in the spring of 1809 and, declared the inspector triumphantly, 'had not lost an ounce of stone'. There was still hesitation in 1809 over tackling a bridge across the Beauly, 160 yards wide at high water, and it was thought better to improve the ferry. Within two years, however, a rethink led to parliament granting the right to charge tolls on the new bridge to be called the Lovat, with five arches and a central span of 60 feet. The Lovat Bridge was eventually completed in October 1814. The combination of high rainfall, frost and thaw was not kind to the new roads and, as the mileage of made surface inched forward, the need for repairs became as much of a concern as construction and, in July 1814, an act designating responsibility for this was passed into law: one quarter of the expense of repairs now fell on the public purse, with the remaining three-quarters being assessed from the county landowners and rent payers. Not before time, thought the Commissioners, who pointed to the example of John Sinclair, 'a most diligent overseer ... with a few good workmen', who arrived in Ardentinny in August 1814 to find that the heavy rain had set the burns in spate and, despite every effort, he and his team could not prevent the collapse of a 12-foot bridge arch over a ravine. The Kyle of Sutherland was bridged between Ardgay and Bonar in 1811–12 by an iron bridge that Telford had cast in Denbighshire and brought north in sections to be assembled *in situ*. Soon after its completion it survived a severe test of its strength: snow and frost in the winter of 1813–14 resulted in a flood surging down the Carron river, charged with ice and logs, 'a formidable instrument of destruction' that failed to dislodge the new structure.[8] Another on the Bonar model was constructed and erected at Craigellachie on the Spey, where it still impresses the traveller.

There were many problems with contractors, some of whom in response to the advertisements that appeared regularly in the newspapers no doubt tendered for jobs beyond their competence. The Contin bridge was destroyed by a flood in 1811, but its replacement, at the time of the Commission's seventh report in 1815, remained not good enough to be acceptable, 'the masonry being insufficient'. The 22 miles of the Achnasheen road were half done and likely to require two more seasons for completion, as the contractor had made an 'imprudent contract'. On Skye, the original contractor for the road from Kylerhea to Sconser had failed to complete to the detriment of his guarantor, John Bayne, an Oban merchant and shipbuilder, who was 'much declined from his former prosperity', and John Grant, who had been ruined.

Telford and his fellow engineers had of course to deal with local interests. On 31 August 1811, a Caithness man called George Sinclair wrote to tell Sir Benjamin Dunbar, the laird of Hempriggs and Ackergill near Wick, how he had spent time with Mr Telford the previous evening in the inn at Berriedale. 'He appears to be sincerely disposed to cooperate in rendering our roads as complete as possible,' said Sinclair, 'and listened to our representations on the subject not only with attention but with an evident desire to take advantage of any useful hints that might be given him.'[9] The diners in the Berriedale inn also thought that a contractor called Darby had proved inefficient and ought to be dismissed, and selected instead a Mr Nicol, who had already been working on the bridge at Helmsdale: 'of whose honesty & activity we spoke in high terms – & who being totally unconnected with Caithness could not be objected to on the score of partiality to the interests of any particular proprietor', in Sinclair's words. On the following day, Sinclair and his colleagues traversed the route for the new road, found it defective and wrote about it to Telford. Later he told Sir Benjamin: 'I see it will be necessary for all the Gentlemen of the County to exert all their activity & circumspection to counteract the idleness of the Labourers and the artifices of the contractors.' The circumspection was not always effective. Another contractor for the road from the Ord to Wick, a man called Leask, was causing the Commission headaches in February 1813; two years later, in April 1815, he was reported to have 'deserted the work much indebted to the Country Workmen employed by him', but now matters had been taken in hand and the road was expected to be finished by the year's end.[10]

Examples of the tenders submitted by road contractors survive among the Dunbar Papers in Caithness. One by William Steven and Alex Leith in March 1825 offered to build a section of road near Wester between Wick and John o' Groats, stating that it would be 18 feet wide, with side drains nine inches deeper than 'the bed of the metal', 15 inches wide in the bottom and sloped on the sides at the rate of 'two [inches] horizontal to one perpendicular'. The stones of the road metal were to be 'roughly but regularly broken to the depth of seven inches in centre and four at the sides'. The cost of this work, in which a large amount of time would be spent simply breaking stones into pieces of the right size, would be 3d per yard for forming, and 1s 3d per yard for the metalling and finishing. If the job was not completed satisfactorily or in the time allowed, the contractors agreed to 'forfeiture of one third of the prices as stated'.[11]

In 1791 the minister of Creich parish, George Rainy, wrote that the local people used to be 'amused from time to time with the hopes that a bridge was to be built over the Kyle'. The drovers had to swim their cattle across or, if the beasts refused to take to the water, ship them to the Ross side in cobles. 'The people pretend to foretell,' wrote Rainy, 'whether they shall have a good market or not, by their readiness to swim.'[12] No doubt many of Rainy's parishioners lived long enough to see what they had joked about become a reality. In 1813 the Commissioners resolved to bypass Little Ferry at the mouth of the Fleet by forming an embankment at the landward end of the wide basin of Loch Fleet to carry the new road.[13] Not building new piers at Little Ferry would save £1,200, 'full enough to make the new road' along the south shore of the basin. New farms laid out on the flat ground between the basin and Golspie had already provided a stretch of new road 'almost in a perfect form'. The estimated cost of the Mound, as the embankment is called, and new bridge came to over £8,400, and an additional benefit came through the finished structure enclosing a large area of swampy strath that would be good for agriculture. In the event, this plan did not fully materialise (the ground is now a flourishing alder wood) but the Mound was built – constructed mainly in 1816 by men from the Sutherland estate under the supervision of William Young and Patrick Sellar – and remains a striking feature on the Sutherland section of the A9. The completion of the Mound encouraged William Young to lay out and build a road from Bonar via Lairg and Altnaharra to Tongue and the residence of Lord Reay.[14]

Just as the new road to the far north was being pushed across the land, there occurred the worst ferry disaster in the region, in the words of a contemporary, 'a most calamitous and awful accident'. On the morning of 16 August 1809, the boat on the Meikle Ferry crossing of the Dornoch Firth left its mooring and headed for the Tain shore. It was the time of the Lammas Fair and the boat was crowded with men, women and children eagerly anticipating the day out. 'The Passage boat . . . in consequence of being imprudently Overloaded, Sunk or upset when about one hundred yards from the Bank on the Sutherland side.' A smaller ferry hauled 11 passengers and one ferryman from the cold water. A twelfth survived by swimming to the shore or clinging to the boat. The rest – 99 people – perished. The dead were mostly from the Dornoch area but there were also a few from Golspie, Rogart and Lairg, men and women, some old, some only infants. A leaflet was soon published to solicit subscriptions to aid those now bereft of breadwinners or resources – many of the victims had been carrying savings to spend or deposit in the bank in Tain – and, in lurid and sensational words, it describes 'mourning crowds searching the shores by night and by day for the mangled remains of the objects of their tenderest affection'. Within weeks, the disaster fund took in around £3,000, almost half of it from Highland exiles in India, the West Indies and South Africa, to distribute among some 176 widows, orphans and parents.[15]

By 1821, when the Commission published its ninth report, the bulk of the road-building had been accomplished; now the north was knit together by some 875 miles of made road, laid in place at an average cost of less than £400 per mile, and many bridges, and the Commission could look on its achievement with some pride. 'The Highland proprietors have so largely experienced the value of their new roads that they are not only ready to go further in expenditure for additional roads,' read the report, 'but have arrived at desiring roads of a quality superior to what we think prudent in point of expense, or for other reasons desirable in the Highlands.'[16] The report went on to explain to any southern readers, and those in parliament, that Highland roads needed special attention – 'the heaviest part of the expense' – to guard against the erosive effects of heavy rainfall.

In 1814 the Commission had taken over the military roads. These, wrote Mitchell, '[had] operated on the whole country like a fructifying and irrigating stream, so sudden and striking was the improvement. The value of lands also rapidly increased. The proprietors, however, were very unwilling to bear the burden of repairs.' The result was that roads deteriorated. 'At last [they] became so intolerably bad as to be almost impassable,' recalled Mitchell, 'and John Duke of Atholl in 1823 applied to the [Commission] to allow my father to arrange for their repair and restoration, the country gentlemen raising funds by tolls and on personal security.' Mitchell was put in charge of reconstructing the military roads in Perthshire and spent around £180,000 on them in the first seven years. 'As the trustees of those roads were the aristocracy of the country,' noted the engineer, 'I found my professional duties very agreeable.' Although this was not always the case, as Mitchell himself wrote. When he had newly taken on his role as a road engineer – in about 1825 – he had to defend himself against an accusation by Grant of Rothiemurchus that his neglect of a stretch of road in Badenoch had led to the death of an elderly woman during a flood.

CHAPTER 10

Destitution roads

'a sufficient wage in money or food . . .'

The famine that resulted from the epidemic of potato blight in the Highlands in the 1840s led to a burst of local road construction in Wester Ross as a means of providing relief to the rural poor. These so-called destitution roads were built by those in need, who received oatmeal rations in return for their labour.

The journalist Robert Somers travelled through the north in autumn 1847 and in the course of his reporting for the *North British Daily Mail* attended a meeting of the Commissioners of Supply in Dingwall. Although his Dickens-esque description of the proceedings is patronising and laboured, he summarised the situation well, describing how the large size of the west coast parishes of Gairloch and Lochbroom had hitherto defeated the capacity or willingness of the local landowners to fund road-building. Only two roads – from Dingwall to Poolewe and to Ullapool – spanned the county, leaving all the intermediate country with what, in Somers' words, had been provided by 'Nature and the occasional tread of footsteps'.[1] Early in 1847 a Central Board of Management for Highland Relief had taken over from the Free Church the leadership of the public effort to alleviate the dreadful dearth resulting from the failure of the potato crop on which the rural people, crowded onto small plots of land, depended. The Board decided that employing the poor in Wester Ross on the construction of roads 'seemed a rational and a beneficial enterprise'. The landowners 'warmly seconded' this proposal, and it was suggested, wrote Somers, that four roads should be made; the Board would pay one-third of the cost of £5,000, the rest coming from the landowners. This provided workers with a basic wage and no more. The Commissioners' Minutes for the meeting, on 26 October 1847, list the four: 14 miles from Loch Broom to Little Loch Broom; 12 miles along the shore of Loch Maree; the six or so miles from Poolewe to Aultbea; and an 11-mile stretch through the property of Alexander Mackenzie in Lochbroom parish. These four sections combine to make what is today the A832 but in 1847 only the first two sections had already been surveyed, and the construction costs were estimated at £100 to £130 per mile.[2] One destitution road was laid in Sutherland in 1847, over the 30 miles between Lairg and Scourie (now the A838), funded by the destitution charities and the Duke of Sutherland in equal part.

As a boy of around seven years old, Osgood Mackenzie could remember the potato famine and the reaction of his mother to the provision of work. She thought ridiculous what had happened in Ireland where road-building had been done to little purpose other than simply to provide work and felt that the men had to receive 'a sufficient wage in money or food to enable them to do good work themselves and to support their dependents'. Osgood himself was given the honour of cutting the first turf on the construction of the Loch Maree road:

How well I remember it, surrounded by a crowd, many of them starving Skye men, for the famine was more sore in Skye and the islands than it was on our part of the mainland. I remember the tiny toy spade and the desperate exertions I had to make to cut my small bit of turf, then came the ringing cheers of the assembled multitude, and I felt myself a great hero.[3]

The road-building had not yet started when Somers jour-
neyed west on the stagecoach that Macleod of Macleod now
ran three times a week between Inverness, Dingwall and
Dunvegan, via Strathpeffer, Strathgarve and Strathbran (now
the route of the A832 and A830), a trip that in fair weather
took 20 hours. 'Taking a seat . . . in this admirable conveyance,
I was carried with unexpected rapidity to what, properly speaking, are the distressed districts,' wrote the journalist.

More than a thousand men found work with the road gangs,
receiving payments often in quantities of oatmeal rather than in
money, and by 1850 they had laid some 90 miles of road along
the western shore, linking Gairloch, Poolewe, Ullapool, Coigach
and Knockan. The relief work 'gave the whole of the coast-line
from the mouth of Loch Torridon to Loch Broom the benefit of
more or less good highways', wrote Osgood Mackenzie, 'which
are all now county roads. How well do I remember the first
wheeled vehicle, a carrier's cart, that ever came to Gairloch, and
the excitement it caused.' In 1851, George Rainy, son of the
Creich minister who had foreseen a bridge over the Kyle of
Sutherland, and now owner of Raasay after making much
money from slave plantations, suggested that poverty could be
relieved by giving men work on the construction of the proposed
railway line to Mallaig, an idea that was stillborn, as another 40
years were to pass before the rail connection to the fishing haven
in Morar became a reality.[4]

CHAPTER 11

The stagecoach

*'the guard in his scarlet coat blew
his bugle loudly and merrily . . .'*

The new roads made possible the extension of stagecoach services throughout the Highlands. Those who had means also now found it much more convenient to keep horse-drawn carriages and that in turn affected social life, boosting convivial gatherings now that they were easier to get to. Inns, too, began to keep chaises for hire, much to the benefit of early tourists. The first issue of the *Inverness Journal* – newspapers and made roads arrived together in the Highlands, two aspects of a burst of modernity – carried an advertisement for the sale of a second-hand gig at Ettles Hotel, 50 guineas, a fashionable, close-panelled vehicle, fitted up in a superior manner.[1] It also had notice of the newly published *Traveller's Guide Through Scotland and Its Islands*, already in its third edition, available for 8s. Public coach services through the central Highlands appear to have started in 1806, with a coach called the *Caledonian* running between Inverness and Perth, a venture initiated by some local businessmen, among them the Inverness solicitor Peter Anderson.[2] It was a short-lived enterprise but also a harbinger. The journey took two and a quarter days, only half the time needed in the days before the road was made. Parts of the main north road were not conducive to easy coach travel; the route south from Inverness, for example, began with a long haul up the steep Drumossie brae, a difficult pull for horses in the best of weather. In fact, Telford had found that the military road that Wade's soldiers had made in 1728–30 out of Inverness was too steep for coaches and had relocated his replacement to the east.[3] But the technology and the times could only get better, and they soon did with the inauguration in June 1807 of a diligence service – a faster coach called the *Duchess of Gordon* in recognition of her role in the launch of the venture.[4] The *Inverness Journal*, which began to be published in 1807, carried regular announcements about the coaches. In April 1809 it was noted that a diligence would henceforth leave Edinburgh at 7 a.m. on Monday mornings, with the expectation of arriving in the Highland town at 4 p.m. on Tuesdays.[5] On 30 June 1809, the paper noted 'a remarkable instance of the celerity with which a person may now travel in the Highlands. Mr Gordon of Carrol ... left Edinburgh, per the Inverness coach, and reached his house in Sutherland, a distance of 215 miles, in forty-seven hours and a half.'[6] The same year saw the start of a coach service north to Tain, and the *Duchess of Gordon* beginning a twice-weekly run between Inverness and the capital. In September, the proprietors announced they would cope with the shortening autumnal day by making overnight stops at Dalwhinnie and Dunkeld.[7] Winter journeys must have caused waiting relatives much anxiety, as when on 14 December 1809 the *Inverness Journal* lamented: 'We fear the Highland road is impassable. The Caledonian Coach which should have arrived on Wednesday evening [the 12th] is still on the road, but where, we know not.' Coach services rapidly increased in frequency to link all the major towns. A mail coach began to ply daily between Inverness and Aberdeen from 5 April 1811 (the inside fare was a substantial £3 13s 6d; a seat outside in the wind and rain only £2 9s), a weekly coach between Inverness and Perth from 3 January 1812. The Caledonian Coaching Company ventured to begin a diligence service five times a week to Edinburgh in the summer of 1811, covering the distance in two days, with a seven-hour overnight stop.

In Rothiemurchus, Elizabeth Grant noted how in the summer of 1813

> a great improvement took place in our postal arrangements; a stagecoach was started to run three days a week between Perth and Inverness. Our bag was made up at Perth and dropped at Lynwilg at Robbie Cumming's, whose little shop soon became a receiving house for more bags than ours. It was quite an event; we used to listen for the horn; on still days and when the wind set that way we could hear it distinctly . . . At one or two breaks in the wooding we could see the coach, a novel sight that made us clap our hands.[8]

A decade earlier it had taken the Grant family three days to bring their carriage from Perth to their house and they had had to cross the Spey by using the carriage-boat at Inverdruie. Then the family had used a coach called a sociable, with leather curtains that failed to keep out heavy rain, and four horses, one of which had the habit of lying down in the shafts and refusing to get up until he was cured of the trick by having lit straw placed under his belly. Coach travel was clearly not for the faint-hearted. Now a coach three times a week was an advance indeed, even although, as Elizabeth recorded, Drumochter remained dreary beyond all. The last stage on the Grant progress was at Pitmain, at the inn that Mrs Grant described as being less than salubrious – 'no carpets on the floors, no cushions in the chairs, no curtains on the windows' – but with 'excellent' food: 'hotch-potch, salmon, fine mutton, grouse, scanty vegetables, bad bread, but good wine'.

The completion of the new road over the Ord allowed a diligence company to begin a coach service between Inverness and Thurso, a journey of more than 24 hours. The timetable for this marathon trip was advertised in the *Inverness Journal* in July

1819. The travellers left Inverness at 6 a.m. and had main stops at Beauly (7.50 a.m.), Dingwall (9.40 a.m., and a 30-minute halt for breakfast), Tain (2.30 p.m., and another 30-minute break for dinner), Golspie (10.05 p.m., and 30 minutes for supper), Berriedale (3.20 a.m.), Wick (7.30 a.m., and breakfast), and at last Thurso post office (11.30 a.m.). The southbound coach left Thurso at 7 a.m. and reached Inverness at 12.30 p.m. on the following day. This works out at an average speed of a little over seven miles per hour. (Coach speeds on easier routes would rise to a dizzy 35 miles per hour by 1863 in the last years before their place began to be taken by the steam-engined trains.) We do not know if any passenger went the whole way – more likely travellers got on and off, and the coach drivers must have worked in shifts – but the experience of crossing the hills of the Ord above the sea in the twilight of a fine summer night, with the calling birds, the jingle of harness and the snorts of the horses, must have been memorable. Joseph Mitchell came to dread it:

> Oh! The misery of a night journey alone by the mail to Caithness. First there are the perils of the Meikle Ferry [still in use for coaches]; then you have to cross the Ord of Caithness ... then to wend your way along that dreary Caithness coast, with the sea on one side seen through the pale moonlight, and the bleak bare country on the other. If the night is gloomy, a solemn loneliness comes over you, rendering the bodily fatigue of travelling still more oppressive.[9]

The new mode of transport had its attendant problems. On 7 May 1819, the advertisement for the daily post coach about to start on the Aberdeen–Inverness run included the wording: 'The proprietors of this new coach rely with confidence on the support of their friends and the public to this undertaking; superior Vehicles, civil and attentive Guards and careful

Coachmen are provided; and any well-founded complaint against their servants of insolence, inebriety or carelessness will instantly ensure the dismissal of the person offending.'[10] That drink-driving could be a difficulty is suggested in a letter that Jessie Anderson in Inverness wrote to her son in October 1818 when she learned that he had arrived safely in Edinburgh: she had heard that the northbound coach had been upset at Dalwhinnie, injuring four passengers, one possibly fatally, and that the accident had been blamed on the driver having taken drink. In defence of the drivers, it must be said that the temptation to swallow a warming dram now and again must have been strong. The *Inverness Journal* reported on 23 July 1819 that a mail coach had overturned twice during the last two years, '... on one of these occasions the driver and [on] the other the driver, guard and several passengers narrowly escaped with their lives, and the coach was shattered to pieces'. On another occasion, 'The mail coach horses, becoming unmanageable, deranged the harness and ran off with the coach in the streets of Inverness ... an outside passenger, alarmed for his personal safety, leaped off.' Near Brora one day in February 1855, one of the horses pulling the northbound mail coach was 'startled by the passing of a horse carrying panniers or side baskets', shied to one side of the road and overturned the coach; the three passengers, all seated on top, and the driver suffered only 'trifling bruises' but the guard, Thomas Peacock, was thrown down and severely injured.[11] On Tuesday, 26 March 1839, the southbound Perth Mail was about five miles north of Dalnacardoch when one rein gave way; the coach ran off the road and overturned. A passenger and the coachman were thrown down a steep brae. The passenger suffered 'a slight contusion to the head', The guard jumped off. None of the four inside passengers was hurt. The coach was only slightly damaged, so it was got back on the road and continued to Perth, where it arrived 'in good time'.[12] In another accident in September 1849, the coach was upset near Moy and tumbled into a swollen burn so that 'the whole insides were very nearly drenched'; the passengers were brought into the nearby toll-house, where they sat shivering for some seven hours before they could proceed on their way.[13]

Coaches began to run daily between Inverness and Perth in June 1825, the southward journey beginning at 5 a.m. from the Caledonian Hotel. This connection was further improved in July 1836 when the daily mail coach began to go as far as Edinburgh. The southbound coach rumbled out of Inverness at 9 a.m. and, after a half-hour break for dinner at Dalwhinnie, reached Perth at 10.30 p.m.; the northward journey was made overnight and must have demanded forbearance, although the newspapers reported cheerily that it was possible to dine in Edinburgh one day and breakfast in Inverness the next.

The inn of Pitmain, where the Grants had stopped, became a frequent halt for coaches. 'Old Pitmain! An abominable hostel,' apostrophised the circuit judge Henry Cockburn in 1844, 'but it served the public, I suppose, at least one hundred years, and all this time had received the sort of welcome which is given by a vessel in distress to the only port it has to repair to.' With a relish for hyperbole, Cockburn wrote about the scene when a coach arrived for a night's stay: '. . . knowing by experience the advantage of first possession, every monster rushed in and seized whatever he could lay his claws upon – meat, drink, the seat next the fire, the best room, the best bed – and awkward-ness or timidity were left to shiver or starve'.[14] In the judge's view, the innkeeper and his staff – 'the savages of the house', he calls them – never had anything in readiness and looked on the hubbub as 'showing the importance of the house'.

Companies now vied with each other to provide the travel-ling public with better services and did not shrink from decry-ing their competitors, such as in an advertisement for the new *Defiance* coach on the route between Edinburgh and Aberdeen via Strathmore.[15] Taking the *Defiance*, ran the argument, would mean you could avoid having to use the Fife coach – cramped, dirty and filled with undesirables – between the ferries on the Forth and Tay. In contrast, the *Defiance* would have only four, not six, passengers inside and ten outside, and would take only 15 hours for the trip, 'which, in the memory of persons yet alive, at one period required four days!'

'As every obstacle which could be devised has been thrown in the way of this Coach being established by a party too contemptible to be brought into public notice,' continued the advertisement, 'the Proprietors confidently expect that the respectable part of the Travelling Community will give this establishment that countenance and support which alone can ensure its permanency . . .'

Families, ladies and children would feel secure on the *Defiance*, readers were told, as the guard and two coachmen had been selected as the best for 'honesty and sobriety . . . and will be distinguished by a Crimson Dress and Grey Hat'.

In 1837, Joseph Mitchell participated in surveys of alternate routes to that followed by the military road through Drumochter Pass and reported on a feasible way, more than ten miles shorter, that ran between Glen Feshie and Glen Bruar. This way, which recalled the ancient routes mentioned in Part 1 (page 14), rose to a higher altitude, over 2,200 feet, and was therefore more liable to be cut off by bad weather in winter, and would have cost, Mitchell estimated, £34,507 to construct. In the event it was never tackled, and the main road stayed at the lower altitude in Drumochter.[16]

The coach network spread. The *Caberfeidh* began to rattle between Inverness and Dingwall in June 1829 to connect with the *Brilliant* for the onward journey to Invergordon.[17] In the same year, coaches began to operate between Oban and Inveraray, one going via Port Sonachan, the other by Dalmally. The *Argyll*, as the former was named, left Oban at 5 a.m. on a Monday to connect with the steamer *Lochgoil* when it departed from Inveraray for Glasgow. The northward journey also set off at 5 a.m., on Tuesdays, to catch the steamers for Staffa and

Inverness. The Lorn coach, following the Dalmally route, travelled northward on Tuesdays and Fridays, southward on
Mondays and Thursdays, and had room for 25 passengers,
suggesting it was an early charabanc with bench seats.[18] A mail
coach began to run three times a week from Inverness to
Dunvegan on Skye in June 1847, the advertisement now recog-
nising the potential for attracting tourists and touting the 'very
fine scenery', 'the wooded lakes and wild moors', 'the seldom
visited hills of Lochalsh' and the 'unrivalled scenery of the
Cuchulin [sic] hills', all to be enjoyed during the 21 bumpy
hours on the road.[19]

When not using the public coach, circuit judge Henry
Cockburn travelled widely around the Highlands in the 1840s
in a chaise or a gig, savouring the scenery but also freely criticis-
ing the infrastructure. 'This ferry, though boasted as the best in
Skye, is detestable, at least for carriages, and as ill conducted as
possible,' he protested, describing a crossing from Glenelg to
Kylerhea in September 1841, continuing: 'But what can a ferry
be for carriages, where ours is only the third that has passed this
year.' The feeling may have been mutual, as the only way to
bring a carriage on board the boat was to assemble a gang of
men, 'all scolding in Erse', recalled Cockburn, to lift the equipage over the side. The return crossing, from Kyleakin to Kyle,
was little better: 'The ferry is ill provided with a boat and
machinery for carriages, but hands, and the hope of whisky, did
the business, though certainly their knocks and jolts, if survived,
are the coachmaker's triumph.' Strome ferry was 'like the rest',
although here the judge was intrigued to see the ferrymen
become excited by the sound of the posthorn as the mail coach
drew towards the village: 'I had forgot in these solitudes that
there was a post.'[20] Three days later, Cockburn was back on the
east coast, staying at the Bogroy Inn, a few miles from Inverness,
and reflecting on his recent journey. Crossing 'the southern end
of Ross-shire', in his words, he had found it to be 'a drive worth
any one's taking. The inns are all comfortable, and as to the

roads, though there may have been about four severe unavoid-
able ascents, we have not come upon one bad quarter of a mile
since we left home; and all the Government roads are uniformly
admirable.'

Osgood Mackenzie recalled in his memoirs the experience of
travelling as a small boy by coach north from Perth in the winter
of 1843–44. 'We managed to get as far as Blair Atholl when a
violent snowstorm started, and a few miles beyond the village
the coach was suddenly brought to a standstill by trees being
blown across the road both in front and behind us.' Someone
ran off to find men with saws and axes but by the time they
arrived the coach had become stuck fast in the snow – 'we got
back to Blair Inn by the help of a very high-wheeled dog-cart'.
When, after several days, it became clear that no thaw was
imminent, the Mackenzies returned to Perth to catch the 'newly
opened railway' to Aberdeen, and the steamer to Inverness.[21]

The growth of public transport peaked around 1848 when
the Highland capital saw six steamer and eight coach depar-
tures daily. In her memoir of life in Inverness in the first half of
the nineteenth century, Isobel Anderson wrote how the Millburn
Road on the east side of the town was a favourite spot for an
afternoon walk, as one could see the *Star* coach tearing away to
Elgin, 'drawn by four horses, while the guard behind in his scarlet coat blew his bugle loudly and merrily'. The fare to Elgin
was 16s inside and 10s 6d outside. This was not cheap – a
housemaid would have to work for possibly six weeks to earn
the price of a ticket. Intermediate journeys could cost a lot less,
as Mrs Anderson explained:

These coaches were always ready to stop and pick up any
passenger by the way, for a short journey. One could get six
miles for a shilling as outside passenger and for eighteen-
pence inside. The inside was anything but comfortable,
particularly if closely packed. The Defiance was perhaps
more roomy than the Star, and it kept to the main road all

the way. The fare inside to Aberdeen was £2, and £1 2s outside.[22]

Mrs Anderson recalls the coaches with some excitement and fondness, but occasionally we have a glimpse of the discomfort, such as in a letter written by a disconsolate traveller in November 1825: 'I was almost starved to death on the outside of the Coach from Tain to Inverness. William Horne his wife and two sisters having the inside – My wish was that they had been inside of a whale's belly.'[23]

'Many a snowstorm and bitter blast and wet jacket I had to endure,' recalled Joseph Mitchell, contrasting his own experience with that of his father. 'I had generally good roads and tolerable inns, with the advantage of youth and health ... during all my journeys, travelling some 7,000 or 8,000 miles a year for about forty-five years I never had an accident.'[24]

Mitchell includes in his memoir how, as the roads improved after 1824, commercial travellers began to give up horses for gigs. They used to be called riders, wrote Mitchell, and they went as far north as Tain: 'portly old gentlemen, with rubicund faces' in top boots and brass-buttoned blue coats, bringing saddlebags with their wares and heavy whips. They were good for conversation and convivial evenings in the inns, before they were replaced by younger men, laments the engineer, who spoke about horses and inns and not much else.[25]

The novelty of the coach and what it symbolised in terms of connection with faraway places is captured in what an anonymous writer remembered of its arrival in Thurso or Wick:

It entirely eclipsed in popular excitement the arrival of a present-day train. Both sides of the street were lined with spectators ... as the guard and driver, both arrayed in red coats, descended ... The driver usually entered the hotel to deliver his way bill, and retail the latest news from the south. The guard's first visit was to the post office to see the safe delivery of the mail bags. And then, what an exciting time it was ... when the fresh horses were being yoked ... the guard got up and shouting to the driver, 'All right, Tom' away went the four fresh horses at the trot or gallop.[26]

To add to the excitement, and possibly to relieve the tedium of their normal routine, it was not unknown for rival coaches to 'race' with each other. On the occasion of Queen Victoria's birthday in 1841, when there was a public holiday and much good cheer, the mail coach from Aberdeen arrived in Inverness 'splendidly decorated with flowers, evergreens and flags ... with a postillion in full dress, the guard in his new scarlet coat, and the bugle sounding a merry and joyous strain' and was surrounded by a cheering crowd. More theatre followed: 'The new rival coaches betwixt Perth and Inverness made their debut on this occasion, and we question if the Highland road ever before witnessed such feats of horsemanship. Both seem to have run at the rate of about twelve miles an hour.' The *Princess Royal* and the *Duke of Wellington* both had amateur gentleman drivers at the reins that day, and they met in the evening to toast their escapade. What the passengers thought – should any innocent of the situation have been aboard that day – has not been recorded.[27]

CHAPTER 12

Trustees and tolls

'*a burden on the county . . .*'

In the early 1820s it became apparent to the Commissioners for Roads and Bridges that the costs of keeping the new transport infrastructure in good repair would be a continuing problem. In Inverness-shire, for example, 'the outlay for 1822 amounted to £2,098; and the maximum assessment provided by the [current] act with the Parliamentary allowance amounted to no more than £901 8s 8d'.[1] Similar deficits pertained in the other mainland counties. To help defray the costs and reduce the assessment laid on the landowners, it was decided to introduce a Bill in Parliament to permit the erection of toll gates on some roads. Another option available to the county authorities, the Commissioners of Supply, was to take over the roads themselves. 'In the latter case,' thought the *Inverness Courier*, 'it would not require of the spirit of prophecy to fortel [*sic*] what would become of all the fine roads and bridges which have been completed ... at such an enormous expense', but it left the question whether or not in such a sparsely populated region as the Highlands tolls would take in enough to cover costs. 'If the deficient sums were provided for by tolls, it would be a great relief,' continued the *Courier* editor. 'If the county of Inverness clears £1,200 a year and the county of Ross £700 it is as much as can reasonably be hoped for.'

Sutherland was the first county in the north to acquire a parliamentary act to establish a turnpike road, in this case from Portinleik (Bonar Bridge) to the Ord. The county road trustees, a number of the freeholders and heritors, met in Dornoch in October 1804 and decided that they would apply for an act to allow assessment for their contribution to match the funds expected from the Commissioners for Roads and Bridges, and seek in the same piece of legislation the authorisation to levy tolls and commute the statute labour into cash contributions. The act was passed on 25 April 1805, to endure for 15 years. It included what were probably quite standard conditions throughout the country. The trustees were given the power to erect turnpike gates on bridges 'and also such Number of Toll Houses as they shall think fit'. The charges could be levied on 'any Coach, Chariot, Berlin, Landau, Curricle, Calash, Waggon, Cart, Sledge or other Carriage whatsoever or any Horse, Mare, Gelding or Cattle whatsoever'. Public coaches, of which at this time there was none in the county, and wagons were charged between 4d and 6s, depending on the number of horses and oxen in the shafts. Lesser charges were laid on animals and droves of livestock. Any person with or without a wagon who made a return journey before midnight on the same day had to pay only once; and no charges were due from vehicles engaged in road repair, traffic between one part and another of the same farm, and anyone going to worship on the Sabbath. In the event the trustees did not implement the erection of toll gates for nearly a decade, until after the Commission engineers had modernised the road along the east coast of the county and had constructed the bridge across the firth at Bonar. Two tolls were set up: one at the north end of the bridge at Bonar, and the other at the east end of the bridge over the Helmsdale river. These were let by public roup at the end of May in 1814: the first toll-keepers were David Ross, alias Don, at Bonar, who paid £34 15s for the rent of the toll, and Robert Clunes at Helmsdale, who bid £21 (both had been given an upset price of £20). Tolls were also considered for Brora, Craigton and the Mound, but these appear never to have been put in place.[2]

Except in Ross-shire, where the farming lobby came out against tolls, there was general agreement in the 1820s to pursue a general act to allow tolls. The bill went through the House of Commons and then the Lords and was given the royal assent on 8 July 1823. Although the county authorities now had the power to levy tolls, little happened for four years until, in the spring of 1827, the Commissioners of Supply in Morayshire let tolls by public roup, and Nairnshire soon followed. It was normal practice to let the toll gates each year by roup, with the successful bidders hoping to make a profit from the collecting rights and at least for the duration of the rental to possess a good cottage for the family. The income depended of course on the amount of traffic and the bids reflected this expectation.[3] In August 1827 it was unanimously resolved at a gathering of townspeople in Inverness Court House to proceed with the erection of toll gates on roads leading from the town[4] and a month later an advertisement appeared under Joseph Mitchell's name on behalf of the Commissioners for Roads and Bridges to inform the public that toll bars would go up on Monday, 24 September at seven places – one on the road to Fort George, one on the road to Beauly, and five between Tomatin and Dalwhinnie.[5]

No sooner were the toll gates in operation than the idea arose among the livestock breeders and buyers of re-opening what was called 'the ancient Drove Road' in the north, so as to retain 'free and uninterrupted, that ancient and peculiar right of way enjoyed beyond the memory of man'.[6] Landowners who formerly had tolerated the passage of herds were now objecting to paying for the upkeep of turnpike roads and the damage to their pasture. Drovers also protested that having to pay tolls, which were like the 'black mail' imposed as protection money in bygone times, would reduce rents in the north and drive up food prices in the south. Some went further and claimed that confining droves to turnpike roads led to cattle arriving at their destination 'in a diseased and foundered state'. The drovers had already had to contend with decreasing access to common land and free grazing at overnight stances. The old way of shifting livestock over long distances was clearly becoming irreconcilable with modern transport systems and a burgeoning proprietorial attitude among landowners, and disputes rumbled on for many years.[7]

In October 1827 discontent in Ross over the tollbars in Inverness-shire roused some of the gentry into action. 'Not only the Northern Counties [Ross, Caithness and Sutherland] but the Northern Burghs ought to join in petition to the Legislature,' protested Hugh Rose of Glastullich at a county meeting in Tain. Mr Rose contrasted the generous spirit manifested by the county of Ross in the construction of the road from Novar to Bonar Bridge that benefited the Sutherland people with the 'illiberal conduct' of their southern neighbours who 'proposed to lay their northern brethren under a heavy contribution for a road [the Highland road from Inverness to Perth] which it was unsafe to travel, and which they would neither improve nor shorten'.[8] Despite the grumbling, the toll bars stayed in place and soon were joined by more in Ross-shire and in Caithness as well. In their 14th report, published in March 1828, the Commissioners stated that the Highland counties would be called upon to contribute £6,000 a year towards the cost of upkeep of the roads, a sum they recognised as a heavy burden and one not easily raised in a thinly populated country. The Commission budget for the year 1827 records an income of £16,994, of which £288 came from Ross-shire tolls at Tain, Novar and Conon, £183 came from the Wick and Thurso tolls, and £5,684 from the county assessments; expenditure on roads and bridges amounted to £5,582, two-thirds of which was spent in Inverness-shire and Ross-shire, and £2,146 on the old military roads.[9] The infrastructure put in place by the army, some of it now nearly a century old, continued to be of concern. For example, a letter to the *Inverness Courier* in 1847 lamented that the old bridges built by General Wade's men were now being allowed to fall into ruin. 'The bold lofty structures [are] now all but deserted for the commodious transit afforded by erections of later date,' noted the correspondent, adding that 'some of the most useful and picturesque ought to be preserved', instancing the old bridge of Carr and the Sluggan bridge in the parish of Duthil.[10]

The road trustees for Ross and Cromarty divided the large county into districts. In 1828 the parish of Lochbroom was designated the eleventh of these. An indication of the condition of the infrastructure can be found in a report the district trustees drafted in the late summer of 1829 for a general meeting to be held soon in Tain. Their concern was the line of road from Garve to Ullapool, most of which lay in their patch. It was in a bad state: their resolution was to make it 'at all times passable for a Horse' but 'moderate' repairs would require an investment of '£400 sterling' which was 'far beyond the present means of the District'. The trustees confined their ambition 'to the removal of loose and pick fast stones, filling up soft and boggy places, and making the Road generally passable' and reckoned they could do this with the £70 at their disposal, if they could hire day labourers, although they were not sure if they had to proceed by means of regular contracts.[11]

A total of 27 road toll gates existed throughout the three counties of Caithness, Ross and Cromarty, and Inverness-shire in 1846 – the Sutherland tolls had lapsed by this time. (See Table 2.) In October 1857 the Muirtown toll, on the only route west along the Beauly Firth, attracted a rental of £295, higher than any other in the Inverness area. As examples of the income from tolls, the net 'take' at Raigmore toll in 1833–34 was £268 9s, and that at Muirtown £162 10s; the total collected in Inverness-shire was £1,053 3s 4d. At the letting of the toll bars, held in the Caledonian Hotel in Inverness in September 1857, four gates commanded an increased rent while the rest stayed at the same level. Two gates – at Holm and Scaniport – were to be discontinued.[12]

The coach companies were major contributors to the income of the toll houses. Judging from the accounts in the 1846–47 *Rental Book of Tolls*, for example, the *Defiance* paid in dues to the toll houses on the roads to Fort George and Nairn for 12 months a total of £154 16s, around 43 per cent of the income. As well as the coaches, some enterprising souls ran omnibuses: one was John Grant, owner of the Caledonian Hotel in Inverness, who maintained a service to the Loch Ness steamer at Dochgarroch with what is described as 'a Break [*sic*] with 2 horses', a route necessitating the payment for five months over the winter of 1847–48 a toll total of £2 3s 6d. The Tulloch Castle omnibus and the Brahan Castle omnibus regularly passed the Strathpeffer bar on the Contin road. The Glencoe coach, which made the long journey from Inverness to its namesake, taking a full day to complete the trip, paid at three toll bars – at Tomnahurich, Drumnadrochit and Lochy Ferry, the amount varying according to the number of horses in the shafts. The Sutherland road trustees had shown a more liberal attitude and had specifically exempted the new Inverness to Thurso coach from having to pay tolls at Helmsdale.

Occasionally there were court cases arising over toll charges, but short-lived altercations and grumbling – 'toll rage' – must have been more frequent. A minor incident took place in Wick in July 1868 when the sheriff court found in favour of a timber merchant called Macewen who had refused to pay on the grounds that his place of business was less than 100 yards from the toll bar and to get to it he had to pass the checkpoint.[13] A much more serious outbreak of public unrest over paying tolls occurred in Dunkeld over the charges for crossing the road bridge over the Tay. Originally built in 1805–09 to a design by Thomas Telford, the construction was funded in part by a government grant but mostly from loans and bonds raised by the Duke of Atholl. The tolls, all of which went to the bridge trustees, who were solely the duke and his heirs, were levied to repay this debt, but as the years went by the locals began to suspect that they were being required to pay 'the duke's bawbee' long after the original debt had been cleared, suspicions fuelled by the absence of any published accounts. Several developments brought matters to a head. One was the opening of the railway station in 1859 in Birnam on the opposite side of the Tay, which meant that every time Dunkeld people went to catch the train they had to stump up a halfpenny for the toll as well as the fare. Then the duke declined to meet a deputation from the Free Church congregation, who wished to be allowed to pass toll-free on the Sabbath. Finally, in November 1867, locals formed a committee to look into the financial status of the bridge. Its convener, Alexander Robertson, a local fuel merchant with the by-name Dundonachie, openly challenged the duke's right to collect tolls. To defuse the situation the duke had the accounts published, but by then no one was willing to accept them and unrest continued. More than 4,000 people attended a public meeting in Perth towards the end of June 1868 to express their anger, and about two weeks later a procession of locals led by pipers and a drummer marched up to the offending toll gate and threw it into the Tay. Alexander Robertson was arrested but let out of prison on bail of £10. A new toll bar appeared on Saturday, 11 July but that evening a mob smashed it to pieces. The police felt powerless to intervene, although one man was hurt on the head. The unrest continued when the toll desk was thrown into the river – the collector's wife fainted from fear. Two men were arrested the following day and on the Monday a detachment of the 42nd Highlanders marched from Perth with the sheriff and the procurator fiscal to cool tempers.[14] At last the dispute went before the Court of Session and after complicated and lengthy legal argument the court ruled that the duke was entitled to continue to exact tolls to cover costs of £16,000, not £60,000 as had first been claimed by the bridge trustees.

The government launched a major inquiry into the maintenance of public roads in Scotland in December 1858 to find out the extent of debt liable on road projects and to show how 'desirable and practicable' it would be to institute an equitable system of assessment to replace the existing combination of tolls and statute labour. Chaired by William Smythe of Methven, it reported a year later, after soliciting information from all the turnpike trusts, burghs and local authorities on revenue and expenditure on the roads in their care, and touring the major towns to hear witnesses. By this time a patchwork of legislation had evolved across the country so that almost every county had a unique mix of road management systems, with various classes of road – military, parliamentary, local or under no management at all.[15] In Bute and Shetland the old system of statute labour brought in by the 1669 Act during the reign of Charles II – thought 'rude and inefficient' by Smythe and his colleagues – still pertained, but everywhere else it had been superseded by a slew of local Acts. In 1845 the General Statute Labour Act, whose chief effect had been to introduce payment of commutation in lieu of actual labour, had incorporated many of these. Road trustees applied commutation charges to raise funds, usually with exemption for property owners or tenants whose holding was valued at less than £5.

It was found that Aberdeenshire had 34 turnpike roads, one of them – at Ballater – still under construction; Banffshire had 17; Elginshire five (one of these was a Banffshire trust, although the road was wholly within Moray); Perthshire had 35, ten of which held roads partly in other counties, all independent of each other with separate staffs; Argyllshire is listed as having none, Ross and Cromarty likewise; Inverness-shire had one, shared with Nairnshire. In Caithness the statute labour had been abolished in 1793 and the roads maintenance paid for by tolls and an assessment on heritors; now the 'great trunk line' from the Ord to Wick and Thurso was under the Commission for Roads and Bridges, as were the 136 miles of turnpike road, a situation that had pertained since 1838 when the county road trustees had persuaded the Commission to take them on. Caithness also had 41 miles of parish roads and some burgh roads in the care of different bodies, for example in Wick under the charge of the British Fisheries Society. The four northern counties all contributed annual sums to pay off the costs of the erection of the new bridge in Inverness in the early 1850s (see page 180).

In summary, the inquiry found that the debt on the various roads amounted to more than £2.3 million, some of it irrecoverable, and in those districts where the railways were now extending and drawing travellers away from roads there was every possibility that toll income in the future might be lower than at present. There is 'no other feasible plan of dealing with debt than debts of each county be valued at real worth and massed into one sum and the gross amount charged as a burden on the county,' concluded Smythe and his fellows. They proposed setting up road boards and one turnpike trust in each county, with uniform rates of toll. These recommendations soon led to a complete change in the governance of roads: under the provisions of the Highland Roads and Bridges Act in 1862, the Commission for Roads and Bridges – with some 930 miles of road and more than 1,000 bridges to its credit – was wound up, officially ceasing to exist in 1863, and its responsibilities were transferred to county road boards or, in the cases of Argyll and Caithness, to existing county road trustees. During its productive lifetime, it had spent £540,000, over half of which had come from the public purse.

Further legislation, in the form of the Roads and Bridges (Scotland) Act in 1878, simplified the administration of the roads, vested it all under the control of county road boards, overseen by county road trustees, and brought an end at last to tolls and statute labour. The Commissioners of Supply of Inverness-shire were summoned to a meeting on the afternoon of 17 January 1879 in Inverness Castle to discuss how they might adopt and implement the new Act.[16] Those who attended included the usual powerbrokers – solicitors, clan chiefs, landowners or their factors – and it was unanimously agreed to adopt the Act – was any other outcome ever likely? – but to reserve intact the Highlands Roads and Bridges Act of 1862, so far as it was necessary, to enable the Commissioners to complete and pay for the road and bridge works still in progress under their charge. The minutes noted a 'diversity of opinion' over how to divide the sprawling county into road districts and it was agreed to seek legal counsel on how to deal with the islands. After the acceptance of the proffered advice and a few minor adjustments at later meetings, nine districts were listed: Inverness itself; Aird, Urquhart and Abertarff; Badenoch; Lochaber; Skye and Raasay; Harris; South Uist; North Uist; and Barra. The four districts comprising the outer isles were counted as one for the purpose of electing officials to the new county road board. It was unanimously agreed in March 1879, after an exchange of views with neighbouring county councils on how to carry out the business, that the board should comprise 30 trustees – five from each district – and that this body should 'consist of trustees in the proportion of three proprietors to two elected trustees'.

Lord Lovat, who had chaired all the meetings to date, was unsurprisingly chosen to be chairman, with Viscount Reidhaven, heir to the Earl of Seafield, immediately below him in the list of trustees. It was not until the formalities of formation had been gone through that the road board in August 1879 got down to dealing with actual road matters; the first item in the Minutes was a request from Alex Fraser of Faillie in Strathnairn to erect a new footbridge to replace one washed away by a flood in 1874 (one has the impression that Fraser had himself elected to the board to see to this outstanding local problem). Other items were a desire from Lord Seafield and Sir John Grant of Rothiemurchus to have a road in the parish of Duthil upgraded to the status of 'highway', and a request from the burgh of Kingussie to have four public streets also declared highways. The Inverness and Argyll county boards agreed to share the purchase price of £1,800 for the pontage (the toll) and bridge of Lochy Bridge.

The board also dealt with the all-important assessments to be levied to raise funds to manage and maintain the roads, and finally fixed these at amounts varying between 3½d in the pound of rental value in North Uist and 7d in Skye and Raasay. No assessment was made for Barra because, noted the clerk, no authentic information had been received. Occupiers and tenants whose property was valued at £4 or less had only to pay half the assessment charge, the other half being met by the landlord.

The road boards had only a decade of life before another change, under the Local Government Act of 1889, created county councils that incorporated the boards into their structure. When this took place in Inverness, we find six individuals from the old road board reappearing on its successor. This half-dozen included Lord Lovat, in his role as Lord Lieutenant, and Lord Abinger, although this time round he had been elected to become one of the 55 Inverness-shire county councillors.[17] On the one hand, continuity of experience; on the other, continuity of power. One of the new councillors, Aeneas Ranald MacDonell, an advocate and owner of Camusdarach, near Mallaig, put forward the motion on 16 October 1890 to petition Parliament, through the MP Charles Fraser Mackintosh, for assistance with road construction to link the remoter parts of the mainland and the islands to the population centres, 'and to urge upon the Government the necessity of opening up those localities in order not only to give employment to the people but also to stimulate and facilitate the resources thereof'. The convener and some other councillors thought the time inopportune, but the matter was put to the vote and carried. Nothing, however, appears to have resulted directly or very quickly from MacDonell's initiative, but the development of roads and bridges was included in the programme of the Congested Districts Board, established in 1897 to administer grants for the Highlands. Based on its predecessor in Ireland, the Highland Board provided funds for development and relief projects in the rural parts of what became known as the seven crofting counties – Argyll, Inverness-shire, Ross and Cromarty, Sutherland, Caithness, Orkney and Shetland. Some funds went towards road-building.

Inverness-shire County Council's estimated expenditure on roads in 1890–91 amounted to £9,400, with South Uist being assigned a miserly £160 and most (£2,199) earmarked for the 2nd District, the Aird lying immediately west of the capital. The council took over the maintenance of several roads in different parts of its jurisdiction and constructed some new pieces of infrastructure, such as a bridge to replace a ford over the Rhue (Rha) river on Skye, and roads to the townships of Herbusta and Peingown.

And then, as if to welcome the new authority to the job it had to do, nature struck again at the Highland infrastructure. January 1892 opened with a very heavy blizzard, possibly the greatest for 30 years, as people said, and it left the whole countryside 'groaning under a massive load of snow'.[18] Roads were effaced from view and movement became almost impossible. Five trains were embedded between Grantown and Dalnaspidal. Six engines and a plough were needed to extricate a goods train that had become entombed in snow on Alvie moor between Kingussie and Aviemore. At Altnabreac on the Caithness county boundary, a south-bound train was stuck for a whole weekend: the ten passengers struggled through the snow to food and warmth at Forsinard, five miles down the line, leaving the road workers living in the district to feed the wagonload of cattle that had had to be abandoned. When the snow at last melted there was a great flood, in every valley from Thurso to Perth, and many bridges and embankments were overcome. The Ness overflowed in the centre of the town, the Beauly river cut 'two serious rents' in the Lovat bridge, the Cannich bridge was swept away, as was the bridge at Bonar. In a domino effect of destruction on the river Glass a series of wooden bridges collapsed, each adding to the debris that sped downstream to batter the next to pieces. On 5 May the Inverness-shire County Council had to approve expenditure of £12,000 to build three new crossings at or near the Lovat Bridge at Beauly, and upstream at Kilmorack and Cannich.[19] At the Kyle of Sutherland, the new Ross-shire and Sutherland county councils likewise had to contemplate the urgent replacement of the crossing at Bonar. The new bridge with three arches of cantilevered iron between pillars of granite was completed in 1893.

Part 4

The growth of shipping

CHAPTER 13

Maritime traffic

'carrying a press of sail . . .'

'I enforced this matter pretty warmly to the secretary, and other members. All these gentlemen expressed their approbation of my proposals . . .' So wrote John Knox in the introduction to his account of a tour through the Highlands in 1786.[1] The gentlemen to whom he referred were the members of the Highland Society of London, and the proposals were Knox's views on how to boost the economy of the far north. The society had been formed towards the end of May in 1778 in the Spring Garden Coffee House. Thirty years had passed since government forces on Drumossie Moor outside Inverness had put an end to the Jacobite dream of regaining the British throne and almost fatally broken the old clan society of the Highlands. The lands of the chieftains and lairds who had turned out in the Stuart cause remained forfeited, while some of the chieftains and lairds themselves had lost their heads or been driven into exile. Now, the gentlemen in the coffee house, some of whom were heirs to these same forfeited acres, were set on regaining their social position (the forfeited estates were to be restored to the heirs in 1784), while enjoying drams, pipe music and poetry, and recalling their native braes in wistful nostalgia.

Knox had retired from running an extremely successful book-selling business in the Strand. In 1764 he had travelled into the

Highlands and Islands on the first of several trips and had been deeply affected by the poverty he saw among the ordinary people. 'I transmitted to the secretary [of the society] . . . a long letter stating the urgent necessity of opening an inland navigation in the Highlands, and also of erecting fishing stations along the coast,' continued the indefatigable stravaiger. It was an imaginative and, on paper at least, a sound scheme, to turn to the sea to build a new economy. At the time the Dutch were more industrious in exploiting the herring shoals. A home-grown fishery would provide employment, cut emigration already running into the tens of thousands, and strengthen the navy and the country's defence through providing a pool of skilled seamen. Knox despised 'the newly devised custom of ejecting fifty or a hundred families at a time, to make room for a stock of sheep'. In his view, 'This practice, with the religious commotions of the last century, nearly depopulated the South of Scotland, from whence it is said 7,000 families transported themselves to the North of Ireland, America, and other parts. The same causes have lately produced the same effects in the Highlands . . .'

The sea's potential led to the establishment of the British Fisheries Society in 1786. Who better for the Highland Society to ask to make a tour to collect the names of potential subscribers than the man who had created this vision. Thus, Knox set out on his last and biggest excursion, from Oban north to Cape Wrath, with a side trip into the Hebrides, along the north coast to Duncansby and south again to the Moray Firth and Edinburgh. He reckoned the distance at over 3,000 miles and his time for completion at six months. Much of it he did on foot or by boat. It was no mean achievement, considering he was in his mid-60s, but he died in Dalkeith in August 1790, too soon to see the realisation of much of his dream.

Knox pointed out 'the comparative insignificancy' of the military roads built in the preceding decades, as none had been made beyond the Great Glen. In the northern counties, he claimed, the inhabitants of each glen were prisoners for much of the year, hemmed in by the mountains and bad weather until the threat of death from famine forced them to venture to the low country in search of meal or fish. Infrastructure – new roads, harbours, even canals – was needed. In his view, there was only one natural harbour on the entire north-west coast, at Loch Eriboll, where a vessel could find shelter at all states of the tide. There were no towns and no dockyards where repairs could be effected. But the potential was there. Oban, he thought, was 'formed by nature' to be a main harbour and a place of trade, a strategic naval base and arsenal to guard the western seas. This was prescient, as in a few years the country would be at war with France, and privateers would harry the northern shipping lanes.

The British Fisheries Society, or to give its proper title 'The British Society for Extending the Fisheries and Improving the Sea Coasts of the Kingdom', built on the work that had been started by the Commissioners for the Annexed Estates and the Board of Trustees for Manufactures and Fisheries. The latter, founded in 1727, had been active mainly in the Lowlands in boosting linen manufacture. The Fisheries Society was to have a much greater impact in the north, founding planned fishing settlements first at Tobermory in 1788, and then at Lochbay on Skye, on the island of Canna, at Ullapool on Loch Broom and, finally and most successfully, at Wick in Caithness in the form of the planned settlement of Pulteneytown.[2]

The efforts of the various public bodies had a reinforcing effect on each other's development projects. A report in 1754, from the surveyor of manufactures in the Highlands to the Commissioners for Improving Fisheries and Manufactures in Scotland, declared that a road from Ullapool to Dingwall fit for wheeled carriages would be too expensive for the county authorities. George Brown, however, surveyed a route to Ullapool in around 1790 and work began on it in the summer of 1792 under Kenneth Mackenzie of Torridon. Thirty-eight miles had been completed by 1797 at a cost of £4,582 and it formed an 'excellent' road, in the view of Roderick Macrae, the Lochbroom minister, 'where lately nothing could be carried but in creels on horseback, carts and carriages can now travel with the greatest ease and expedition'.[3] The decision of the British Fisheries Society to initiate a fishing port at Ullapool was influenced by the existence of this road. The minister's successor in the pulpit was less enamoured of the road when he wrote about it in 1835: 'being a new thing in the Highlands', the road had 'astonished the natives not a little', but the line followed by the builders had been so 'absurd' and the execution so 'wretched' that the road had been for a long time 'not only useless but dangerous' to both walkers and riders, and to wheeled carriages 'almost impassable' – the reader feels that the minister is speaking here from experience.[4] Some of bridges had been 'carried away', and a new road would be 'an immense improvement'. The Commissioners for Roads and Bridges undertook just such a project between 1839 and 1850.

Victorian photographers have bequeathed to us breathtaking sepia panoramas of the harbours on the east coast of the country, the basins and quays packed with boats, and masts and sails rising like a forest from thickets of people and barrels. These are the classic images of the great nineteenth-century herring fishery encouraged by the efforts of the British Fisheries Society. Among the fishing boats, we see the occasional schooner or full-rigged barque, the workhorses of maritime commerce. The volume of coastal shipping received a great boost from the herring fishery but it was already on the increase before that. The tonnage of shipping owned in Scottish ports increased during the eighteenth century almost fourfold until in 1791 it stood around 140,000 tons.[5] Most of this expansion took place in the last decades of the century, and in the years immediately following the Treaty of Union in 1707 seaborne trade had continued at first much as it had done in the previous century. The letters of the Inverness merchant John Steuart, written

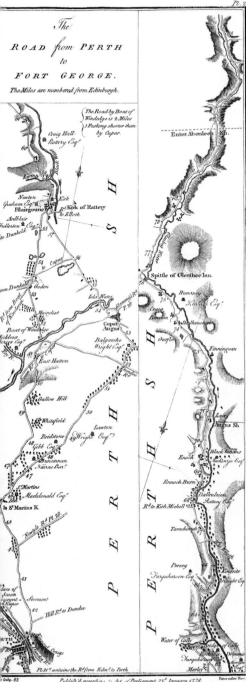

PLATE 1. Thomas Bowen was a London mapmaker with an inventive approach. He devised road maps as a series of strips depicting a route; this one from 1776 shows the north road, now the A93, from Perth via Blairgowrie and Glenshee. (Author collection)

PLATE 2. *Right*. D.G. Moir's map of old paths and tracks, published in *Scottish Hill Tracks* (1947), shows, for this part of the south-west Highlands, a denser network than that of the present road system. (Author collection)

PLATE 3. *Below*. The packhorse bridge at Carrbridge survives as a precarious arch. Built by mason John Niccolsone in 1717, it was badly damaged by floodwaters in the eighteenth century and in 1829. (Author collection)

PLATE 4. *Bottom*. An early nineteenth-century engraving of the bridge over the Tay at Dunkeld. The poet Robert Southey thought that this was his friend Thomas Telford's finest Highland bridge. It was built in 1803–05 under the direction of engineers Patrick Brown and John Simpson. (Author collection)

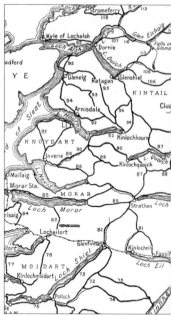

PLATE 5. Schooners and steamships jostle for quay space in Wick harbour in the late nineteenth century. (Johnstone Collection, Wick Society)

PLATE 6. The *St Ola*, the first of three vessels to carry the name, ran between Scrabster in Caithness and Stromness in Orkney for 59 years from 1892. In the 1939 Powell-Pressburger movie *The Spy in Black*, she was 'sunk', but in fact she steamed on until she was scrapped in 1951. (Author collection)

PLATE 7. The paddle steamer *Iona* on the Glasgow to Oban run. She was built for MacBrayne in 1864 at Clydebank to replace a predecessor and namesake sold to the United States to be a blockade runner during the American Civil War. The *Iona* served the south-west coast until the summer of 1935 and was broken up the following year. (Author collection)

NATIONAL HOTEL,

DINGWALL.

JOHN SINCLAIR, Proprietor.

THE above large and commodious Hotel is beautifully situated near to the Railway Station, and within five miles of the far-famed Strathpeffer Wells. The splendid Tourist Coaches DEFIANCE and WELLINGTON leave the National Hotel every lawful morning direct for Skye, Lochmaree, and Gairloch. The above Coaches, which are well horsed, have no connection with Mail Gigs, and are the only Coaches having any connection with Lochmaree, Gairloch, and Ullapool.

Families would do well to secure seats beforehand. The scenery on this route is well known to be by far the finest in Scotland.

Parties leaving Glasgow or Edinburgh in the morning can be in Dingwall same evening.

Carriages, Waggonettes, &c., kept for hire or job.

Letters for rooms, coach-seats, or conveyances, punctually attended to.

PLATE 8. Competition for tourist custom has long been strong in the Highlands, as displayed in th advertisement for the coach services offered by the National Hotel in Dingwall in the early nineteenth century. The phrase 'lawful morning' is a reminder that there are no coaches on the Sabbath. (Author collection)

PLATE 9. The post wagon at the Rhiconich Hotel, Sutherland, about 1906. (Courtesy of Willie and Jennifer Morrison)

PLATE 10. *Above*. The worst rail accident in the Highlands occurred at Carrbridge on 18 June 1914. A thunderstorm of unprecedented severity led to a great spate rushing down the Baddengorm burn just as a train was crossing a bridge over a gorge on the outskirts of the village. The water tore away the bridge foundation and the fourth carriage in the train fell into the spate. Five passengers were drowned. (© Highland Railway Society)

PLATE 11. *Left*. A nineteenth-century railway conductor. (Johnstone Collection, Wick Society)

PLATE 12. *Top.* The coffeepot loco, as it was known, at Dornoch in 1936. This tank engine worked on the branch line between the Mound and Dornoch for over 50 years, almost the entire time the branch was open. (Courtesy of William and Jennifer Morrison)

PLATE 13. *Above.* A locomotive tries to batter through deep snow at Scotscalder in Caithness. (Johnstone Collection, Wick Society)

PLATE 14. *Right.* Cycling became popular in the late nineteenth century and had a liberating effect on society. (Johnstone Collection, Wick Society)

ᴛᴇ 15. A scene scarcely credible now – a flock of sheep on the A9 near the Drumochter Pass, 1930s. ᴀthor collection)

ᴛᴇ 16. The Fergie, economical and tough, was a boon to hundreds of farmers and crofters ᴛoughout the Highlands. This one, in Dunnet in Caithness, is equipped with a back delivery for ᴛting hay. (Author collection)

ᴛᴇ 17. The vehicle ferry across Loch Duich in the 1930s. Eilean Donan castle rises in the ᴀkground.(Courtesy of Willie and Jennifer Morrison)

PLATE 18. *Right.* Ted Fresson and islanders on the occasion of the opening of an airmail service to North Ronaldsay. (Highland Photographic Archive, Inverness Museum & Art Gallery, High Life Highland)

PLATE 19. *Right.* Lorries in the Highlands can be adapted to carry anything. Here a small house is being transported on the Black Isle. The founder of the transport company, Hugh Fraser (left), was proud of the slogan painted on the vehicle front: 'Anyware Anywhere'. (Courtesy of the Fraser family)

PLATE 20. Large trucks with heavy loads, such as this timber lorry crossing the Easter Fearn burn in Ross-shire, can be a serious test of infrastructure not designed with such use in mind. (Author collection)

PLATE 21. *Left*. In his 1718 map of the far north, Hermann Moll indicated roads with a double or a single line according to their importance and gave mileages. (Reproduced by permission of the National Library of Scotland)

PLATE 22. *Below*. The A9 at Navidale on the approach to the Ord of Caithness. The old track that Bishop Forbes followed in 1762 and the road constructed in the early 1800s by the Commission for Roads and Bridges were superseded by this long ribbon of tarmac built between 2004 and 2006. (Author collection)

PLATE 23. The Wade Stone stands beside the A9 a few miles south of the Drumochter Pass. Erected 1729, it marks the completion of the military road through Glengarry. There is a tradition of leaving coins on its top. (Author collection)

PLATE 24. General Wade considered this bridge over the Tay at Aberfeldy his finest achievement. (Courtesy of Mairi Stewart)

PLATE 25. *Left*. The inscribed stone at the Well of the Lecht, commemorating the construction of the road by companies of the 33rd Regiment in 1754. (Author collection)

PLATE 26. *Below*. The clapper bridge at Aultbea, one of two examples in Wester Ross of this type of construction. (Author collection)

PLATE 27. This gang of workmen erected the new bridge at Bonar in 1893 after its predecessor had been destroyed by a flood. Note the diver in the centre. (Courtesy of Willie and Jennifer Morrison)

PLATE 28. The present bridge at Bonar, the third on the site. The monument celebrates the work of the Commission for Roads and Bridges. (Author collection)

PLATE 29. Inverness railway station in its heyday, during the days of steam.
(Courtesy of David Henderson)

PLATE 30. A lone cyclist waits at Lairg station for the train southbound to Inverness.
(Author collection)

PLATE 31. The course of the old road over the Devil's Elbow can be seen in surviving ox-bows of tarmac. (Author collection)

THE DEVILS ELBOW (THE HIGHEST PUBLIC ROAD IN GREAT BRITAIN, 2199 FT ABOVE SEA LE

R. 217504

PLATE 32. The Devil's Elbow hairpin must have been daunting to drivers in the early days of motoring.(Highland Photographic Archive, Inverness Museum & Art Gallery, High Life Highland

ATE 33. A Highland Airways De Havilland DH84 Dragon I flies over Scapa Flow in the mid-1930s. ourtesy of Andrew Rae)

ATE 34. The *Iona*, the first roll-on roll-off ferry in the Caledonian MacBrayne fleet. Introduced in o, she could load vehicles at bow, stern and aft beam. (© The Olivia G James Collection courtesy he Highland Archive Service (Skye and Lochalsh))

PLATE 35. The Berriedale braes in Caithness are a notorious traffic chokepoint on the A9. The road has steep descents on both sides of the narrow valley, with the hairpin bend on the north brae being the worst for long juggernauts. (Courtesy of Elizabeth-Anne Mackay)

PLATE 36. Diamonds, the sign for a passing place, seem to be forever. There are several stretches of single-track road in the north-west Highlands. (Author collection)

between 1715 and 1752, refer to the movement of goods throughout the North Sea and the Baltic. One cargo vessel, the *Margaret* of 50 tons, is recorded as carrying salmon, herring, timber and iron to and fro between Danzig, Rotterdam, Hamburg, Portsoy, Yarmouth and London in the ten years before she was grounded and wrecked on a sandbar outside Montrose in December 1725. This little saga of commerce was probably typical of what could befall a trading vessel; the *Margaret* had even been plundered by Swedish privateers in the Kattegat. Of his goods lost in the Montrose wreck, Steuart lamented that all he had left was 'a barrell of pitch'.[6]

Between 1734 and 1744, an enterprising merchant called Colin Campbell ran a trading business, relying on coastal shipping, from Inveresragan on the northern shore of Loch Etive. This was called the Loch Etive Trading Company and handled both everyday practical goods and consumer items. Campbell corresponded with merchants in Glasgow and Leith, and with clients closer to home in Lorne and Appin. It appears that some of the districts on the west coast remained without local ownership of seagoing vessels right through the eighteenth century. There were small craft used for fishing and inshore work in every coastal community, but the tacksmen in Durness also kept two sloops based in Rispond for trade in fish.[7] Drawing on records that have survived in Orkney, Ian Hustwick has described in detail the trading life of an Orcadian sloop, the *Peggy and Isabella*, over a period of some 30 years; such vessels formed the backbone of coastal commerce at the time.[8]

In 1750 Murdoch Mackenzie, a Kirkwall schoolmaster turned surveyor, published his atlas of coastal waters. Beginning in his native islands, where he waited for a winter frost to provide him with the opportunity to measure an accurate, level baseline for his triangulation on the ice of the Loch of Stenness, Mackenzie surveyed Orkney and the Pentland Firth.[9] Never before had such accurate charts with data on currents and tides been available to seafarers. Instead of remaining a turbulent gut of whirlpools and surf with a reputation to make mariners tremble, the Pentland Firth became a feasible route between the North Sea and the Atlantic, cutting hours if not days off the long, northabout sweep beyond Orkney or Shetland that deep-sea vessels had hitherto felt obliged to follow. Mackenzie went on to survey the Hebrides, the west coasts of Britain and the coast of Ireland for the Admiralty, and was followed in his post by his nephew of the same name. Other surveys followed: John Ainslie and Murdo Downie produced charts for the east coast in 1785 and 1792 respectively; Joseph Huddart, Robert Laurie and James Whittle covered the west coast in two charts published in 1794; and the Admiralty launched a complete new survey of Scottish waters in 1825.

With the increasing maritime traffic came a rise in the number of casualties. Comprehensive information, apart from some anecdotes, is lacking for the years before 1700 but the early nineteenth century shows a clear rise in wrecks and marine accidents. In his studies of wrecks on the north-east coast and in the northern islands, David Ferguson found that shipping losses showed an upward trend during the 1700s, a high level between 1800 and 1850, and a steady decline after that.[10] The fall in maritime accidents after 1850 was attrib-uted to the gradual replacement of sail by steam. Another factor helped. Hard on the heels of the publication of the new charts came another aid to safe navigation – lighthouses. The need for these was frequently expressed and led to the estab-lishment by act of Parliament in 1786 of the Commissioners of Northern Lighthouses. From its headquarters in Edinburgh, it oversaw the construction of lighthouses at key locations. Initially, there were four: Kinnaird Head (1787), the Mull of Kintyre (1788), and North Ronaldsay and Eilean Glas (1789). Other lights soon followed: on Pladda in 1790, the Pentland Skerries in 1794 and the Bell Rock in 1811. In the view of the Commissioners of Supply for Nairnshire, shipwreck losses in the Moray Firth arose from the want of lighthouses: 'Vessels running from the South to take Shelter in Cromarty Bay – the only port of safety on the east coast of Scotland – are frequently foundered or stranded for want of lights to guide their Course up the Firth – and during the present winter no less than sixteen vessels foundered or were stranded on the coasts of the Moray Firth and all the crew, excepting two, perished.'[11] They resolved to write to the Northern Lighthouse Commissioners on the subject, suggesting that two light-houses – on Tarbat Ness and on the Skerries near Stotfield – would serve to alleviate the problems. Altogether by 1850 the Board would build more than 30 coastal beacons and continued to add others after that date. The wars with the French also played their part in encouraging the growth of coastal shipping. Privateers threatened to pick off merchant vessels and, to counter this threat to trade, the government and the Royal Navy put into place a convoy system. In the north the assembly point for any merchant ship wishing to sail in convoy to Scandinavia was established at Longhope, and to get to Longhope the shipmasters had to navigate into waters which they may have otherwise given a wide berth. A fearful place to strangers, admitted Murdoch Mackenzie's nephew Graeme Spence, trying in 1812 to persuade the Admiralty to open a naval base at Scapa Flow, but the locals 'would think light of it'.[12]

The founding in 1824 of the National Institution for the Preservation of Life from Shipwreck – the name changed to the Royal National Lifeboat Institution in 1854 – contributed to a reduction in the loss of life around the coast. Yet, with nothing beyond their experience to advise seafarers of the weather, the dangers in the days of sail remained extreme, especially on a lee shore where wind direction could overcome the best sail handling to drive a ship to disaster. The press of the period has chilling reports of many tragedies and it will suffice to quote from one, from 28 September 1861, when an unknown vessel was wrecked at the entrance to Wick bay:

At 6 pm the [harbour] Pilot on watch observed a schooner
up from the North on the port tack, carrying a press of
sail ... [it] soon became evident to those onshore that the
vessel was fast running to destruction ... At 6.30 pm the
vessel struck very heavily and remained a few seconds, did
not broach to or fall off, her sails remained full, the press of
sail and action of the waves forcing her over the sunken
rocks into deep water ... when in less than twenty seconds
she sank under full sail, bow down and disappeared.'

The local lifeboat and a steamer searched in vain for survivors, and it was not until the following day that it was discovered the hapless schooner had been a Prussian vessel, the *Arnold*,
with a crew of four. Two weeks after his death, the body of the
captain was washed ashore and interred in the local
kirkyard.[13]

At Stornoway in 1785 Knox found 13 vessels at anchor.
There was no quay worth the name, he wrote, and the boats
used the beach to load and unload, a practice that was to
continue in some places until modern times. The famous Clyde
puffers that brought coal and general cargo to the Hebrides in
the early twentieth century were designed with beaching in
mind. Despite the absence of port facilities, Stornoway had
trade links with Scandinavia, Ireland, Holland and France, and
made a handy port of call for ships sailing between the west of
England and the Baltic.[14] 'There are very few vessels belonging
to Assynt,' wrote the Revd William Mackenzie, 'Mr Macdonald,
Lochinver, has one or two', but the lairds and tacksmen in the
district overcame the lack by hiring ships from Leith to come
yearly to carry away their stocks of cured salmon and herring.[15]
Lochinver was to gain a pier in 1837, but it was frequently the
resort of herring busses before that date. In the south-west
Highlands, there were active harbours at Oban, Tarbert,
Campbeltown and Inveraray.[16] Oban had its birth with the
establishment of a base there by a Renfrew trading company in

around 1713; a customs house opened in 1764 and in the next 20 years the little town began to grow rapidly. In 1792 it had 15 to 20 sloops involved in fishing and coastal trade, and one vessel plying to the Baltic. Writing that year, the minister noted that 'the traders ... labour under great inconvenience for want of a proper quay to discharge their goods'.[17] Inveraray had a poor harbour in the 1790s, according to its minister, but it was home to one vessel employed in foreign trade and six in coastal commerce.[18] Tarbert, situated on an isthmus, was ideally suited to act as a communications nexus, with weekly packets to what the minister called 'the low country' and to the Western Isles, and a post delivery three times a week; 'Many of the young men' in the place were 'seamen employed in vessels belonging to the parish, or to the ports of Rothsay, Cambeltoun and Greenock'.[19] Thomas Pennant observed in 1774: 'It is not very long since vessels of nine or ten tons were drawn by horses out of the west loch into that of the east, to avoid the dangers of the Mull of Cantyre, so dreaded and so little known was the navigation round the promontory.'[20] Some thought was given to cutting a canal across the mile-wide isthmus between the east and west sea-lochs. An application to Parliament for a bill to permit such a scheme was advertised in November 1845 but it was never to be dug.[21] Campbeltown's 'excellent harbour' also allowed regular sea connections with the Clyde and was home to an important herring fishery; in the 1790s it had 33 sloops and schooners and one ship of 500 tons carrying timber from Canada.[22]

At Thurso, in the 1790s there had been a gradual increase in coasting trade during the previous 20 years and now it was 'pretty considerable', with 16 decked vessels calling regularly, eight of which belonged to the town.[23] On the east coast of Caithness, at Wick, the herring fishery was still on a modest scale, awaiting the construction by the British Fisheries Society of the new harbour, and exports of grain customarily took place from the nearby haven of Staxigoe. Orkney and Shetland, where the voes cutting deep into the island landmasses provided a choice of sheltered havens and anchorages, had their small locally owned merchant brigs and sloops for trading. Lobster smacks traded along all the northern coasts for shellfish to be brought quickly to the urban markets in the south. Stromness had become an established harbour during the eighteenth century, almost a crossroads of the northern seas, and the last stop in Britain for Arctic-bound whalers and the ships of the Hudson's Bay Company. Some 300 vessels anchored in its sheltered water every year, a total that had dropped a little since the Pentland Firth had become better known, and some captains now chose to sail onward without bothering to heave to. On the north side of the Orkney mainland Kirkwall had a growing trade built around the export of raw produce and the import of consumer and manufactured goods; the number of ships had grown from 17 in 1770, representing some 825 tons, to 33 in 1790, or 2,000 tons, recorded the minister in his contribution to the *Statistical Account of Scotland*. Shetland had a similar trade, and exported some 800 tons of dried white fish every year to Hamburg, Ireland and the Catholic Mediterranean countries; the herring fishery at this time was still largely in the hands of the Dutch, who sent fleets of boats every season to the northern islands, a state of affairs that was soon to change. The northernmost archipelago in the British Isles, Shetland lay normally about six days' sail north of Leith, but storms in winter and the fog common in the summer could make a journey last considerably longer: John Mill, a parish minister in the islands, recorded in his diary how one voyage in August 1765 took ten days and in Bressay Sound, within sight of their destination, the vessel was in danger of being driven to Norway 'had not kind Providence changed the wind'.[24]

On the east coast, the main ports were Cromarty, where a pier had been built in 1785 to accommodate the regular trade with London, Leith and Aberdeen; Findhorn, home to several coastal trading vessels; and Inverness, a centre for trade both domestic and international since the Middle Ages, with seven vessels of 400 to 500 tons. The harbour at Banff towards the eastern corner of the Moray Firth had expanded bit by bit since 1625, and had a home fleet of 22 sloops and brigantines varying from 60 to 210 tons. Aberdeen remained the principal northern port, with dozens of vessels sailing in and out of the estuary of the Dee every year. A new pier erected by John Smeaton in 1775–80 could accommodate ships up to 200 tons. The *Statistical Account* noted a sharp fall in foreign ships between 1788 and 1794 but an almost twofold increase in coastal vessels, another manifestation of the general rise in shipping in this period.

CHAPTER 14

Canals

'It is hardly possible to express the astonishing advantages . . .'

Several people before Knox had thought about the construction of canals. In 1716, when the first surveys of Inverness were being drawn by military engineers, the town's minister, Robert Baillie, noted how they were talking of a canal to Fort William 'but that is no easy matter'.[1] On his first venture into the Highlands in 1762, Bishop Robert Forbes fell into conversation with some local men in Fort William, or Maryburgh, as he called it:

> I observed what an easy matter it might be to cut a Canal from Loch Lochy to Loch Oich,' he wrote, 'and from there to Loch Ness and, by deepening the River of Ness, to promote a navigation from Inverness to the West Seas ... They acknowledged all this to be true, and that some had actually been proposing such a Plan, and had been taking a View of the Ground with that Intent.[2]

The late eighteenth century was the time of the canal. Although some rivers had been 'improved' to permit navigation in earlier times, the first canals with systems of locks and basins designed specifically to allow barges to move with bulk cargoes – mainly coal in the early years – were constructed in the late

1750s. The Sankey Canal between St Helens and the Mersey opened in 1757, and the Bridgewater Canal two years later. Work began on the Forth and Clyde Canal across the waist of Scotland in 1768 and on the Monkland Canal in the 1770s. The spread of the network of navigable waterways across the industrialising parts of England stimulated what could be called 'canal-mindedness' among the public. The first canal in the Highlands, linking Ardrishaig to Crinan in Argyllshire, was surveyed in 1771 but for another two decades it remained only an intention. The minister of the parish of Kilmartin, where vessels could wait in Loch Crinan for weeks for a fair wind to round the Mull of Kintyre, observed in 1790 how Mr John Rennie, the eminent engineer who had surveyed the route, was of the opinion that it could be made 'at a very moderate expence, and with plenty of water for boats and barges as well as large vessels'.[3]

A private company to proceed with a canal was empowered by the Crinan Canal Act in 1793. Work went ahead, under Rennie's direction, and the completed waterway, nine miles long, opened to traffic eight years later, in July 1801, considerably delayed by problems with labour and the terrain. The engineer's original estimate of £103,000 proved inadequate and a government loan, on the security of the expected income from tolls, had to be sought to allow completion of the work. Not for the last time in the Highlands was a large infrastructure project made to carry a heavy burden of hope. 'It is hardly possible to express the astonishing advantages . . . to the people,' wrote the Kilmartin minister, Hugh Campbell. 'It will not only enable the inhabitants to avoid the very dangerous passage around the Mull of Kintyre but, by affording a ready market for all the productions of the Western Isles, it will invite people to pursue a variety of kinds of industry to which they have hitherto been strangers.' Campbell foresaw the easy importation of salt and coals, the former essential to the growth of herring fishing, and, as a result, 'the people [would become] as happy as they are now miserable, and they would be under no temptation of leaving their native soil to try their fortunes in America'. How to tackle the economic and social development of the Highlands was already metamorphosing into the 'Highland question'. Emigration to America from some Argyll parishes had been heavy in the 1770s and was rising again as Campbell was writing. What could be done to keep people at home and provide them with a decent standard of living? The investment in infrastructure projects was widely seen as one answer to the socioeconomic problems emerging in the Highlands, a concept still alive in our own time.

The need to bring in revenue brought forward the opening of the Crinan Canal. This haste led to problems. In January 1805 a stretch of bank on boggy terrain a few miles from Ardrishaig collapsed and necessitated a re-routing of the waterway, and a storm in 1811 burst the banks to release a flood of water, rocks and earth. By 1814, the canal company was in debt for £67,810 'exclusive of interest'.[4] Another government loan was secured in 1816 and resulted in major renovation work being undertaken under the expert eye of Thomas Telford in 1817. Soon afterwards, the canal was in effect nationalised, taken under government control, and its management placed in the hands of the Commissioners for the Caledonian Canal. 'After the above repair, the annual revenue of the canal has been sufficient for its support, and for improvements and renewal of works,' noted the Revd Alexander Mackenzie, who was not only the parish minister of South Knapdale but also involved in canal management. In the view of some commentators, the canal had been built 50 years too soon, for it proved too narrow to handle many of the steamships that began to ply the shipping routes in the 1820s.[5] Although the larger steamers were still obliged to keep to the sea, the number of passengers travelling via smaller steam vessels on the canal increased from 2,400 in 1820 to 21,406 in 1837. They also benefited from a scenic, leisurely route to the west coast and, like its later and more famous partner in the Great Glen, the Crinan Canal came into its own in the late twentieth century as a major recreational resource. Queen Victoria and Prince Albert came by in August 1847: 'We and our people drove through the little village [Lochgilphead] to the Crinan Canal where we entered a most magnificently decorated barge drawn by three horses, ridden by postilions in scarlet,' recorded the Queen in her journal. She enthused about the scenery but was less enamoured by the actual voyage and the two and half hours it lasted: 'the eleven locks we had to go through – (a very curious process, first passing several by rising, and then others by going down) – were tedious'. Twenty-five years later, when Victoria, now a widow, passed along the Caledonian Canal she was still complaining of the boring necessity of locks.[6] The royal visit, of course, was advertised to boost the burgeoning Highland tourist industry and passengers flocked to follow the so-dubbed 'Royal Route' from Glasgow to Oban. In 1866, a trim little steamer, the *Linnet*, began what would become 65 years of service, carrying tourists and locals during the summer months.

The Commissioners of the Forfeited Estates, the government body who had managed the lands confiscated from those lairds and clan chiefs who had come out for the Jacobite cause in 1745 and had acquired considerable sums for re-investment in public works, appointed James Watt in 1773 to survey the proposed route for the Caledonian Canal. Watt envisaged a canal ten feet deep. A report published in the *Scots Magazine* in 1806 on the monies left from the forfeited estates also included £4,500 earmarked for a 37-mile canal from the Tay to Lochearn, but it was never to be built.[7] In the summer of 1801, Thomas Telford and William Jessop worked on a survey for the route of the Caledonian Canal and felt it to be a feasible undertaking: 'The line is very direct and I have observed no serious obstacle in any part of it,' wrote Telford. He reckoned that it would require seven years for construction and would cost £350,000, assuming half of the funds to come from the landowners who would benefit from its passage through their estates. In the event the government decided to fund all the costs of the canal, a move that has led A.D. Cameron, a historian of the project, to dub it 'the first nationalised enterprise'.[8] Telford proposed that the canal should be 15 feet deep and 50 feet wide at the bottom but these dimensions were soon altered to accommodate naval frigates. The contemporary war with Napoleon also had bearing on the decision to build the canal, in that its existence would mean merchant shipping could avoid not only the turbulence of the Pentland Firth but also the guns of any privateers.

The labour began in 1803, with the digging of trial pits along the proposed line. Telford, forever on the move, supervising the wide range of engineering projects happening across the country under his direction, gathered an expert team for the hands-on work. Matthew Davidson, like Telford himself originally a stonemason from Langholm, took up the post of resident engineer at the north end at Clachnaharry; and John Telford, no relation to Thomas, filled the equivalent position at Fort William. Each man received a salary of £200, a house and a horse. Local men were also brought on board, notably John Mitchell from Forres, whom we have met already. Telford spent only six to eight weeks in the year on the canal and the Highland roads, inspecting, advising and planning, taking John Mitchell with him in a gig where the roads were ready, in the saddle where they were not. When John Mitchell died in 1824, Telford handed the father's job to the son, Joseph, who began his own working life as a stonemason on the Caledonian Canal and, as we have seen, went on to achieve fame as an engineer in the north.

The early 1800s must have been a good time to be a qualified mason, with the canal and the road-building programmes in progress. The opportunities drew men from a wide area, from the four corners of Britain and from Ireland, sometimes on a seasonal basis. 'As the spring of the year came round,' recalled Joseph Mitchell, 'these [masons from Moray] might be seen in parties of eight or ten, wending their way, with burdens of apparel and tools, to fulfil their season's engagement.'[9] Other types of worker were also needed in large numbers – carpenters, carters, horsemen, blacksmiths and, above all, labourers who could wield a shovel or a pick with some skill or push a laden barrow. There was valuable spin-off to other local industries – to the quarries who supplied the stone, to owners of woods who could supply timber, to farmers, butchers and bakers who had to feed the workforce – and in 1809 a new foundry was established in Inverness to make iron rails. The local Highlanders, unused to the demands of industry, were unreliable timekeepers and would occasionally take time off to do some job at home. Among a few, whose forebears had fought at their chief's bidding and lifted cattle for sport, there may have lingered a feeling that digging earth was hardly a fit occupation for a gentleman. Matthew Davidson, who died in 1819 before his work on the canal was done, was remembered by Joseph Mitchell as 'a cynical humourist, very clever, very kind, a great reader; if he hated anybody he hated Highlanders for their inert ways – or said he hated them, for I am sure he did not'. They may not always have been ideal workers but to the Highlanders the money was useful, indeed needed among the growing population, and the piecework rates – 6d a cubic yard for earthwork, 2s a cubic yard for cutting out rock in the Corpach basin – must have been attractive. The basic day wage remained at the usual Highland rate of 1s 6d, with oatmeal for subsistence. Telford himself received three guineas a day as long as he was engaged on the project, and his superintending staff between £52 10s and £157 10s a year. By the summer of 1804, almost 200 men were at work on each of the basins at Corpach and Clachnaharry, but this total grew quickly and had passed 1,000 by the end of 1805. One Highland habit – the drinking of whisky in preference to beer – persisted despite efforts by the authorities to alter the custom.

The newspapers published regular reports on the progress of the great enterprise and on the social changes it wrought. 'The increased assiduity of the Labourers and Workmen (who are nearly all Highlanders) may partly be ascribed to their experience of regular payment every four weeks, without the delay of a single day,' observed the *Inverness Journal*, which had started publication in August 1807, only a few months before these words were written.[10] There were, of course, problems – delays caused by bad weather, flooding of the excavations, a few, though only a few, complaints about pay and conditions, and so on – but also moments of excitement such as when in January 1808 the workers dug up a massive silver chain from a cairn at Torvean.[11] To prevent the canal water from leaking away through the porous glacial gravels in the vicinity of Inverness, the bottom and sides had to be lined with puddled clay, a laborious, mucky process in the days of hand tools. The substrate at Corpach was solid rock but that presented its own difficulties. At Torvean the road had to be shifted; the bed of the Ness itself had to be altered and embanked to accommodate the canal; a stretch of the Oich was diverted and its old bed used for the canal; and at Clachnaharry, to provide the required constant depth through the shallow mudbanks of the Firth until the main sea channel was reached, a mound had to be laid out into the sea for 900 yards. At Lower Banavie a culvert was constructed to allow a burn and a farm track to pass under the canal. By and large, the local landowners cooperated and accepted the proposed sums as compensation for the disruption to their property; Cameron of Lochiel was content with the £2,000 he received. Alastair MacDonell of Glengarry, as was his wont, was happy to sell timber to the engineers from his forests while maintaining a flow of complaints – he wanted vessels to keep to the south shore of Loch Oich away from his house, and he disputed the value of the land he gave up to the project.[12]

By the end of 1807, the Muirtown basin had been dug out; by December 1809, the locks were in place. In 1811, work began at Fort Augustus. The ladder of locks at Banavie, dubbed Neptune's Staircase, where the water level rises 60 feet in some

500 yards, was completed by 1812. Steam pumps were brought into action and a steam dredger began to puff and dig at Dochfour. In the summer of 1818 the canal was open to traffic as far as Loch Ness. In 1821, the Laggan locks were completed.

During 1819, some 265 vessels used the new waterway: 'no difficulty has been encountered, nor damage sustained by any of them', reported the *Inverness Courier*, 'and the doubt formerly entertained as to the practicability of this navigation no longer appears to exist.'[13]

A steam boat had by this time made the return trip between Inverness and Fort Augustus six times. The newspaper was a firm supporter of improved connectivity: 'Nothing more forcibly shews the rapid improvement of this country, and the enterprising commercial spirit spread abroad among the people,' noted the correspondent, adding that a new smack, the *Jane Mackenzie*, starting on the coastal service to Leith, and coach services were also now daily at Inverness, which 'very few years back, no public vehicle approached, and which within the memory of living men seemed as unapproachable as Stornoway or Lerwick.' Even Stornoway's remoteness was about to be dented, for the Hebridean town was also soon to receive a steamboat service. 'A traveller by a private stage coach may reach Edinburgh twenty hours sooner than a letter put into the post office of Inverness at the same hour he departs,' noted the *Courier*, implying that there was still much room for improvement in certain quarters. 'How would the grey-haired sires of former days, leading their strings of little garrons, loaded with packs and going in a sort of caravan to avoid the exploits of the Borlums and John Gunns of those days,' mused the editor, 'how would they have stared to hear of a coach running from Inverness to Perth in one day!' [14]

The canal had its official opening at last on 23 October 1822, when the steam yacht *Lochness* cast off at Muirtown to enthusiastic cheers and cannon shots from a crowd of sightseers. Scarcely a breath of wind disturbed the water, and the smoke from the guns drifted upwards undispersed. The Inverness Militia band turned out to play 'God Save the King' and, aboard the yacht, all the local dignitaries assembled in jovial company. The Right Honourable Charles Grant MP was there, several lairds from various parts of the Highlands, the provost and baillies of the town, and more landowners and gentlemen, including MacDonell of Glengarry, unembarrassed by the trouble he had caused, were expected to join the vessel en route to Fort William. More spectators flocked to the banks along the way.

Unsurprisingly, the Caledonian Canal proved to be a very costly undertaking and the Commissioners were moved to defend themselves against their critics by making wild overestimates of the revenue that was expected from the tolls paid by ships using the new route. 'After a labour of nearly twenty years ... the country will feel a great degree of satisfaction in hearing of the completion,' noted the editor of the *Inverness Courier*, in a mixture of condescension and sympathy. He continues:

> It has afforded ... employment for the population of those forlorn wastes through which it passes; and not only mitigated the hardships consequent on the late rapid changes of our country, which have chiefly affected the lower classes, but aroused them from a state of inactivity, and by joining with those skilful workmen who resorted to it from all parts of the kingdom, they have acquired habits of industry, and other advantages, which will last while they are a people. [15]

Commenting in 1824, John Macculloch, a doctor and a friend of Sir Walter Scott, wrote 'The Caledonian canal is finished: at last. What shall I say ... What, except that I wish, since the object was to spend money, that it has been built on arches, like the Pont du Gard; that posterity too might have some enjoyment for its expense ...' [16]

In the event, the toll income remained for many years less than one-tenth of the projections. It was also unsurprising that over the length of time it took to complete the construction the costs rose, although the bulk of that expenditure was recycled into the local economy, providing a stimulus to many local enterprises and further development. In the end, although the amount is subject to debate, the project consumed somewhere between £650,000 and £900,000 of government funds. Public investment of this sort did not please everyone – the *Inverness Courier* held firmly to the view that 'the prime mover of all true improvement' was 'individual interest'.[17]

To navigate the canal, ships paid according to their size and the distance they travelled, the charge for a steam packet going the full distance from the Inverness Firth to Loch Linnhe being initially 10s. Sailing vessels relied, of course, on the wind but in adverse conditions horses could be hired to tow boats at two miles per hour. The rate of calculation began at a farthing (¼d) per ton per mile for the full passage. This was doubled to a half-penny (½d) per ton per mile in 1825. What probably did not escape the Commissioners was the fact that, apart from light-house dues, the passage of the Pentland Firth was free and, as maritime technology and navigation improved, becoming less and less dangerous. To boost traffic, the Commissioners resorted to advertising and, in 1828, reduced the toll to the original farthing.

CHAPTER 15

Fishing and smuggling

Ship News

While eyes in the central Highlands were gazing in admiration on the canal, those in Caithness were fixed on a new harbour and planned town taking shape at Wick under the aegis of the British Fisheries Society.

In 1790 the society had asked Thomas Telford to survey the ports in the Moray Firth to see which could be capable of improvement for a new herring port. Telford concluded that Wick should be the place. Accordingly, after long negotiation, the society reached an agreement with the local landowner, Sir Benjamin Dunbar of Hempriggs, on 11 March 1803, to feu 390 acres of land on the south side of the rivermouth at Wick. This was the site for Pulteneytown, named after Sir William Pulteney, the governor of the society. Construction began with the replacement of the wooden bridge over the Wick river by one of stone, and in short order work proceeded on the harbour and a planned grid of streets. The new town grew quickly and soon became home to an assorted population of fishermen, fishcurers, tradesmen, merchants, artisans and their families. The catching and processing of herring reached an annual peak in the late summer when the teeming shoals of the silver darlings passed along the coast. In the first 20 years of its existence the catch in Wick leapt from 10,000 to almost 200,000 barrels of salt herring per year. All the other havens around the Firth were swept up in the bonanza. For example, Helmsdale produced over 5,300 barrels in 1815 and 46,571 barrels in 1839.[1]

The fishing and the increased coastal trade spurred a burst of harbour building, new stone piers and quays to replace the wooden piers and beaching shores of earlier days. Portsoy's harbour dates to 1701 and Findhorn's to 1778, but many of the others were first constructed in the early 1800s, including Avoch, Cullen, Burghead, Nairn, Invergordon, Fortrose, Portmahomack, Portree, Kirkwall, Helmsdale, Brora, Lochinver, Castletown, Scalloway, Mallaig and Kinlochbervie.[2] Joseph Mitchell turned his hand to this activity with his plans for new harbours at Findhorn and Lossiemouth in 1827, and at Burghead a decade later; he was appointed in 1828 to be the engineer in charge of the British Fisheries Society harbours. Another notable harbour engineer was James Bremner from Caithness; Bremner also established a reputation as an ingenious salvager of wrecked ships and was summoned to rescue Isambard Kingdom Brunel's steamer *Great Britain* when she went aground in Dundrum Bay in Ireland in 1846.[3] The development of coastal infrastructure continued throughout the century. Portmahomack had an old haven dating from 1698 but the Commission for Roads and Bridges replaced it in 1815. Bonar Bridge made do with a wooden pier from the 1830s and had it replaced with a stone one in 1877. The government supported the construction of small harbours on Islay, Jura, Colonsay and Gigha as relief works during the 1846–47 potato famine.[4]

The Caledonian Canal traffic was greatly boosted by the herring fishing in the north. During the winter months regular and frequent shipments of salt herring from the northern curing stations to markets in the south-west, to Liverpool, Bristol, Belfast, Dublin and other ports on the Irish coast, made their way through the Great Glen. As the nineteenth century wore on, herring shipments to northern European ports and the Baltic increased in number, with sailing schooners, smacks and three-masters linking harbours all around the North Sea. At the height of the annual activity, in the autumn after the fish had been laid tightly and snugly in salt and before the winter gales set in, it is typical to read in the local papers about the *Margaret* from Boddam, the *Sarah* from Wick or the *Eliza* from Helmsdale arriving in Hamburg, Cuxhaven, Elsinore, Danzig, Memel, Stettin or Konigsberg. Local papers in Caithness carried regular news about events in Prussia and the exchange rates with the mark and the rouble.

The growth in coastal shipping and fishing stimulated ship-building.[5] During the seventeenth and eighteenth centuries it was common to find small sailing vessels being built in the settlements around the Moray Firth, at Inverness and Garmouth and Findhorn. This was the high point in a tradition with a very long, if intermittent, pedigree: one famous record exists for an oceangoing ship being constructed in Inverness in 1249 for Hugh de Châtillon, Count of St Pol, for voyaging to the Crusades, an occurrence that is unlikely to have been unique.[6] The building of smacks, brigs, schooners and other vessels seems to have resumed in Inverness in 1828 and again, after a short gap, in 1863, when two schooners for the coastal trade were on the stocks. The last schooner built in Inverness was probably the *Hilda*, from Robert Stewart's yard, for a Beauly merchant called Maclennan, who intended to use her in the Baltic trade. Robert Stewart's daughter Elisa christened the ship before she slid into the water on 20 October 1879, as a band on the opposite bank of the Ness struck up what the newspaper called 'a lively air'.[7]

What made shipbuilding on any scale feasible on this coast was the ready source of good timber from the forests in the surrounding hills. The Spey and the Ness flowed seaward from well-wooded straths, and the Dee draining the eastern Cairngorms likewise provided yards in Aberdeen with the timber they needed. A comparable resource did not exist on the northern and western coasts. Exploitation of the Strathspey forests on a large scale began in the 1730s under the direction of the York Building Company. Felled trees could be floated down the Spey to be exported from Garmouth to the naval shipyards in England. Increasing demand for ships in the late 1700s led two timber merchants from Hull, Ralph Dodsworth and William Osbourne, to think of establishing a yard closer to the source of the material they were handling. In 1786 they bought the Glenmore Forest from the Duke of Gordon for £10,000, formed the Glenmore Company, recruited shipwrights to move north and opened a yard at the mouth of the Spey. The coast here is a notoriously shifting maze of sandbars and hardly had they set up shop than the river took a swerve to the east. Undaunted, the entrepreneurs dug a canal to maintain access to the river. William Osbourne's cousin, Thomas Hustwick, a Dover shipwright, was placed in charge of the yard. The earliest record we have of a ship built in the yard is for a 700-ton vessel whose launching is reported in the *Aberdeen Journal* on 28 April 1795. In his seminal work on the subject of Moray Firth shipbuilding, Ian Hustwick lists more than 600 ships built at Speymouth between 1780 and 1895, with significant numbers also being launched from yards in Banff, Buckie, Clachnaharry, Findhorn, Inverness and other ports. Harbours further to the north, such as Wick, tended to focus on the construction of fishing boats, but they too turned out schooners. Even some small havens joined in to launch the occasional vessel, such as the sloop *Elizabeth McKenzie* at Dingwall in 1842, and the two sloops the *Catharine* and the *Jane Arnott* at Meikle Ferry in 1830 and 1843 respectively. Such sloops were small vessels, perhaps 30 feet long and capable of carrying 20 tons of cargo, but they played a part out of proportion to their stature in the coastal trade of the period. The tonnage built in the Moray Firth yards peaked in the 1860s and declined thereafter, as it became increasingly necessary in the later decades to import timber from the Baltic. Among the last vessels to be built at Speymouth was the schooner *Janet Storm* in 1890.

The first issue of the *Inverness Journal*, on 7 August 1807, had a brief section headed 'Ship News'. It informed readers that the *Banff*, under Captain Strachan, the *Peace and Plenty*, Captain Fowler, and the *Three Friends*, Captain Steven, had all arrived in Leith with cargoes of grain from Cromarty and Findhorn.[8] The shipping news also recorded the arrival in Inverness of coal, meal, hemp, timber, salt or just 'goods' from other British ports and from the Baltic. These weekly snippets of what the paper came to call 'maritime intelligence' can be read to build up a picture, albeit fragmented, of a steady traffic around the coast and further afield. For example, on 29 January 1813, we find an advertisement that the *George*, under Walter Strachan's command, probably the same Strachan who skippered the *Banff* some years before, 'will sail from this place [Inverness] on Saturday the 30th curr, and from Cromarty on Monday the 8th February, and call off Findhorn and Burghead on Tuesday the 9th, wind and weather permitting.' A week later, the *Inverness Packet*, captained by John Mann, was due to make the passage from Cromarty to the Carron Wharf in London. Some vessels were described in the advertisements as armed, a selling point at a time when the privateers lurked in the offing. The *Ploughman*, a 'Fast Sailing and Armed Brigantine', was set to sail from Aberdeen on 16 March to join a convoy for Halifax and Pictou.

The nineteenth century saw a great growth in coastal passenger services. Ships began to stand out weekly from Inverness for London: the Inverness packet, as it was called, began service in 1804 and is first noted in the local paper in 1810. In February 1815 the northbound packet reached Burghead in the record time of 70 hours from Gravesend, a day and a half faster than the time needed to make the same journey by coach. In May 1835, the packet did the return trip between Burghead and London in just nine days, a feat worthy of much comment at the time. Some of the skippers who regularly commanded the coastal boats became well known and it was customary to include their names in advertisements. One such was Alex Clark, the skipper of one of the smacks on the London run, the *Fame*, who died in January 1837 in Cromarty at the age of 76. Joseph Mitchell recalled how he had taken a lively interest in the careers of the young men who travelled with him to London. Clark's own life reads like an adventure novel. As a young fisherman working out of Covesea, now Lossiemouth, he had been pressed into the Royal Navy on HMS *Fortitude*, had fought against the Dutch and the Americans, and had come home to be a smuggler until he saw the error of his ways and went into legitimate trade. Once, on the *Fame*, on passage to London, he fought off a French privateer.

On the Caithness coasts near to the Pentland Firth, a number of local fishermen began to work as pilots, guiding strange vessels safely between the North Sea and the Atlantic on this increasingly used maritime shortcut. Fiercely independent individuals, the pilots watched to see if any approaching sail needed their services and, when one stood in to land in search of assistance, they raced with each other in their small boats to be the first to claim the job. It was a dangerous game and lives were lost – it was not unknown for a merchant captain eager to get on not to pause after successful navigation of the Firth to allow the pilot to leave his vessel – but the rewards were also considerable.

Smuggling was one long-standing maritime practice that now became less common. Joseph Mitchell recalled seeing a cave on the west coast stacked with kegs of smuggled spirits but could also record that the last illicit cargo 'run' in the Moray Firth took place in 1825, when Donald Mackay with the help of fishermen from Campbelltown (Ardersier) brought a shipment of drink from Holland. Mitchell also recalled how in 1821 two shipping companies operating clipper smacks vied to provide passenger services between Aberdeen and London. This kept fares low – he found that the cost of his passage, for cabin and maintenance, which could last up to ten days but on this occasion took six, was 21s. Mitchell was sailing south to begin an apprenticeship in Thomas Telford's London office. 'We had about 20 passengers, ladies and gentlemen. I was sick for a day and a half but then got well and greatly enjoyed the life on board. We had breakfast at nine, bread and cheese and beer at twelve, an excellent dinner at four, when the gentlemen had wine and toddy, and at nine p.m. cold meat etc.'[9]

CHAPTER 16

Steam at sea

'The facilities for communication now existing in the north . . .'

'Except the post, the only communication Inverness had with London was by smacks, three or four vessels about one hundred and sixty tons each,' stated Mitchell about the early 1820s.[1]

The Caledonian Canal and the steamboat arrived more or less together, two embodiments of progress and modernity that engendered great excitement. The possibilities offered by placing steam engines in ships had been realised by several engineers and inventors on both sides of the Atlantic during the late eighteenth century, but it took years of experimentation before the concept became a commercial reality. The prize goes to Robert Fulton, who inaugurated a commercial service on the Hudson between New York City and Albany in 1807. Fulton had visited Britain and conferred with, among others, the Scottish pioneer of seaborne steam, Henry Bell.

Born in 1767 into a family of engineers and millwrights in West Lothian, Bell learned about ship design at an early age in Bo'ness. In 1800 he conveyed his ideas for steam power to the Admiralty but, despite Lord Nelson's support, the sea lords were less than impressed. The undaunted Bell built his *Comet* and in 1812 sailed her – if that is the right word – from Port Glasgow to the Broomielaw and then back to Greenock, all of 24 miles at a speed of five miles an hour against a head wind.

Five years later the *Marion* began the first regular steamship service on Loch Lomond. In 1818 a steamer called the *Rob Roy* operated for a short time between Greenock and Belfast, with a stop at Campbeltown; a weekly Londonderry to Glasgow steamer began to run in 1824.[2]

On 22 June 1820, the *Inverness Courier* informed its readers that a steamboat had been spotted off Lossiemouth passing west 'in fine style', before continuing: 'We could not help reflecting how well suited a vessel of that description is for opening up the intercourse of the upper end of this Firth where nature has interposed so many barriers in the way of travelling.'[3] To increase the excitement, Mr Bell himself was understood to be on board, encouraging the *Courier* to hope that some local gentlemen would seek Mr Bell's advice to start a steamboat service – 'And if so constructed as to take in 25 to 30 tons of goods, in addition to passengers, there is not a doubt of its success.' In July 1820, the new steamer began to ply between Inverness and Fort Augustus four times a week – 'elegantly and commodiously fitted up ... refreshments of every description, of the best quality, will be sold on board, on reasonable terms; and Books and Music will be provided.'

It was not a cheap service. A cabin cost 5s, the steerage 3s 6d. Dogs were charged half-fare. A carriage met the boat at Fort Augustus and conveyed onward passengers to Fort William to catch another steamer to Glasgow. Advertisements informed the public of the fares of each stage of a journey from Inverness to Edinburgh, Liverpool, London and Belfast. It was a new era. And now that it was easier and more comfortable to travel, more people began to do it. As if to remind the public, however, the elements saw to it that plans did not always work out. On 10 August 1820, the *Inverness Courier* carried an advertisement that a steamboat called the *Stirling* would make a trip on the 15th from the sea-lock at Clachnaharry to Wick in Caithness, calling on the way at Fort George, Cromarty, Nairn, Findhorn, Burghead and Brora, a prodigious and ambitious excursion at the best of times. Two weeks later, the newspaper reported how 'The Steam Boat did not go the length of Caithness . . . owing to the tempestuous state of the weather', and neither could it call at every port, disappointing several gentlemen in Nairn, who had gathered with the intention of making the trip.[4]

The original *Comet* came to grief on 13 December 1820 off Craignish Point near Oban, where the passengers were taken off safely but the vessel became a total wreck. Henry Bell had a successor constructed with the same name, and this vessel appeared in the Great Glen in 1823, plying between Glasgow and Fort William for the season; the *Loch Ness* steamboat began to chug from Inverness at 7 a.m. every Friday morning to connect with her for the southbound voyage to the Clyde.[5] The second *Comet* also offered trips from Fort William to see the curious Fingal's Cave on Staffa and the religious sites of Iona. The *Comet* and another Bell steamer, the *Stirling Castle*, sailed on the Inverness–Glasgow route from 1822. The *Stirling Castle* went from Inverness to Fort Augustus every Monday and Wednesday, making the return voyage on Tuesday and Thursday. On Fridays she carried on through the canal to Corpach to meet the *Comet* and returned to Inverness on Saturdays. Under the headline 'Cheap and Expeditious Travelling', she was described as having 'excellent accommodation . . . an attentive Steward, and a careful, steady Captain and Crew'.[6]

Before long – in 1823 – a steamboat was being built at Inverness; the *Malvina*, she was launched on the canal on 29 July. By the end of 1828 a steam ferry was plying the firth at Kessock, and four years later three steamers were passing through the canal on a regular link with Glasgow. It was not long before they began to operate on the east coast open-sea route, amongst the first being the *Duchess of Sutherland*, plying between Inverness and London from March 1836. The *Duchess* continued on the route after she was sold to the Aberdeen Steam Navigation Company in 1838 and became a familiar sight. In 1845, the three-day passage to London on the *Duchess* cost £4

3s. Other steamers that regularly called at Inverness in the 1840s were *North Star*, the *Duke of Richmond* and the *Maid of Morven*. The owners of the *Maid of Morven* were so pleased at the end of 1829 with the 'very liberal encouragement' they had received for their regular service to Glasgow that on Monday, 7 December they offered a free cruise to the Cromarty Firth and back, leaving from Kessock at 9 a.m.[7]

A packet boat, carrying passengers and livestock as well as mail, began to sail between Poolewe and Stornoway in 1759 in response to a plea to the postmaster general.[8] In the 1820s, it appears that the packet acquired a skipper from Gravesend, 'a regular bird of the Thames', in Joseph Mitchell's words, who had come to the Hebrides in command of a cod smack and had stayed on.

The Poolewe–Stornoway packet, the *Glenelg*, disappeared in bad weather one morning in November 1824 or 1825 when she put to sea on the insistence of a minister anxious to return to Stornoway before the Sabbath. The skipper reluctantly agreed to go, and the smack was last seen leaving Loch Ewe for the turbulent open sea. The minister, two other passengers and the three-man crew perished; a box belonging to one of the passengers was later washed ashore at Scoraig in mute testimony to their fate.[9] Gradually, after the advent of steam propulsion, regular services made their appearance in the Western Isles. Among the first were a steamer in 1819 connecting Glasgow to Oban via the Crinan Canal and in 1822 the *Argyll*, sailing as far as Stornoway.

In 1828 the *Ben Nevis*, which normally sailed between Glasgow and Portree, began to make regular runs to Stornoway. Several other shipowners initiated west-coast services in the following decades. For example, Sir James Matheson, co-founder of the Jardine Matheson trading company based in Hong Kong, bought the island of Lewis in 1844 and launched a steamer service with the *Falcon* between Ardrossan and Stornoway in the following year. The *Falcon* unfortunately caught fire and had to be scuttled, and in 1846 Sir James put the paddle steamer *Mary Jane*, named after his wife, on to the route. Built with the lines of a yacht, her original *raison d'être*, the *Mary Jane* made her first passage from Glasgow to Stornoway in 28 hours in early 1846. She continued under the Matheson flag to provide good service for another decade, calling en route between the Clyde and the Long Island at Oban, Tobermory and several harbours on Skye, and in time making a foray to Lochinver and Balmacara near Kyle once a fortnight to connect with the mail coach to Dingwall. Sold in 1857 and thereafter altered and renamed, the *Mary Jane* stayed on the west coast until she was finally broken up in 1931.[10]

By 1855 an extensive steam packet service connected coastal settlements. On the east coast, the *Martello*, under Captain William Hodge, sailed 'unless prevented by unforeseen circumstance' from Inverness every Thursday evening at 8 p.m. and from Invergordon on every Friday morning at 6 a.m., calling off Fort George, Cromarty, Nairn, Findhorn, Lossiemouth, Cullen and Banff, before setting course for Granton, whence she set out on the return northward voyage every Tuesday morning at 10 a.m. Horses, cattle and vehicles, the public was warned, were shipped and carried at the proprietors' risk. Reserving a state room between Inverness and Edinburgh cost 16s, a second-class berth only 6s. In the same issue of the newspaper, an echo of older days persisted with the 'fast-sailing' schooner *Kinloss* that was touting for cargo for her forthcoming departure from Hore's Wharf at Wapping, London, bound for the inner Moray Firth harbours.[11] The Aberdeen, Leith and Clyde Company was running the steamer *Sovereign* weekly between Granton, Aberdeen, Wick and Kirkwall, the clipper schooner *Fairy* between Aberdeen and Lerwick, and the 'remarkably fast-sailing coppered Cutter' *Cock of the North* between Kirkwall and the North Isles. Possibly in view of the potential turbulence of northern seas, the company made it clear that it would 'not be responsible for Leakage, Breakage of glass, china, earthernware, furniture, cheese or similar brittle articles', and this was only one warning in a long list of the accidents that could befall. A few steamer services catered for travel over quite short distances, probably a reflection on the slow nature of land travel and the discomfort of a crowded coach: for example, the steamer *Sampson* ran between Inverness and Beauly once a week, and also made regular sailings to Muir of Ord on market days and to Dingwall via the Cromarty Firth.[12]

Shipping news occupied many column inches in the northern press, sadly often on the subject of wrecks, fog and loss of life – the *Martello* was wrecked on the coast of Fife early in December 1857[13] – but also at times with good news, such as in February 1858 when it was reported how the Wick schooner *Vapour*, under Captain John Sutherland, had made a swift passage with a cargo of coal from Shields Bar to Cromarty in only 29 hours, thanks to a strong southerly wind.[14] The Great West of Scotland Fishery Company operated a screw steamer called the *Islesman* that carried cargo and passengers between a string of ports along the west coast as far north as Lochinver from 1859; in 1868 she was sold to an owner in Barbados and later was lost in a storm off Martinique.[15]

The condition of the Crinan Canal, now under the jurisdiction of the Commissioners for the Caledonian Canal, was giving concern in 1833.[16] Urgent repairs were needed, reported inspectors in May that year, to a total cost of over £5,000. Telford's opinion on what should be done is included in the minutes of the meeting of the Commissioners in June 1834, including the construction of an additional pier for steamboats at the Loch Gilp entrance, a fishing boat slip and a small lighthouse or beacon, deepening of entrances, replacement of decayed lock gates, and the cutting of projecting rocks – the works amounted to a major renovation of the whole canal. Heavy rain and floods in the autumn of 1834 caused damage to the Caledonian Canal, and masonry at Fort Augustus gave way in 1837; these problems and others accrued until in 1843 an extensive overhaul of the structure was initiated under the direction of the engineer James Walker. The canal re-opened from sea to sea on 1 May 1847, by which time James Barron, the editor of the *Inverness Courier*, estimated that the costs had soared to £1,300,000.

'As an illustration of what may be done with the facilities for communication now existing in the north, we may here mention that Mr Walker, being on express Government business to Ireland ... proceeded in one of the Canal steam-tugs ... from Corpach direct to Belfast. The passage was made in seventeen hours ...'[17]

The canal now had four steam tugs ready to tow vessels and speed their passage, but the improvements were just too late to have much effect in increasing revenue. On a brighter note, as commercial traffic declined, some of which was already being lost to railways, passenger and tourist services increased. In 1873 Queen Victoria travelled the length of the canal in the steamer *Gondolier* and found the tedium of the passage relieved by amusement at how the crew worked the locks.

Maritime transport was crucial in bringing the north into regular commercial contact with the outside world, promoting the movement of people, goods and livestock. Travellers did not always appreciate what this could imply. In August 1857, a very disgruntled passenger on the *Clansman* was moved to vent his feelings on how he and others were shifted to make room for sheep:

On Monday ... I, in common with many other passengers, left Stornoway on board the *Clansman* for the south ... we were carried to ... Loch Seaforth. We were there ordered off the deck and quarter-deck. The vessel was then filled from stem to stern with sheep – about 1,000 ... after a delay of some hours, we started for Glenelg ... where we landed our unpleasant companions ... such conduct on the part of the steamboat officials was alike unjust to us as passengers by a public conveyance and insulting to us as gentlemen. I am, your obedient servt, Roderick Nicolson.[18]

In the mid-1800s the shipping services in the Western Isles fell largely under the control of one company owned by the brothers George and James Burns. One of the employees of the company in its Glasgow headquarters was the Burns' nephew, David MacBrayne, who in February 1851 in partnership with David and Alexander Hutcheson formed a new company to take over the firm's Hebridean operations. In the 1870s, after the Hutcheson brothers retired, MacBrayne stayed on, changed the name of the business and, as the famous parody of Psalm 24 has it, acquired the Western Isles:

> *The earth belongs unto the Lord*
> *And all that it contains,*
> *Except the Western Islands,*
> *And they are David MacBrayne's.*[19]

David MacBrayne eventually retired himself in 1906.

The names of the many Hutcheson/MacBrayne ships regularly ploughing the Hebridean seas became as familiar among the islanders as those of their relatives. The first one on the Stornoway route, the *Chevalier*, was a paddle steamer launched in March 1853; she was replaced by another paddle steamer, the *Clansman*, on which Mr Nicolson had his annoying encounter with sheep, in 1855. The fleet expanded considerably as the century progressed until, on the eve of the First World War, more than 30 ships sported the MacBrayne livery of red funnel and red lion rampant on a yellow disc, including cargo vessels and excursion boats, as well as the regular passenger ferries.

As MacBrayne was to the Hebrides, so the North boats were in relation to Orkney and Shetland – in this case, North being an abbreviation for the North of Scotland, Orkney and Shetland

Shipping Company. Just as MacBrayne linked the west coast to the Clyde, so the North boats connected the northern archipelagos, and for a time Caithness, to Aberdeen and Leith. In his history of the firm, Alastair McRobb traces its origin to the Leith & Clyde Shipping Company in the 1790s, when vessels sailing between these two destinations, although they were only some 40 miles apart as the gull flies, had to take the northabout course through the Pentland Firth or between Orkney and Shetland.[20]

The extension of a postal service to Shetland came about with a packet vessel called the *Isabella* in 1758, but this remained for a long time intermittent and irregular.[21] In 1823 a group of Lerwick businessmen formed the Leith and Shetland Shipping Company and operated a schooner *Norna* for some years. The Aberdeen, Leith and Clyde company gradually extended its services until Inverness, Wick and Kirkwall were brought into the schedule by 1833, and then Lerwick by 1836, though at first only once a fortnight and in summer, with the paddle steamer *Sovereign*. As the trade grew, year-round services were only a matter of time, and were introduced for Inverness in 1848, Wick in 1850, and Orkney and Shetland in 1858. The ships could also call at Banff, Cullen, Lossiemouth and other Moray Firth ports as required.

In 1875, the North of Scotland, Orkney and Shetland Steam Navigation Company was born and the naming of the steamers after saints (the *Saint Clair*, launched in 1868, was the first) became the normal practice.

The golden age of coastal shipping services brought the people of the islands into full social and commercial contact with their mainland neighbours, and by the end of the nineteenth century all the large ports in the Highlands and Islands were also partaking in coastal and foreign trade to some degree, the latter concerned mostly with commerce in herring and timber with the Baltic. Captain George Macdonald even floated the idea in 1881 of launching a twice-weekly steam-packet service between Inverness and Norway to carry goods all year and tourists in the summer months, but sadly this continental link was never established.[22] Yet it was notable that steam had not achieved a monopoly on power and a considerable number of boats still relied on sail until the time of the First World War.

PART 5

The new iron roads

CHAPTER 17

The first railways

'the country is an asylum of railway lunatics . . .'

The concept of laying rails along which wheeled vehicles could move had a long pedigree before iron succeeded wood as the material for rails in the 1790s and steam locomotives took over from horses. The famed *Puffing Billy* first ran on the tramway between Stockton and Darlington in 1813, and a year later George Stephenson introduced an improved locomotive, the *Blücher*, on the same route. At the same time, the first railway in Scotland was built to carry coal from the Kilmarnock pits to the port of Troon. Its conception illustrated the revolution in transport that was just beginning, as the owner had first thought of a canal to replace the transport provided by horses and carts before he realised the advantages of a rail line.

The Kilmarnock and Troon Railway was approved by Act of Parliament on 27 May 1808 and, built under the direction of the engineer William Jessop, opened for traffic in July 1812. Its horse-drawn wagons were soon carrying passengers as well as coal. A steam locomotive, *The Duke*, arrived in 1817.

The most significant development in the story of travel and transport in the Highlands during the nineteenth century now came about: the arrival of the steam engine. While steam-powered ships chugged into our story in 1820, as told in the previous chapter, it took a few more decades to bring north the steam locomotive.

In the interval, nature continued to throw challenges in the way of the engineers. A major test for the road network laid out by the Commission for Highland Roads and Bridges arose in 1829 in the form of floods of Noah-like proportions. Before the rain, however, the summer was unnaturally dry and hot all through May, June and July. In Moray vegetation shrivelled; and on one Sunday in the centre of Ross-shire, at Kinlochluichart, as if in an ominous omen, what appears to have been a mudflow precipitated a 'moving mountain of soil, stones and trees, coming slowly but steadily down the deep worn course of the little stream' to destroy a bridge, houses and crops. Sir Thomas Dick Lauder, whose book described it thus, wrote that the simple people attributed the catastrophe to divine punishment on their landlord for having voted in Parliament for Catholic emancipation.[1] On 3–4 August heavy rain from the north-east deluged the coastlands of the Moray Firth and the central Highlands. At Huntly Lodge, the gardener measured a rainfall of three inches in 24 hours, one-sixth of the expected annual amount. Bridges and buildings were tumbled and crops washed out in the catchment areas of the Blackwater, Alness, Beauly, Nairn, Findhorn, Divie, Lossie, Spey, Nethy, Dulnain, Deveron, and the Don and Dee rivers, all thrown into surging spate. Remarkably only eight people lost their lives amid the turmoil. A few had remarkable escapes. Among them were the driver and guard of the mail coach from Banff to Inverness who, disdaining the option of a safe diversion, tried to cross the Deveron on the flooded bridge after their passengers had wisely opted to get off. Scorning the shouted advice of all the onlookers, the driver urged the four horses forward into the spate. They did not get far before the whole equipage was overturned and swept away. The coach smashed against a building, the four horses struggled and reared and fought against the efforts of some hardy souls in a boat who tried to cut them free with the result that only one survived. The coachman managed to hang grimly on to a lamp-post until he and the guard, who had clung to the top of the coach, and the mails were rescued. 'Great indignation' was expressed by the onlookers, recorded Lauder, who acknowledged that, although servants of the royal mail were expected to persevere 'in defiance of risk', in this case their zeal had 'proved to have been mistaken'. Overall, the transport network was severely disrupted: 'The flood has so completely broken up the communication that the arrangements regarding the coaches have been overthrown, and the time of the mails rendered quite precarious,' wrote Lauder. When the bad news of the flood reached the ears of Joseph Mitchell in Thurso, he left for the south on the coach, covering as quickly as he could the 200 miles to Craigellachie, where his assistant, Dallas, led a team to secure the iron bridge.[2] The ability of Loch Ness to absorb a considerable input of water probably saved Inverness from severe harm on that occasion; its turn would come 20 years later.

The ramifying railway lines in the low country created a satisfying demand for Highland timber for sleepers but, otherwise, the north remained for a time unaffected by the brash new form of transport. In the south, however, the railway was taken up in a whirl of anticipation and enthusiasm. During this period of 'railway mania' – 'the country is an asylum of railway lunatics', observed Lord Cockburn[3] – many companies were formed, lived dangerously and died through takeover or amalgamation before a few major firms emerged. In his memoirs, Joseph Mitchell says that 620 companies were registered in 1845, with a united capital of over £560,000; speculation was particularly rife in Perth, and when the bubble burst about half the well-to-do people in the city were financially damaged or ruined. The various boards of directors of the companies usually comprised landowners and merchants, with a handful of engineers and lawyers, providing social weight and expertise enough to attract shareholders. In influential articles in *The Scotsman,* the editor

Charles MacLaren foresaw two lines connecting Scotland to England, one in the west linking Glasgow via Dumfries to Carlisle, and the other in the east joining Edinburgh to Berwick. During the 1820s and '30s, many local lines were laid in the Central Belt. In February 1842, the first 'inter-city' line opened between Edinburgh and Glasgow. In May 1847, the Dundee and Perth railway opened, to Barnhill on the east bank of the Tay, and in the following year Aberdeen and Perth became the northernmost termini on the expanding network.[4]

In May 1844, a number of 'gentlemen connected with the northern districts of the country' assembled in the Town House in Inverness at the invitation of the provost to consider the construction of a railway line to Perth along the route of the main highway through Strathspey, Badenoch and Atholl.[5] Joseph Mitchell told the assembly how he had already taken levels along much of the way and found a feasible course for the line to follow; other gentlemen laid out statistical data on population and probable traffic levels to prove how the venture would be worthwhile. Shortly after this, at a meeting in Badenoch, Major Macpherson of Glentruim declared he was ready to give up without charge some of his property to accommodate the line, provided other gentlemen would do likewise. The local press were firmly behind this scheme: 'This is truly in the spirit in which we trust to see this enterprise taken up ... by all classes of people in the Highlands, as a matter of common concern in which the whole north country is deeply interested.'[6] Such spirit in the north, thought the editor of the *Inverness Courier*, would convince southern capitalists how wise it would be to invest in 'this remarkable feature of our times – railway communication'. The Earl of Cawdor made a donation of £20 and other gentlemen also gave liberal sums towards funding the railway. 'We beg to say to all our readers – "Do thou likewise",' enthused the *Inverness Courier*, where there soon appeared on all its railway advertisements an image of a smoke-stacked loco pulling a coal tender and two passenger wagons. Along with the exhortations to raise funds for major infrastructure by subscription, the newspaper columns ran darker stories of accidents and injuries on the southern railways.

Not all landowners were as charitable as Major Macpherson. Many declared their support in public but otherwise sought to minimise disruption to their own interests in farming, shooting and privacy, and where possible to obtain compensation, often precipitating lengthy correspondence over the minutiae of routes and boundaries. A few strenuously opposed the railway, at least in the beginning. The Earl of Seafield was appalled by the thought of 20 miles of track passing through his lands in Strathspey, and his wife 'hated railways' because they brought together such an objectionable variety of people; to her the ideal method of travelling was to post in a four-horse carriage, a mode of transport that no doubt, in her view, effectively kept the undesirable at home or on foot.[7]

As long as the weather held in the autumn of 1844, Joseph Mitchell sent out parties of surveyors, some 20 all told, paid at up to five guineas a day, owing to the demand for their skills throughout the country, to map out a route for the line, and concluded that it should cross the Findhorn river at Farness, pass east of Lochindorb and Grantown and down into Strathspey; such a route rose to an elevation 260 feet lower than the Slochd, where the road ran.[8] This was not the only rail story in the northern papers. Hardly had the doors closed on the meeting in Inverness than word came from Aberdeen, in the form of an article in the *Aberdeen Journal*, that none of the proposed railroads were of 'half so much importance to Aberdeen' as that which connects to Inverness, and it could be built with facility and economy using gentle gradients.[9] Only bridging the mighty Spey would incur some expense. The advantages of such a line to the north were manifest: no harbour on the Moray Firth enjoyed Aberdeen's steamer connections and all the people taking the train to catch them would greatly increase Aberdeen harbour's revenue; in addition, Inverness, perched on the eastern tip of the Caledonian Canal, would become the centre for trade between the east and west coasts of Britain and Ireland 'from which it must derive the greatest advantages'.

In February 1845, the Great North Railway put its shares on sale at £50 each: not only was the plan to connect Aberdeen to Inverness but also to lay three branch lines to Banff and Portsoy, Speymouth and Lossiemouth. This would cost under £1,100,000, and the revenue based on reports from 'competent parties' would result in a dividend of about 7 per cent.[10] Meanwhile meetings to discuss and promote the so-called Inverness and Elgin Railway took place in Elgin, Forres and Nairn, and its promoters published in March its sale of shares – at £20 each. A lively dispute over 'railway poaching' took place in the newspaper columns, as the various companies vied with each other over the merits of their respective proposals. The stramash served as good publicity and stirred a flurry of speculation and share-buying.

Notices appeared towards the end of October 1845 to inform the public that in the next session of Parliament applications would be presented for bills to allow the construction of both the Perth and Inverness and the Inverness and Elgin railways. There also appeared a proposal for a Wick and Thurso Railway to be built to connect the two Caithness towns, for a company to advance the north line as far as Tain and to carry lines through the interior of Caithness and Sutherland, and for a Deeside railway, a branch line from Inverurie to Banff, and another from Dyce to Peterhead. Ambition was now fast outrunning resources. The money market fell into a depression, share prices dropped, but the enthusiasm appeared to wane only a little. A gentleman who contributed to the *Inverness Courier* – and took the view that he was 'almost singular among the men of the north' in adhering to the opinion that a rail line from Perth to the Pentland Firth would not pay – was labelled as displaying 'antiquated feeling' and the 'caustic humour of Jonathan Oldbuck', Sir Walter Scott's character in *The Antiquary*.[11] There was neither the population nor the industry in the north to support such a scheme: 'the brains of the community seem to be disordered by a monomania', thought the writer.

A month later, readers of the papers would have come across a story that may have induced them to agree with the resident Oldbuck. Just as schemes for the north were being proposed, equivalent plans were being laid for lines in the south-west Highlands. Several companies were put together to further these schemes but, with objections pointing to the rugged landscape and the low population, neither conducive to successful railway operations, some of the plans did not progress far. In September 1845, the Scottish Western Railway (SWR) conceived a line starting from Oban to connect with the Caledonian Railway network at Callander, and by a branch south from Crianlarich via Glen Falloch and Loch Lomondside, also to connect at Balloch with another part of the Caledonian network. The Caledonian Railway was already establishing itself as a principal operator in the Central Belt. Very soon after the SWR publicised its proposals, a rival company, the Scottish Grand Junction, came forward with ambition to build a line along almost exactly the same route. (The Grand Junction also conceived a line running east from Tyndrum through Glen Ericht to connect with the Perth and Inverness line at Dalwhinnie, an idea that has remained on paper to this day.) The SWR withdrew to leave the field to the Grand Junction.

Another firm now stepped onto a somewhat confusing stage: Caledonian Northern Direct. It submitted a plan to run from the Caledonian–Dumbarton line near Milngavie via Strathblane and Strathendrick, Aberfoyle and the Trossachs, Glen Falloch and Glen Dochart to Tyndrum, to connect with the proposed Oban–Callander and Tyndrum–Dalwhinnie lines.

Rivalries between the various companies assumed a comic turn when the surveyors for Northern Direct, whose chairman was the Duke of Montrose, were assaulted in Glen Falloch by tenants of the Marquis of Breadalbane and the laird of Glen

Falloch, both prominent Campbells in the Grand Junction company, and tumbled into a ditch with their equipment: 'we hear it was a well-fought battle, gallantly sustained by the engineers against fearful odds', reported the *Perthshire Courier* in a story gleefully copied in the *Inverness Courier*.[12] Rivalry between railway companies and steamship operators flared up from time to time throughout the Victorian period over conflicts of interest in a tight marketplace that nevertheless tended to militate against the best interests of the region. A late example occurred when the Highland Railway company, fearing loss of trade from their line to Kyle of Lochalsh, objected, in the event unsuccessfully, to the extension of the West Highland line to Mallaig.

By the end of 1845 the speculation in railway schemes was winding down. After a winter of contemplation a few wise heads decided not to proceed further with the Perth and Inverness plan, and at a meeting in the George Inn in Perth at the end of March 1846 it was decided, albeit by a minority of the interested parties, to return deposits to the shareholders. The supporters of the railway were now divided over what to do until a select committee of the House of Commons, meeting in May to take evidence about the north rail schemes, rejected the Perth and Inverness application. In the eyes of the select committee, the engineering problems presented by the nature of the high country tipped the decision. They felt that the altitude and the gradients were too much for the locomotives to overcome easily: 'Mr Mitchell,' it was said by one member, to laughter, 'was the greatest mountain climber that had ever been heard of. He beat Napoleon outright and quite eclipsed Hannibal.'[13] The committee did, however, state that the project could be reconsidered after more experience of operating lines in a similar environment. During the same hearings, the promoters of the Aberdeen, Banff and Elgin line, campaigning for a coastal route that would link the towns and villages along the Moray Firth, withdrew their application. In the end, the committee approved the plan of the Great North of Scotland railway to build a more direct line from Aberdeen to Inverness, and the Act received the royal assent on 26 June 1846.

By the end of the 1840s Perth, lying strategically in the gap where the Tay flowed between the Ochils and the Sidlaws, had become a hub for rail lines seeking to reach to the north of the country. The Dundee and Perth line approached the town along the north side of the Firth of Tay and in May 1847 terminated at Barnhill on the east side of the river opposite the town centre; a wooden viaduct, completed in March 1849, allowed it to continue to the main Perth station. Other lines coming in from the south united at Hilton Junction near Craigend on the south side of the town and ran on into the main station, built by the Scottish Central Railway in 1848 as the terminus of its line from Glasgow. Five of the seven platforms in the station were designed to allow trains to pass through to the north. The Scottish Midland Junction line opened in August 1848 to connect Perth to Forfar. Meanwhile the Aberdeen Railway was pushed south to connect with a short local line running between Forfar and Arbroath. These lines united in 1856 as a new company called Scottish North Eastern.

In the far north, interest in the iron tracks ebbed for a time: failure of the potato crop and the resulting dearth in the west Highlands occupied the public mind instead. And then a natural catastrophe unprecedented in local memory struck Inverness in January 1849.

A week of intense rain to the west of the Great Glen flooded the catchment area. Loch Ness itself was measured to be 14 feet above its normal level. 'Never was the Ness seen in such fearful volume and flood,' recorded the *Inverness Courier*.[14] The river burst its banks as it flowed through the town, inundating a swathe of housing on both sides and pulling apart the bridge originally built in the 1680s. The local authorities did sterling work in rescuing and looking after the victims – and no lives were lost – but now the main road artery to the north had been cut. In 1808 another bridge across the Ness had been completed, a wooden structure dubbed the Black Bridge due to the dark colour of the timber (now the Waterloo Bridge), but its link lay to the suburb of Merkinch and the Kessock ferry to the Black Isle and it could not replace the Ness Bridge indefinitely. The engineer James Rendel, advising the Commission for Roads and Bridges, came out in favour of an iron girder structure costing £16,000 on the same site. The government promised aid in the form of half the required funding, with the balance coming from local resources. Debate over design and costs ensued until in January 1851, two years after the initial disaster, the town council plumped for a suspension bridge which was now costed at £18,000. Work started in June 1852 but two consecutive contractors who took on the job failed and another two years passed without completion of the essential transport link. Twenty masons went on strike in June 1854, demanding an increase in pay from one guinea to 24s per hour. James Rendel and Joseph Mitchell fell out over the latter's report on the nature of the riverbed; Rendel blamed the delay in part on Mitchell's failure to represent the true nature of the substrate. At last, late in August 1855, the new Ness Bridge opened to traffic – with commendable accuracy, the newspapers reported the final cost as £23,365 1s 1d.

The newspapers from the middle of the nineteenth century reveal the beginnings of local public transport. Hitherto, travellers had to hire individually a horse or a cab, the forerunner of the taxi, but on 28 August 1844 the *Inverness Courier* noted the existence of the Kessock omnibus – 'for all'. In his history of the Highland bus company, W.J. Milne states that the two-horse omnibus began to operate between the Exchange, the area in front of the Town House, and Kessock in 1836, and that a horse omnibus also ran on the Black Isle to connect Cromarty to the Kessock ferry.[15] This was not long after omnibuses had appeared on the streets of Paris and had then been adopted in some other cities. The early ones were essentially long coaches, drawn by usually a pair of horses, with benches for seating; the essential feature of the service was that the coach plied back and forth on a regular short route, and passengers could get on and off at different places without having to book in advance. The omnibus in Inverness connected the centre of the town with the ferry at Kessock, a distance of about two miles. It must have been a welcome development for the country people who crossed regularly from the Black Isle with produce for the market. In his reminiscences of Inverness life, published in 1905 but referring to the first half of the previous century, John Fraser makes no mention of the omnibus but calls the ferry traffic on market days 'marvellous' with 'crowded boats [crossing] from daylight to dark'.[16] Fraser foresaw that some future railway might take traffic from the ferry but did not imagine that a bridge would one day span the Firth. The 'Brahan Castle' omnibus began in July 1847 to run twice a day between the Caledonian Hotel in Dingwall and Strathpeffer, already becoming famous as a spa with sulphurous waters that offered miraculous healing. The advertisement declared:

> This omnibus is capable of holding 14 inside and 7 out, besides the Driver, and is built on a new and improved plan, and is neatly fitted up. As there will always be steady Horses and careful Drivers employed, Parties visiting Strathpeffer will find this conveyance superior to anything of the sort yet attempted and the charges exceedingly moderate.[17]

The words hint at the common complaints from those who had experienced coach travel. On the Black Isle, an entrepreneur called Mackintosh in Fortrose began to run an omnibus to Cromarty, connecting with the ferry, and advertised it as passing within one mile of the Invergordon ferry across the Cromarty Firth – thus were transport networks forming throughout the region.[18]

CHAPTER 18

New connections

'the train launched forth upon its first trip . . .'

In December 1851, interest in railways sparked up again with the announcement that the Great North of Scotland Railway Company had overcome the financial troubles that had beset it in the aftermath of the mania period and was now about to build a line from Aberdeen to Keith as the first stage in its ambition to complete a route all the way to Inverness. There had been talk of connecting Aberdeen to Inverness for some time, a prospect that did not appeal to every regular traveller: one dissenter was Lord Cockburn, who feared such a railway would 'destroy the posting and the inns on what has hitherto been called the Highland road, and will compel us to be conveyed like parcels – speed alone considered, and seeing excluded'.[1]

Before work began in Aberdeen, however, the prize for the opening of the first line in the north went to the tiny Morayshire Railway Company, which built a six-mile track between Elgin and Lossiemouth. The nine months it took to construct the line over relatively easy terrain must have been a time of some excitement and worry. The navvies – some 300 in number – went on strike, fell a-rioting and otherwise disturbed the peace. But the job was completed, and the line was ready on 10 August 1852. The scheme had been conceived by the prominent Elgin solicitor and businessman James Grant – he was also part-owner of the

Glen Grant distillery and later became provost – who steered the project through a decade of setbacks before it achieved reality. To the cheers of a large crowd and the firing of cannon, Mrs Grant cut the first divot for the construction of the line on the outskirts of Elgin. A larger ceremony marked the opening and was granted a half-page picture in *The Illustrated London News*. A holiday was declared throughout the district, the great and the good processed through Elgin to board the train and rode to Lossiemouth to eat, drink and listen to speeches in a marquee set up overlooking the new station. Around 3,000 passengers enjoyed the jaunts on the line before midnight.[2]

A few months later, the Great North of Scotland workforce set to their shovels and wheelbarrows to build the line from Kittybrewster on the north side of Aberdeen to Inverurie. There was also a revival of interest in the direct Perth–Inverness scheme backed by the Inverness-shire county authorities[3] but before progress had been made on that front a smaller, much more local initiative came to fruition. In November 1853, the prospectus for a line between Inverness and Nairn was issued. The Countess of Seafield – her husband, the Earl of Seafield, was a prominent supporter of the line, holding a view of railways very different to that of his father – cut the ceremonial first sod on 21 September 1854 to inaugurate the construction. This great event inspired a composer, C.H. Morine, to dedicate to the countess a piece of music called 'The Inverness and Nairn Railway Waltzes' which went on sale for 3s.[4] As the 15-mile distance lay over relatively gentle terrain, the work went ahead quickly and, despite some delays brought about by the need to bring in plant and equipment by sea, opened for traffic on 8 November 1855.

'By noon everything was in readiness,' wrote the *Courier* correspondent:

> The carriages were crammed by nearly 800 people, and the provost and Magistrates with the directors, headed by Raigmore and Aldourie (their names by the way being

appropriately bestowed upon the two locomotives) had taken their seats. The doors of the carriages were then closed, and after two or three whistles from either end of the train, Mr Dougall, the manager of the line, gave the final order to start . . . A couple of small guns were fired; a row of flags . . . were hitched some yards higher, and amidst deafening cheers the train launched forth upon its first trip.

The contractors, Messrs Brassey and Falshaw, had estimated the cost at £4,000 per mile.

Before a single train had run to Nairn, the Earl of Seafield and his colleagues were thinking of connecting with the Great North of Scotland line, pushing westward, and formed a company, the Inverness and Aberdeen Junction Railway, to bring about the link. A deputation from Inverness met the directors of the Great North company to discuss how they could cooperate and resolved to withdraw temporarily their parliamentary bills. The delay in furthering the project was blamed by the press on uncooperative landowners and 'men of business throughout the northern counties'.[5]

The House of Commons approved the scheme in July 1856. In October that year the line from Aberdeen reached its planned destination at Keith. It was now possible to travel to London from Inverness quicker than ever, albeit along a complicated route that required some endurance and heaving around of luggage: a train to Nairn, a coach to Keith, a train to Aberdeen, a train overnight to King's Cross. In 1857, the marathon was timed to begin in Inverness at 1.30 p.m. and end in London at 4.30 the following afternoon.

The line from Elgin to the Spey was completed in the summer of 1858 and at last a locomotive steamed across the mighty river – the bridge was to prove very troublesome, but that did not detract from the significance of the moment – and inaugurated 'the new era, which it is scarcely an exaggeration to say has thus commenced in the Highlands'.[6] With little fuss, some of the company officials and Joseph Mitchell went along for an occasion in which they could take pride. 'In many places the works were barely ready to receive the engine,' noted the *Inverness Courier*, which presumably had a correspondent on the spot, 'and progress was very slow except at points where the line has been for some time in common use.' More than a thousand men had been labouring night and day in the previous four weeks to complete the section. The temporary bridge was 'severely tested' but it stayed up and 'running at full speed or slowly, the locomotive and waggons attached did not seem to cause the slightest vibration'.

The full route crossed four major rivers. Two of these, the Nairn and the Lossie, were bridged by stone structures. On the wider Findhorn and on the Spey itself the engineers had opted for tubular iron viaducts. The Findhorn viaduct – 485 feet long, and containing some 400 tons of iron – was complete in the middle of October 1858 and passed as safe by the Board of Trade inspector a week later. The safety inspection involved running trains back and fore across the structure at different speeds and measuring any movement or deflection in the track. The viaduct over the Spey, 70 feet in height, caused some problems: 'a formidable and difficult work, costing in all £34,482', it comprised an iron girder 230 feet long, with six stone side arches to ease the passage of floodwater.

In Joseph Mitchell's view, the directors were in too much of a hurry to complete the line:

Twice did they bring the Government inspectors on the ground without my sanction, and twice were the works rejected as incomplete. The Board of Trade would not sanction the opening of the line for carrying the traffic over the scaffolding erected for the construction of the Spey Bridge. The directors, however, determined to take their own way notwithstanding, and they opened the line and carried on the traffic on the timber scaffolding.

Mitchell noticed that the weight of the girders and the vibration of the trains made the scaffolding sink, and he made it clear that he would not be held responsible for any accident. Until the problem was fixed to the satisfaction of the Board of Trade inspectors, the company directors came up with a solution – passengers had to disembark at one end of the viaduct, walk across the road on the adjacent suspension bridge while the empty train puffed alongside them, then climb aboard again once on unyielding ground.[7] Local newspapers who supported the railway kept quiet about this development.

The directors of the Inverness and Aberdeen Junction company had their names cast in iron on a plaque fixed to the Spey Bridge (the plaque can now be seen in Inverness station). The chairman, Sir Alexander Matheson, had started life in reduced circumstances but had made a fortune under the aegis of his uncle, James Matheson, co-founder of the Jardine-Matheson company in Hong Kong which built its success on trading – opium prominent on their list of goods – into China. Alexander had returned to the Highlands in 1840 to accumulate a large estate, including the 60,000 acres in Easter Ross where he built Ardross Castle. The vice-chairman was Thomas Charles Bruce, a lawyer and the youngest son of the seventh Earl of Elgin of Marbles fame. Among the other board members were five earls and baronets, four lairds, a barrister and John Blaikie, whose father had been five times Lord Provost of Aberdeen and ran a family business with an interest in railway engineering. Bruce had actually stood against another board member, Sir James Elphinstone, in the general election in Portsmouth in 1859 but had come third in the poll. They were all men with north connections of long standing, probably the last such group who were able to fund a major infrastructure project – and they also used their social position to bolster guarantees to investors when money was not forthcoming.[8] Not that they were poor men – three of them had made stacks of money in India, and many had relatives who had done well out of sugar estates in the West Indies and other imperial investments. The Marquis of Stafford was MP for Sutherland between 1852 and 1861, the year he inherited the dukedom of Sutherland from his father; he was a railway enthusiast and was to fund his own line and part of the Sutherland and Caithness Railway. Incidentally, the Duke of Richmond was awarded £2,500 compensation by the House of Lords for loss of bridge tolls over the Spey.

The engineers who guided the construction of the railways became local celebrities. Joseph Mitchell was foremost among them, and not least because he left an entertaining memoir about his career. We know much less about the labour force who constructed the north lines, the navvies. Some of them were Irish, from the itinerant population of labourers who moved from job to job all over Britain, digging canals and tunnels before tackling the rail lines. In 1845, some 200,000 navvies were labouring on the railway lines under construction mostly in the south of the country.[9] Seldom were they welcome.

The workforce on the Border railways at this time were one-third Irish, one-third English and one-third Scots. With plenty of drink and swagger, there was always the risk of fighting and what the papers often called riots could quickly break out between gangs of labourers from different parts of the country. Reports such as the one in the *Inverness Courier* on 8 June 1847 of a riot between Irish and Highland labourers on a section of railway at 'Gallstown' (Galston, Ayrshire), where 5,000 of the 8,000-strong labour force were described as 'strangers', were not a good advertisement for new rail projects in the north.

Wages varied according to a man's skill and the generosity of the contractor: a mason, bricklayer or carpenter could command 21s a week in 1843, whereas the fellow who plied a shovel got 15s. Irish navvies predominated on the West Highland line in the 1890s where the average weekly pay, some of it supplied in food that the men cooked for themselves, fell between 15s and 21s.

It was a rough, hard-drinking life in the hutted encampments close to the work; by the 1890s, at least, a few attempts were being made to alleviate the hardships by providing first-aid posts and a basic insurance fund to dispense benefit in case of injury. And as was the custom in the Victorian age, concerned citizens and the Church made an effort to bring some civilisation to the camps by running reading rooms and recreational facilities of a more uplifting nature than could be found in the drinking and gambling dens. In the mid-1800s, the workforce seems to have included numbers of local men, as is implied in the advertisement in the *Inverness Courier* from the Alford Valley Railway in April 1858: 'WANTED 300 or 400 men for the WORKS of this RAILWAY between Kintore and Whitehouse. Liberal wages will be given to good workmen.'[10]

In April 1862, a navvy at Forres had an accident and is named as John Holms from Brackla, near Nairn.[11] That accidents were sadly common is implied in the report describing the construction of the viaduct over the Findhorn in 1858, where the writer deemed it newsworthy to say that there had been none.[12]

The men building the piers for the viaduct had had a close shave the previous year. They were working behind a coffer dam and were 11 feet below the water level, two steam engines pumping to keep the space dry, when a spate came down and they scarcely had time to scramble out before the flood hit the site. In the event, only trifling damage was done and the men joked that the spate had in fact been a help, as it had carried away 300 tons of gravel that they would otherwise have had to dig.[13]

In the early years of the railway, the newspapers regularly carried facts and figures on the volumes of traffic. For example, we learn that in the week ending 17 March 1855, the Great North of Scotland company took in revenue of £640 17s 9½d, about two-thirds of it from goods, parcels and livestock, with the remainder being paid by the 2,795 passengers.[14] Four years later, for the week ending 9 April 1859, revenue had increased to £1,615 4s 10d and the passenger numbers had risen to 8,742.

In the same week, the Inverness and Aberdeen Junction Railway carried 5,213 passengers and earned revenue of £586 2s 6½d (it counted horses, carriages and dogs in its figures). Ease of travel was encouraging more people to make journeys. 'We believe that all classes are now cognisant of the benefits,' opined the *Elgin Courier* breezily in April 1859. 'The traffic . . . is fully up to, if not beyond, the expectations of the promoters; while all engaged in business or bent on pleasure experience the advantages.'[15]

Excursions, with special fares on Saturdays, featured from the beginning. In June 1857, the people of Inverness could spend their free day on a visit to Nairn for a 2s ticket in first class and only 1s in third (there was no second class on offer). Captain Turner was also offering pleasure trips on Loch Ness in the steamer *Edinburgh Castle*, with dining, music and dancing on the return voyage from Foyers; a first-class cabin cost 3s, a second-class 2s.[16] Reduced season tickets were available to keen sea bathers to visit the beach at Nairn, ranging from 7s 6d for one week (third class) to £3 12s for three months for weekday travel.[17]

In December 1856, a group of local landowners in Easter Ross met in the Tain courthouse to declare themselves in favour of a line through their area. The traffic estimates were judged to offer a reasonable return and, curiously, in view of what was to occur, it was deemed possible to bridge the Dornoch Firth from Ardachie Point – 'a detour by Bonar Bridge is quite out of the question', reads the newspaper report.[18] James Bremner from Wick had stated some years before that the Firth could be bridged for around £20,000, and the alternative crossing, Meikle Ferry, had not shaken off the bad reputation made worse by the disaster in 1809: 'In the miserable state in which this ferry has ever been managed, it is seldom that any passengers who are not compelled by business run the risk of encountering it.'[19]

The first turf for the building of the Ross-shire track was cut in September 1860 and the line opened between Inverness and Dingwall on 11 June 1862. A viaduct carried the track over the Ness river; Joseph Mitchell regarded this piece of work as 'a source of pride and satisfaction'. Long viaducts were also needed to bridge the Beauly and the Conon rivers before the line reached Dingwall. The advance to Invergordon was completed on 25 March 1863 and to Meikle Ferry on 1 June 1864. The construction of the Dornoch Firth bridge, however, was to remain a paper dream.[20]

The engineers and entrepreneurs in Inverness continued to pursue the ambition to have a more direct line from their town to Perth, avoiding the need always to be travelling via the long road – 60 miles longer, in fact – round by Aberdeen. The revival of the proposal in July 1860 caused a stir of excitement. It was now estimated that the construction would not exceed £6,000 a mile, and that half the capital had already been secured.[21] The *Inverness Courier* hailed the project and pointed out the historical significance of the route:

> [It] has been in all time the great highway or thoroughfare betwixt the South and North. To keep it clear and open extensive forests used of old to be set on fire, and when the means of commanding and improving the Highlands began to be considered, the first great military road northward for the principal part of the line was precisely the route now selected.

Neither tunnel nor difficult rock-cutting would be required, and the long miles through the mountains would boost tourism. 'A great opportunity is now presented to us of permanently benefiting the whole North. Let us work heart and hand to have it accomplished.'

A major opponent of the project at the start was the Duke of Atholl. The same nobleman in 1847 had roused a *cause célèbre* when he had tried to slap a ban on public use of the right of way through Glen Tilt.[22] On that occasion the normally compliant public had risen in opposition to the duke's wish, and the town council of Perth had condemned it as an interruption that annoyed travellers and tourists, and militated against the interests of the community. That conflict had been brought to an end when the court backed the case of the Association for the Protection of Public Rights of Roadway, founded in 1845, and the forerunner of the Scottish Rights of Way Society, after it had organised a mass walk-in, defying the duke and his gillies, who tried to bar their way. If the duke had been upset by people walking through Glen Tilt, how much more would he object to a noisy locomotive breathing smoke and sparks?

Joseph Mitchell described his grace as 'manly, kind hearted and upright, proud of his dignity, of his magnificent estates, and people. He was no politician, and whatever wayward and impulsive eccentricities he displayed arose very much from imperfect education and training.' This powerful figure of imperfect education, who owned a vast acreage in the upper Tay catchment through which any direct rail line would have to pass, had to be brought to the correct point of view and, with that purpose in mind, Mitchell and a few of his colleagues visited Blair Castle in September 1860. The duchess was the 'beau-ideal of a Scotch lady of high rank', in Mitchell's opinion; his tactic seemed to be to get her on side and her husband would follow. And so it turned out. Accepting the engineer's assurances that the landscape he loved would not be too much despoiled, the duke, says Mitchell, 'took a great interest in the works ... and would have proved a valuable man of business' had he not been stricken by a fatal cancer that ended his life soon after the line had been completed.[23]

The Act for the Inverness–Perth line was passed on 22 July 1861. Mitchell divided the full distance of 104 miles between Dunkeld and Forres into nine sections, awarding each to a different contractor. Lady Seafield once again performed the ceremonial divot-cutting on 17 October. The mountainous country and its remoteness from settlements of any size presented the construction gangs with special problems of access and supply, but gradually the track took form. The stretch between Dunkeld and Pitlochry was completed on 1 June 1863, the Forres–Aviemore section at the beginning of August. By early September the railway was ready and on the 9th it was passed by the Board of Trade inspectors. Contrary to the assurance confidently given in 1860, two tunnels had been required, albeit for only the short distance of 300 yards in each case, one at Dunkeld and the other at the entrance to the Pass of Killiecrankie, where the minutes in echoing darkness only enhanced the passenger's experience: 'issuing from it, the whole romantic beauty of this wild Highland gorge bursts upon the traveller'.[24]

In Mitchell's view the opening of the line was rushed, as the directors in their desire to catch the tail end of the tourist season ignored some technical problems. The result was that the first train to tackle the northbound journey almost failed to make it, as a string of heavy goods wagons sapped the power of the locomotive on the long gradient up Glen Garry from Struan to Dalnacardoch and brought it to a halt. Efforts to re-start simply blew off steam. Finally, the driver let the fire out, rekindled it, refilled the boiler and waited for the pressure to rise again before the whole assemblage could rumble onward. The passengers sat looking out at the dark hills and listening to the distant splash of the Falls of Garry, an experience not unknown to the traveller on the Highland line today. Meanwhile, as snags with the telegraph connections between stations had not been dealt with, the southbound train waited in ignorance at Aviemore before it could be allowed to proceed.

These misfortunes did little to mar the occasion. The *Inverness Courier* rushed a second edition off the press for the morning of Friday, 11 September with the full report of the celebrations and junketing surrounding the presentation of the Freedom of the Burgh to the Honourable T.C. Bruce and Mr Matheson of Ardross MP, chairmen respectively of the Inverness–Perth and the Inverness–Aberdeen Junction Railway companies. It was now possible to leave Thurso on the midday coach, catch the train at 4.50 a.m. at Invergordon the following morning, change trains in Inverness at 6.20 a.m., change again in Forres at 7.30 a.m., at Perth at 1.15 p.m. and, depending on whether one went via Edinburgh or Glasgow, roll into London early in the morning less than 48 hours after leaving home. A third-class ticket from Inverness to London was priced at 42s 6d. Another instance of the speed of modern travel was recorded by Lord Cockburn, who wrote that in 1843 it had become possible for the 'romantic tourist pinched for time' to journey from Fort William to Edinburgh in 'one long hot day', catching the 6 a.m. coach south to Tarbet and then a steamer to Glasgow in time to board the 5 p.m. train to the capital. 'Spirits of Fingal and Rob Roy! What say ye to this?' the judge was moved to ask.[25]

CHAPTER 19

Road versus rail

'the last of the old stage coach . . .'

The advent of the 'iron horse' spelt doom for the stagecoach, although not immediately and not in every place. The coach operators probably realised that their glory days were over when they began to lose the all-important mail contracts. The news first broke in July 1856 that the mail from the south was to be taken from the coach on the Highland road and sent to Inverness by train from Aberdeen. After much protest, however, the Post Office relented and reversed its decision, and from January 1857 the coaches between Perth and Inverness resumed the carrying of the mail for another few years. Coaches also found a new importance in providing feeder services to the railway, for example on the Inverness and Aberdeen line where, until the bridge over the Spey was ready late in 1858, passengers disembarked and travelled by coach between Fochabers and Keith. And as long as the direct rail line between Inverness and Perth remained a paper dream, the coach companies could still boast, as they did in capital letters in their advertisements, that only they could enable the traveller to cover the distance from the Highland capital to either Edinburgh or Glasgow in one day 'WITHOUT TRAVELLING ALL NIGHT!! QUICKEST AND CHEAPEST ROUTE!!' An outside third-class coach ticket from Inverness to Glasgow cost 32s 2d in March 1858, but it

was a long day, leaving the north at 5 a.m., bumping and slew-
ing over Drumochter, transferring to the train in Perth and
steaming into the Clyde city at 9 p.m. Under the heading
'UNPRECEDENTED TRAVELLING', one company advertised
the introduction of a new coach in December 1858 with inside
lights and seats with arms 'like railway carriages', with room
for seven travellers inside and out. In the effort to compete with
the train, the coach operators also cut their fares, sometimes by
nearly 50 per cent.[1] It was, however, a contest they were doomed
to lose. Although the public no doubt thrilled at the courage
and devotion of the coachmen – such as, in January 1863, when
snow had prevented the mail coach proceeding north from
Dalnacardoch and the guard had ridden with the mailbags to
Dalwhinnie – and although coach speeds had risen to 35 miles
per hour on some roads, the mass of travellers came to prefer
the train, even if one could be plagued by smoke and get coal
grit in one's eye. The mail contracts were awarded to the rail
companies on 30 April 1863 and this time the decision was not
reversed.

Hardly anyone was around to see the departure of the last
Highland mail coach from Inverness at six o'clock on the morning of Sunday, 27 September 1863. Or at least no one who
thought to give the equipage and the prancing horses a loving
farewell. Some other coaches were sent on their way with recognition of what they had achieved. The last mail coach to leave
Wick was seen off with a cheer from a crowd gathered to see it
go and an innkeeper blowing 'Auld Lang Syne' on the cornet:
'Mr Alexander Bannerman drove south last night, with Mr
Duncan Ross as guard – the former exchanging coaches with
Mr Grassick about Berriedale and returning to Wick, with Mr
Donald Murray as guard.' Bannerman drove into Lybster to be
met by a party of well-wishers and what the record notes as 'a
small jollification' ensued. 'The toast – "the last of the old stage
coach" – was drunk with romantic and mournful regret.'[2] When
the first rails and sleepers had been laid, the coachmen had been

defiantly cheerful, confident that an iron horse would never pay its way, but the Victorian era of progress had caught up with them. They could, however, remember with pride how they had done their utmost in many a Highland winter to get the mails through.

The early nineteenth century had seen an expansion of the mail service, with the opening of post offices in many villages and small towns, and more frequent deliveries. In the autumn of 1830 post riders began to deliver mail from Golspie twice a week to Tongue, Assynt, Lairg and Lochinver, the result of an application to the Post Office by James Loch MP.[3] Ill-planned changes could understandably raise the ire of the public. A gentleman who called himself Verax protested about what he labelled a 'most absurd' arrangement for the post runners in his district in a letter to the *Inverness Journal* in 1827: in response to a petition the Post Office had introduced a runner to carry mail from Blair Atholl over Drumochter to Badenoch but, at the same time, and on their own initiative, had withdrawn the runner between Badenoch and Grantown, so that a letter posted to Inverness from Kingussie had to take what Verax called a 'jaunt' via 'Dunkeld, Perth, Dundee, Arbroath, Montrose, Aberdeen ... doubling the postage and more than tripling the time ... No man of business in Inverness can expect an answer to a letter from any part of Badenoch in less than from 14 to 16 days.' The latest issue of the *Journal* had taken seven days to reach Verax, who caustically referred to port wine improving during a voyage to India but 'we never heard of a newspaper sent three hundred miles round to render it more palatable to the readers'. There was more correspondence on this problem until at last in early April the Post Office resumed the Badenoch to Grantown link on its 'former footing'[4]

In the early 1840s, the Post Office was considering how best to introduce a year-round mail connection to Orkney and decided that a steamer from Thurso (Scrabster), although expensive, would be more reliable than the current arrangement whereby mails were carried from Wick to Kirkwall. The modern system of universal delivery, whereby postal charges are paid by the sender in advance and are fixed irrespective of distance, came in with the introduction of the penny post.

Coaches continued in places away from the rail line or in the provision of connections to and from rail heads for some years until motor road traffic came along. In 1869, a young Robert Louis Stevenson, returning to Edinburgh from Wick, where he had been subject to an unsuccessful effort by his family to turn him into an engineer, caught the night mail to Golspie on the first stage of his journey and described it in terms of mystery and romance. They stopped at Lybster, 15 miles south of Wick, the first stage and the first change of horses. 'A Roman Catholic priest travelling within, knowing that I was delicate, made me take his seat inside for the next stage,' recalled Stevenson. He dozed on and off, and woke as they descended the steep brae into the glen of Berriedale, and another change of horses. 'When I and the priest had lit our pipes,' wrote Stevenson, 'we crossed the streams, now speckled with the moonlight that filtered through the trees, and walked to the top of the Ord. There the coach overtook us and away we went for a stage, over great, bleak mountains, with here and there a hanging wood of silver birches and here and there a long look of the moonlit sea, the white ribbon of the road marked far in front by the newly erected telegraph posts.' The third stage of the journey was reached at Helmsdale, the fourth at a place Stevenson could not name (possibly Kintradwell), and he finally reached Golspie in time for breakfast before the departure of the train.[5]

Some coach services deliberately appealed to the tourist market and the increasing numbers of people who came to the Highlands in search of beauty and heritage, an aspect of travel still exploited by the railways today. Such an experience was offered by the 'expeditious and safe conveyance through the Highlands between Glasgow, Fort William and Inverness by the splendid new coaches "The Marquis of Breadalbane" via the

Banks of the Clyde, Dumbarton, Loch Lomond, Lochaber and Fort Augustus'.[6] The route combined a passage by steamboat along Loch Lomond and Loch Ness, with coach along the rest of the way, and listed all the attractions, including the Marquis of Breadalbane's lead mines, Rannoch Moor, Glencoe, Ossian's cave, the parallel roads of Glenroy and the monument in Glenfinnan that showed Prince Charles 'waiting for the gathering of the Clans' (an error still repeated – the figure on the Glenfinnan column is a representative Highlander, not Charlie himself). 'There is not in Europe another line of communication of equal distance which combines a more varied, a more beautiful, a grander or more sublime description of scenery,' boasted the advertisement, not expanding on the fact that some of the listed attractions lay rather far from the actual line of travel.

John S. Banks, a native of John o' Groats born in around 1891, could remember the mail coaches that connected the district to Wick during his boyhood. These were wagonettes, usually pulled by a single horse. Through force of habit, one horse always stopped at the inn in Keiss, about halfway through the journey, but when a traveller, a stranger, asked if this was where the driver changed horses was told, 'No, no, no, this is where we change our breath'; that is, had a strengthening dram. It was also the custom for the driver of another vehicle on this route, a covered coach called the *Barrogill*, a kind of omnibus, to summon second-class passengers to get down and push when faced with a steep brae – those in first class were allowed to stay aboard.[7]

As is often the case in these matters, the last stagecoach to run in the Highlands was on the road longer than anyone may have predicted. The *Caberfeidh* continued to ply between Kingussie and Fort William until the outbreak of the First World War; the last coach driver, James Gillies of Laggan Bridge, died in 1951.[8]

CHAPTER 20

Highland lines

'a gradual but complete revolution . . .'

The most famous of the railway companies in the Highlands was born in February 1865, from a series of amalgamations among its forebears. This was the Highland Railway Company (HR). Its headquarters at Station Square in Inverness faced the Station Hotel and the entrance to the railway station itself – three sides of the plaza were thus dedicated to modern travel. HR had some 250 miles of track in its transport empire, connecting the country from Bonar Bridge south to Stanley Junction near Perth, and east to Keith, a geographical reach that still left tempting unconquered territory to the north and west. Extensions to the north to Caithness and to the west towards Skye were in prospect, the public was told at the shareholders' meeting in October 1865.[1]

By the mid-nineteenth century, the social changes wrought by the railway were becoming clear: much improved communication with the south and between local centres; increasing availability and range of mass-manufactured goods cheaper than anything locally made; a greater buzz of commerce, with new buildings and even streets being erected to accommodate offices and shops; swelling numbers of visitors and tourists, with knock-on effects on hotels. In the midst of the stir, a few older heads lamented the passing of quieter, more self-contained times. Isobel Anderson was one of them: 'Since the opening of the Inverness and Nairn railway in 1855,' she wrote, '[there has been] a gradual but complete revolution in the ways of what had for many years been a quiet exclusive little town.'[2]

The Duke of Sutherland was a great enthusiast of railways. He had his own station erected at Dunrobin, to be handy for his castle home, and liked to drive his own train, once taking the controls to bring Queen Victoria herself north on an excursion. In 1865, he founded his own company to build a line from Ardgay, where the Highland Railway terminated, to Brora. An independent attempt to build a line in the far north had been launched 20 years before, in 1845, between Wick and Thurso, but that had gone nowhere and now this idea had also been revived. The supporters of the Caithness line brought in Joseph Mitchell to survey a route, but he had to admit defeat in the shadow of the Ord; there was no way, he found, to build a railway north from Helmsdale at reasonable cost except by making a long detour inland, up the valley of the Helmsdale river to a point where it became feasible to surmount the county march, a remote, relatively high and bare moorland with limited road access. Mitchell and his partner Murdoch Paterson recommended leaving Sutherland at Forsinard and proceeding in the direction of Halkirk and easy access to the Caithness plain. This did not please the Caithness businessmen for the simple reason that, unlike the road made 30 years earlier, the proposed rail line would bypass the thriving fishing villages along the Caithness coast and instead run through a wild, bleak stretch of moorland where no one lived. (Some of this moorland was to re-enter the public consciousness in the 1980s as the Flow Country, but as late as the 1970s locals still referred to it as 'miles and miles o' bugger all'.)

Work started on the Sutherland railway in late 1865, the dilemma of the Ord still unresolved. There ensued much discussion and argument over where the rail line should run and how it should be funded, some of it petty and riven with parochial rivalries, until at last a Sutherland and Caithness Railway bill received the nod from Parliament in July 1871.[3] By this time, the Duke of Sutherland had brought his railway as far as Helmsdale. To improve transport links with the north-west, the duke had the line routed via Lairg, towards the centre of the vast county from whose name he took his title. Work began on the final miles of the far north line for the Sutherland and Caithness Railway Company in November 1871, under the direction of William Baxter in Sutherland and Murdoch Paterson in Caithness.[4]

The ascent of the Strath of Kildonan, following the Helmsdale river, a natural corridor running inland for some 20 miles, was fairly straightforward. Construction work on the Caithness lowlands likewise presented little technical difficulty after it began in March 1872. The trouble came when the navvies approached the county march. Much effort had to be expended simply to get materials to the work sites: the men had to carry in their accommodation huts on their own backs, and horses had to drag cartloads of equipment through the boggy terrain. To produce a roadway, first for the import of the construction material and then for the railbed itself, it was necessary in places to excavate moss to a depth of several feet and backfill with sand and gravel. Winter blizzards, wind and rain added to the hardships the workers had to contend with but heroically they struggled on and laid the last rails on 7 July 1874. Two days later the Duke of Sutherland drove his guests, who included the editor of *The Times* from London, from Helmsdale to Thurso and Wick where, ironically, it arrived half an hour earlier than expected in a station echoingly empty. Regular train services for the public began on 28 July.

Before the rails began to be laid to reach the northernmost corner of the country, another new line had been built west from Dingwall. This scheme had been seriously mooted in 1864 but had been delayed by funding difficulties that led to Strome on Loch Carron becoming the terminus rather than Kyle of

Lochalsh, directly opposite Kyleakin and Skye. There were also problems from landowners. Instead of choosing Muir of Ord, and the lower valley of the Conon for the first few miles of track, it was decided to opt for Dingwall as the point of divergence from the main north line. Again, objections from a landowner led to Strathpeffer, despite being an obvious destination with its spa traffic, being effectively bypassed, creating a dogleg in the route in the valley of the Peffer and a steep ascent for four miles through the mountainous terrain of Raven's Rock. Twenty thousand cubic feet of rock had to be blasted apart here to cut a gorge to accommodate the line.

The Kyle line, as it is now known, was opened on 19 August 1870. At Strome the traveller was offered a choice of steamer connections, daily to Portree or three times a week to Stornoway. Noting that it was now possible to travel from Edinburgh to Portree in only 15 hours, the *Scotsman* correspondent wrote, a trifle condescendingly: 'In the opinion of many of the West coast Highlanders this is a marvellous feat, and ranks in their estimation as one of the wonders of the age.'[5] The original ambition to terminate at Kyle was eventually realised, almost 30 years later, in November 1897.

The new transport, harnessing the power of steam, was hailed as a great boon but from time to time the public was reminded that it brought attendant dangers, all the more perilous from the greater speeds and forces now in human hands. A very grave accident occurred at the beginning of September 1858 on the Inverness–Aberdeen line only weeks after its triumphant opening. Returning from Keith to collect a brake-van left earlier after a derailment on the incline between Mulben and the Spey, the driver ran his engine off the end of a siding and crushed four of his companions between it and the tender; three died from terrible injuries.[6] There was a bad rail accident at Forgandenny station near Perth early in January 1870, when couplings broke and delayed a train that was then rammed 'with terrible force' by a northbound mail train. The smash happened late at night and the rescuers had to kindle fires from the splintered carriage wood to light what they were doing; several passengers were injured, and two were killed.[7] In another incident at Culloden, an elderly woman stepped from the train while it was still in motion, fell into the space beside the platform and almost lost a hand when she was run over. In June 1870 a train on the Beauly line struck a herd of straying cattle, killing two of the beasts.[8]

These terrible occurrences may have given some people pause, and no doubt fuelled many a parlour discourse on human frailty and hubris, but the railway was now an irreversible and expanding presence. For many, economic well-being came to depend on access to the network, and connections by sea and by road would no longer suffice.

The first plans to connect to Oban were formulated in the early 1840s by a number of companies, but these soon fell by the wayside, unable to overcome problems with finance and the terrain. For example, in July 1846 the Scottish Grand Junction Railway was given clearance by Parliament to build a 45-mile line from Oban to Crianlarich, with a branch to the north end of Loch Lomond, but no progress was made and the company was allowed to wind up its affairs in 1852, when it was observed that 'its construction is not considered a matter of much importance as far as local interests are concerned'.[9] The Callander and Oban Railway company was formed in 1864 with the intention of constructing an east–west link through the Trossachs and the northern Argyllshire hills, and received authorisation a year later, only to run into serious financial problems partly arising from the difficulty of the terrain. By 1870 the company had only managed to lay some 17 miles of track before work ground to a halt in Glen Ogle. Even getting this far had required a considerable engineering effort; the line hangs on the side of the glen, all the while climbing on a 1:60 gradient, and at the north end exits over an impressive viaduct.[10] Then, with more money in the kitty, construction resumed and brought the railhead to Tyndrum and then, at last, in 1880, to Oban.

In April that year a party of directors and friends celebrated with a return train journey between Dalmally and Oban to lunch in the Great Western Hotel, and in the first week of July passenger traffic began. 'The undertaking is one of vast importance to the West of Scotland,' noted the *Inverness Courier*. 'The completed line will form a main artery to which routes already in existence, and probably others which will suggest themselves, will be valuable contributories.'[11] The new line did much to boost tourism and also brought better access to southern markets for local produce. At the same time as the hard-wrought Oban line opened for business, the Glasgow and North-West Railway Company published a more ambitious scheme to build a line all the way from Glasgow to Inverness that would run by Loch Lomond, over Rannoch Moor, and through Glencoe and the Great Glen. Estimates of the cost of this massive undertaking fell between £1.5 and £2 million. Opposition to the proposal was also massive, from the existing railway and steamer companies who wished for no more competition in a market already becoming crowded, and in May 1883 Parliament threw out the plan. Ironically a good part of the route was soon to be built by others. Formed in 1887, the West Highland Railway Company announced their plan to lay a line to Fort William. This was approved by Parliament in July 1889.

The West Highland line was a tremendous undertaking, in the way the engineers and navvies overcame the obstacles thrown in their path by the landscape and the climate, fully in the mould of the lines that had preceded it. The engineer in charge was Charles de Neuville Forman, Glasgow born and bred; in its notice of his death in February 1901, *The Scotsman* called him 'one of the foremost and best known civil engineers of this country'.[12] Forman brought to the West Highland line a formidable body of experience acquired in building railways in central Scotland, but the work was possibly too much for him and may have contributed to his death at the age of only 48. At one point some 5,000 navvies – many of them Irish, because of the low indigenous population – were labouring on the line, working out of camps at Craigendoran, Arrochar, Inveruglas, Crianlarich and other sites where material could be brought in by sea or rail to reach the inaccessible glens and moors over which they had to lay the track. By this time, the men had steam shovels and dynamite to ease the labour but much was still achieved by sheer sweat and effort. To keep construction costs down, the surveyors resorted to contouring the line rather than asking for cuttings and tunnels, the prime example of the approach being on the flanks of Ben Doran where the line almost doubles back on itself in a great horse-shoe-shaped curve. On Rannoch Moor, to cross stretches of bog, sections of line had to be laid on a floating platform of turf and brushwood, and another piece of bog north of Rannoch station had to be bridged by nine 70-foot leaps of a viaduct. The great work was completed by the driving of the last spike on Rannoch Moor on 5 September 1893. The official opening ceremony followed nearly a year later in Fort William on 11 August 1894.

In the mid-1880s the Great North of Scotland Railway company constructed a line along the Moray coast, linking the fishing towns and villages between Portsoy and the mouth of the Spey. At the west end it connected with the Lossie–Elgin branch, and Highland Railway added another connection between Keith and Portessie. The line has now gone, but it has left two impressive reminders of its existence, in the stone viaduct that dominates the approach to Cullen and in the tremendous iron viaduct across the Spey at Garmouth. Here, nearing its debouchment into the Moray Firth, the Spey flows through a shifting maze of sandbanks; to solve the problem of spanning the unpredictable course, the engineers built three sections of viaduct of rivetted iron latticework, a total length of some 950 feet, with the central span crowned by a great bow of steel. The line opened, first for goods trains and three weeks later for passengers, in April 1886.

The spread of railway lines in the north was now almost complete and only a handful of extensions were to be added in the years before the First World War. Strathpeffer gained its own branch and rail station in June 1885, a line from Muir of Ord to Fortrose was completed in February 1894, branch lines were laid to Hopeman from Burghead (1892), Fort George from Gollanfield (1899), Fochabers from Orbliston (1893), Dornoch from the Mound (1902), and Lybster from Wick (1903). The Mallaig line was opened on 1 April 1901, that to Fort Augustus in July 1903. The Callander and Oban company opened a branch line to Ballachulish, including a bridge spanning the mouth of Loch Etive at Connel, in 1903. As in the story of the military roads, some lines were mooted but remained only paper dreams. One of the most notable omissions from a railway map of the Highlands is any line between Garve and Ullapool. Four attempts were made to build one but each came to naught, through failure to attract investment, rivalry between railway companies – Highland Railway opposed a Great North of Scotland Railway plan in 1892 – and in the instance of the fourth and final attempt in 1918 through the refusal of a landowner to cooperate with the Rural Transport (Scotland) Committee.[13] The latter committee also considered a rail line from Culrain to Lochinver, lines on the islands of Skye and Lewis, and extensions to existing lines such as from Thurso to Scrabster, Lybster to Dunbeath, and Conon to Cromarty.[14]

The brief period at the end of the First World War was arguably the last moment when new railway lines were the default solution to transport – the few years before the attraction of the internal-combustion engine in the form of the bus, car and lorry bequeathed the future to the road.

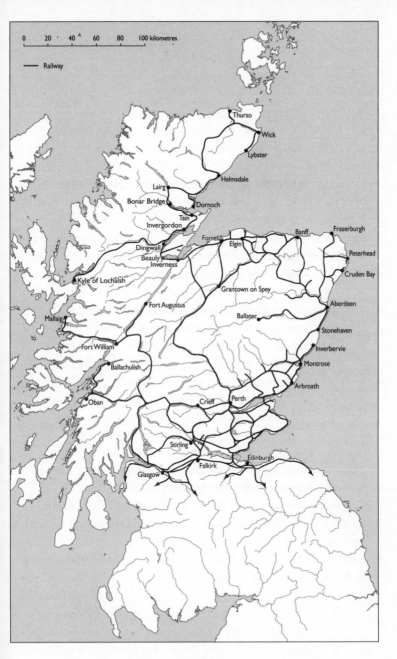

Map 7. Map of the railways in northern Scotland at their maximum extent.

CHAPTER 21

Tourists and an end to droving

*'increased facilities of intercourse between
the Highlands and the Lowlands . . .'*

The steam engine brought an end to the droving trade. Animals
were first shipped out by sea; for example, in March 1836 the
steamer *Duchess of Sutherland* left Inverness with 30 cattle and
60 sheep on board, and took on 30 more at Lossiemouth.[1] As
early as 1858, the livestock dealers were taking advantage of
the new opportunity to send animals quickly over long distance
by rail. In one week at the end of October that year, 70 wagons
with cattle and sheep rattled away from Muir of Ord to the
southern markets.[2] After observing one day in the spring of
1859 how cattle sold to southern buyers would be in Aberdeen
'almost by the time the market stance was cleared', the *Elgin
Courant* noted that 'this branch of traffic is but yet in its infancy
in the north; and ere long we may reasonably expect it to be
very greatly increased'.[3]

By the 1880s, livestock accounted for 80 per cent of the goods
revenue of Highland Railway, and the railway station and the
auction mart, the modern replacement of the tryst, became close
neighbours in many towns. The herding of skittish stirks on to
railway wagons and the cleaning out of the same wagons
became regular if smelly work for railway employees. Highland
Railway also offered passes to drovers accompanying livestock,

one to every three wagons, but they had to ride in the guard's van or a third-class carriage, where they would not disturb the better class of passenger, and pay no more than a third-class fare or sometimes, with their dogs, go free.[4] In 1890, Highland carried almost half a million sheep to the south, herded aboard in bleating flocks at stations that included Lairg, Dalwhinnie, Perth, Muir of Ord, Nairn and Grantown.[5] Lairg came to host – and still does – the largest one-day lamb sale in Europe. Access to the railway was the key to this development.

Made roads harmed the hooves of the animals, and cattle had to be shod like horses, but, as noted earlier, increasing restrictions on movement, arising from new attitudes to property and from the introduction of turnpike roads, also contributed to finish droving not long after it had reached its economic peak between 1825 and 1850. Farmers became less tolerant of large herds of cattle and sheep passing through a countryside where they were enclosing fields, sowing new crops of grass and investing in dykes and ditches. Landowners became jealous of their glens as hunting preserves. In 1844, when a newspaper correspondent wrote a pen portrait of the activity, the Falkirk tryst was still going strong, a bustling trade fair where bankers and drovers argued, cursed, shook hands and exchanged drams over deals involving thousands of animals that had been driven from all airts in the north: 'The men who have accompanied, and tend the lot, are so dissimilar in tongue, dress and aspect that it is difficult to believe they own the same Sovereign and belong to the same country as their Lothian brethren.'[6] Droving lingered on as a rural activity in parts of the country far from rail lines, and some drovers in their old age became subjects of nostalgic reminiscence. In the museum devoted to droving at the mart near Dingwall, there is a letter dated 2006. It reads:

About 65 years ago, I met a 95 year old Drover at a farm sale in Glenlivet . . . he told me he had been in a drove from Glenlivet to Falkirk when he was about 15 [this would have been in the 1860s]. They had slept in the open ... he had woken one morning with his shoulder and right arm frozen to the ground ... 80 years later his arm was still semi-paralyzed.[7]

The railway was also a vital ingredient in the growth in the Highlands of the seasonal game shooting. In July and August, sleeper trains left London nightly with families bound for the big houses on the Highland estates, fully equipped for weeks of hunting, shooting and fishing. The *Inverness Courier* took pride in publishing lists of arrivals of these wealthy holidaymakers. Professor John Stuart Blackie, Celtic scholar and supporter of the crofters in their campaign for land reform, commented in 1885 on how the 'increased facilities of intercourse between the Highlands and the Lowlands which steam communication and the railroads now so amply afford' was eroding the indigenous Gaelic culture and affecting the use of the Gaelic language itself.[8] The professor's caution over the invasion of modernity and the losses it represented was hardly in the same mould as the objections of the old clan chieftains to Wade's road, but it was an echo nevertheless of regret for old ways passing.

A humble yet highly significant form of personal transport appeared in the 1860s – the bicycle, or velocipede as it was earlier termed. At first it was taken up by some sporting enthusiasts. The Velocipede Club in Inverness advertised races, such as one in April 1870 from Millburn to the fifth milestone on the Aberdeen road and back, a distance of nine miles; there were four entrants on this occasion, on a fine afternoon, and the winner completed the course in 50 minutes.[9] There were now a number of 'velocipedists' in the town. 'Could anyone coin a less awkward name?' protested the editor of the *Inverness Courier*. Racing remained a popular sport, but more and more the machine became a simple, easily maintained form of transport available to everyone with a reasonable sense of balance. The bicycle also proved to be almost infinitely flexible in its capacity for adaptation, being able to carry all manner of goods and even livestock. Its importance is easily underestimated but, for the first time, an ordinary working man or woman could own their own means of transport that did not require fuel or feeding and find themselves, in what leisure time they were allowed, free to explore over longer distances than a pedestrian could contemplate. And it affected social attitudes, dress and courtship patterns, as young people began to form cycling clubs and make jaunts during their leisure hours. The cost of a bike was low – in 1901 second-hand machines were being advertised in the *People's Journal* for £3, and a new one could be bought for weekly instalments of 2s 6d, quite within the means of someone with a steady job.[10]

As the nineteenth century drew to a close, the traveller could reflect on how much the Highlands had opened to the rest of the world. In the space of 100 years, new modes of public transport – stagecoach, rail, steamships – had created an increasingly inter-connected globe.

The telegraph had made its entry in the 1860s and the telephone in the 1890s. New threads of communication linked every corner of the Empire, then approaching its height, and it was now almost taken for granted that the Post Office could deliver a letter or a package posted in, say, Lerwick to friends or relatives in Canada, South Africa, Australia or Malaya. It was a remarkable social transformation. And there was more to come.

PART 6

Cars, trains and planes

CHAPTER 22

The motor car

'the dust and grit of the road . . .'

Anyone standing on the Ord of Caithness in the late summer of 1860 may have witnessed a significant event – the passing of the Earl of Caithness and his good lady in a steam car. What the bishop Robert Forbes in 1762 had called, with his tongue in his cheek, 'the finest road in the world' was still a daunting prospect for the traveller, and for a smoking horseless carriage to bump over its surface was a remarkable occurrence indeed.

In 1859, the Marquis of Stafford had ordered for himself a steam car from the Castle Foundry in Buckingham, where the manager Thomas Rickett left off his normal tasks of manufacturing agricultural implements and steam engines to turn a car out for the enterprising northern nobleman. The steam car had a seat in front for the driver and passengers, where they sat with their backs to the boiler on its platform between two great wheels and a funnel high enough to let the smoke blow over their heads, if they were lucky. On a narrow platform at the rear rode the stoker, who kept the boiler working and the steam pressure at the correct level. The Marquis drove his Rickett steam car on the roads of Sutherland and, not to be outdone, the Earl of Caithness resolved to get one himself (James Calder, in his history of Caithness, itches to credit the earl with its actual invention).[1] Driving it from Inverness to Barrogill Castle (now

the Castle of Mey) on the shore of the Pentland Firth was a
worthy achievement, and that is what the earl did, at a speed of
around eight miles an hour, arriving in Wick to loud cheers
from the townsfolk.

The steam car consumed about one hundredweight of coal
during a 20-mile trip, but this was held to be acceptable on
common roads. 'A journey of 140 miles made in two days, at
a cost of less than 1d per mile for fuel, proves this,' wrote
Calder, quoting from an article in the *Parlour Journal*, 'and the
fact that no accident to man or beast was caused by the steam
carriage during the whole journey answers the objections as to
frightening horses.' The two noble pioneers were probably
aware that an early car of the type they drove with enthusiasm
had been made nearly a century before, a steam-powered road
vehicle built by William Murdoch for his boss, none other
than the illustrious James Watt himself, who used it in
Cornwall.[2]

Steam cars were too cumbersome to catch on with the public,
but they foreshadowed the advent of the form of transport that
has changed the world – the motor car powered by the internal-
combustion engine. The Austro-Hungarian inventor Siegfried
Marcus is credited with installing such an engine on a wheeled
vehicle for the first time in about 1870. The first petrol-powered
automobile followed in 1886 from the workshops of Karl Benz
in Mannheim. Scots played a prominent role in the early days of
motor manufacture; the first British-built car was produced in
1895 by a Glaswegian locomotive engineer, George Johnston,
who based his machine on continental models. Johnston also
has the distinction of being the first motorist to collect a speeding fine; almost as soon as he had taken to the road, he was
fined 2s 6d for driving at a startling 17 miles per hour. The 1865
Locomotive Act stipulated that road vehicles observe a maximum speed of 2 miles per hour in urban areas and that a man
brandishing a red flag should walk in front of any vehicle haul-
ing wagons. A later Act gave short shrift to the red flag and

raised the speed limit to 14 miles per hour, but not soon enough for Johnston.

The pace of development of the new mode of transport was impressively quick, and by 1900 ten different brands of Scottish car were chugging from the workshops. The Caledonian Cycle and Motor Company, based in Aberdeen, produced a four-seat dogcart between 1899 and 1906 which sold for £200. As far as is known, no motor cars were manufactured in the Highlands.[3]

Registration for road vehicles was introduced in 1903. In Inverness-shire, nine motor cars and motorbikes were entered in the big ledger kept for the job before the end of December. The first – listed as a grey and black tonneau French model, owned by Granville Hugh Baillie – was duly marked in as ST1 two days before Christmas.[4] The number grew: 37 were registered in 1904, 20 in 1905, 34 in 1906 and, eventually, in 1913, on the eve of the First World War, 132. Car owners at this time tended to be professional men, such as doctors, or toffs, or, in a few cases where officialdom helped with funds, provosts; and many of these owners did not do their own driving but employed chauffeurs. Advertisements in 1910 quote Humber cars as costing from £285 but already there were dealers in these models in Inverness, Nairn, Dingwall and other towns.[5] Fashion was affected very early; in 1905, the Edinburgh department store of Patrick Thomson was advertising 'the new motor cap', on sale for 1s to over 5s, as the correct thing in outdoor headwear – 'It is fast replacing the tam o'shanter everywhere . . .'[6] The young man desirous of mobility for less cost in that year could choose between spending eight guineas on a new Humber bicycle or saving £40 to purchase a Humber motorbike. Newspapers began to note that the railway locomotive was starting to lose its iconic status as the fastest machine on land.

As the inter-war years progressed, the price of cars fell in relation to income: in 1925 Wolseleys were available in several models, ranging from £225 for a two-seater to £1,200 for a

Landaulet De Luxe,[7] but by the end of the decade a 7 hp Austin could be bought for £140 and second-hand cars for less than £100 – a Ford 7.5 ton lorry cost only £15 in 1929.[8]

It did not take long for motorists to appreciate what the Highlands had to offer. The western branch of the Scottish Automobile Club began to stage annual reliability trials, at first in the form of a non-stop run from Glasgow to London but then, in 1905, for the first time, over a more testing route through the Cairngorms. Forty-four cars entered that year to display their endurance over a course of 595 miles in four days. In the first stage, the entrants set off from Blythswood Square in Glasgow at half-minute intervals and had to reach Dundee via Edinburgh, Stirling and Perth as quickly as they could within the allotted limit of 7 hours 20 minutes. Twenty-five cars managed to complete the non-stop drive, first place going to a 16 hp Albion Tonneau in 6 hours 17 minutes. Day two was more demanding of drivers and engines – over the Spital of Glenshee and the Devil's Elbow to Braemar and down Deeside to Aberdeen; on day three, the route ran west to Keith, up into the hills at Tomintoul, and then down Strathspey and over Drumochter to Pitlochry; and the fourth day saw the survivors roar through the Perthshire glens, via Aberfeldy and Crieff, west to Dalmally and south via Loch Lomondside to Glasgow. Two hill climbs were included – at the Devil's Elbow and near Aberfeldy. It was great fun, and the thrill can be felt in the words of the correspondent from the *People's Journal* who rode as a passenger in one of the cars:

> my ears are still resounding with the hum of machinery, my face and hands still burn with the effects of sun and wind, the dust and grit of the road have not yet been thoroughly eradicated from the roots of my hair, and my whole frame has scarcely recovered its normal equilibrium. But I would willingly go through the same experience at a couple of hours' notice ...

Fifteen cars survived the four non-stop runs.[9]

It would have been fairly reassuring for the early motorist to enter such an event with a team of mechanics and supporters as back-up. The individual driver required more courage but there were many who showed they had it, such was the lure of the open road, albeit a road potholed and dusty, where punctures were a fact of life. One man, remaining anonymous and again writing in the *People's Journal*, which had a wide readership throughout the north, described in lyrical terms how he had seen more of his native land than ever before in a fortnight's tour and not once had he stepped on board a train.[10] With one companion, our hero – possibly starting from Dundee, where the newspaper was published – drove first up the A9, though it was not yet so labelled, to Inverness. 'We traversed roads good, bad and indifferent, never turning aside in face of danger,' he boasted, going on to taunt his readers with, 'Ah but the scoffer knows not and, not knowing, cannot understand the harmony of a car's whirl when it is averaging 20 miles an hour, and never giving its lucky driver cause for a moment's anxiety.' A puncture, conveniently happening only a few streets from the centre of Inverness and the garage of Macrae & Dick, where it was fixed 'within less than a quarter of an hour', did not lessen the enthusiasm. Despite the loose gravel on patches of the road at Drumochter, the writer found 'the Highland highway far ahead of many other Inverness-shire roads in construction'. It took courage to drive over the Lecht on a road the writer called a 'fiendish sheep track'; the descent to Bridge of Brown was a 'nightmare', with brakes about to burst into flames and water boiling in the radiator. 'I daresay it is a fine boast to say that you have taken your car over a road compared to which the Devil's Elbow is child's play, but I cannot imagine any normally consti-tuted motorist repeating the experiment.'

The weather was another thing. The travellers were caught in a torrential downpour between Fort Augustus and Banavie that found its way through their layers of clothing, 'blinding the driver, and temporarily converting an ordinarily passable road into a mountain torrent of water, gravel and clay'. Beside Loch Lochy the swollen burns 'foamed across the roadway, and in and out of their deep tracks we bounded, anxiously speculating as to when the end would come and we should have to swim clear of the water-logged remains of the car'. The end did not come but the experience had been alarming enough to keep the driver awake for a while that night, vowing to be considerate of his 'faithful motor' in future and reaching for metaphor to convey his feelings: 'No war lord ever acquired greater affection for his charger in the thick of battle than did the driver of my 7 hp Swift through these perils of the North.'

Who could resist such publicity for adventure and the new mode of travel? Not all, though, had such a stirring time and were probably grateful for that. The journey, in August 1907, made by a 20-year-old business secretary called Joseph Ruddlesden and his companions when they drove a 46 hp Napier from Leeds to Strathspey is sedate in comparison with the hardy men in the Swift. From Wetherby, they motored via Morpeth and Alnwick to Edinburgh to pick up the north road. Twenty miles south of Perth they ran over a terrier that bolted unexpectedly from a lodge gate (the dog survived the experience), and near Killiecrankie one of the car doors opened to strew a trail of parcels along the road. When they stopped at Kingussie to ask the way, the car would not restart until they replaced a broken drive chain. By this time they were close to their destination near Kincraig. The journey had taken five days and they had reached speeds up to 20 miles per hour.[11]

The speed of the noisy monsters on the road was beginning to cause concern. A trial motorcycle rally took place in 1906, a six-day event on the route between Land's End and John o' Groats: 'At no part of the journey will competitors be allowed to exceed twenty miles an hour,' warned the newspapers, 'while the minimum schedule pace is fifteen miles an hour.'[12]

The advent of the motorcar presented opportunities for local firms already in the business of transport. A prime example of this is the company still active today and known throughout the Highlands as Macrae & Dick. The founders, Roderick Macrae in Beauly and William George Dick from Redcastle on the Black Isle, formed a partnership in 1878 to set up a horse and carriage hire company in Inverness. Among their customers were the landowners who resorted to the glens every autumn to hunt, shoot and fish, a lucrative clientele for the Inverness firm that at one time had as many as 300 horses in their stable.[13] It was natural to switch from running carriages to motor vehicles, and later to branch out into road haulage and tourism. This was a pattern of development replicated throughout the north, as smiddies became garages and filling stations, garden sheds grew into bicycle repair shops, and carters turned themselves into bus owners.

The density of traffic was becoming a problem in the south of England by the end of 1905 – in the previous three years the number of vehicles in Britain had risen from some 8,000 to 80,000 – and there was discussion of building roads dedicated to accommodate only motor vehicles.[14] In the north of Scotland traffic density remained low but was still gradually increasing. The makers of early cars were naturally keen to showcase their work and rarely missed a trick to impress the public. Henry Alexander drove a standard Ford Model T (registration S1871) to the summit of Ben Nevis on 15 May 1911. The hardy motorist got bogged down several times and at 3,000 feet had to cut a path through snow, but the objective was achieved, never mind that it took a gang of men weeks to prepare the route and that the final drive lasted for five days.

CHAPTER 23

New roads needed

'the ever increasing mechanical traffic . . .'

The first half of the twentieth century saw some expansion of the road network, but essentially the pattern created by Telford and his colleagues continued to serve the region. Roads were now in the care of the various local authorities, and expenditure on construction and maintenance was limited by what the county or burgh council could raise through the rates, the local property tax, supplemented by grants from central government. The road estimates for the Mid-Ross district in Ross and Cromarty for the financial year 1912–13 are probably typical for the rural authority: the department would need a budget in that period of £5,278 15s 8d, which included £230 for the road surveyor's salary and £75 for his clerk; a grant was expected from the National Road Board of £311, and this would leave £4,524 18s 5d to be raised from the ratepayers.[1] After the First World War, the budget for roads in Mid-Ross had to be greatly increased to resolve new problems. The road surveyor Charles Hogg submitted the following to the council in October 1919: 'Beyond the ordinary maintenance of the Roads and Bridges in the District, during the next 18 months the sum of £10,765 has to be expended in Reconstruction and repair of damage done by Timber Haulage.' During the war years, the carting of timber cut down by Canadian and Newfoundland soldiers for the country's needs had damaged the road surfaces in places; Hogg mentioned some 40 miles of roadway on the Garve–Ullapool, Conon–Findon and Alness–Boath routes. 'Owing to the unsettled state of labour and the remoteness of some of the roads involved I recommend that these works be carried out by direct labour under the Road Surveyor,' advised Hogg. At least now he had some mechanical aids to call on, and he listed desirable items of plant: a Baxter Patent Portable Stonebreaker, a Barford & Perkins water ballast motor road roller, vans for the workmen to sleep in, a back-tipping motor lorry, an Aveling & Porter compound traction engine convertible to a 12-ton steam roller with attached scarifier, and a 200-gallon one-horse hand tarring machine from the Municipal Appliances company. The plant would be needed anyway in the future to keep the west coast roads in order and provide the extra strength to cope with 'the ever increasing mechanical traffic'. Better to convince the canny councillors to approve his expenditure, the surveyor explained that the portable stonebreaker could spit out 45 tons of road metal in a day for only 2s 6d a ton, much more economical than the 3s 6d to 4s a ton needed to pay a man to break stones. The Barford & Perkins motor road roller was also a bargain: it could rumble on for a nine-hour day on seven gallons of paraffin, cheaper than a steam roller even without considering the problem of carting coal to the west coast. This equipment would cost £4,067: '[This] appears a large [sum] for such a small district,' wrote Hogg, 'but with a promised grant of 5/sevenths of the initial cost from the Ministry of Transport, only about £1,162 would have to be raised from the rates . . .' In the event, Hogg proved to be correct: in October 1919, the Scottish Advisory Committee agreed to pay over £6,000 to the council, including the roads grant and compensation for damage done by timber haulage.

The classification of roads started before the First World War but had to be resumed in 1919 by the then new Ministry of Transport. The Highlands were assigned to two zones for the numbering of the roads: zone 8, comprising the Hebrides and all of the mainland west of the Great Glen; and zone 9, with the north-east, Orkney, Shetland and areas north of the A8 and east of the A9. The A9, the great north road itself, became the boundary between the zones and was defined first as extending from Edinburgh to Inverness and, from 16 May 1935, to John o' Groats. (From 1 April 1997, it was redefined as having Scrabster as its northern terminus, with the section from Latheronwheel via Wick to John o' Groats being re-designated the A99, a reduction in status that has resulted in local grumbling.) Trunk roads, through routes of national strategic importance, were defined and created by Act of Parliament in 1936 and came into official existence from 1 April in the following year. The Ministry of Transport assumed responsibility for their upkeep, leaving other roads mostly in the care of county or burgh councils. Only five trunk roads were created in the Highlands: the A9, the A882 (Wick–Scrabster), A82 (Glasgow–Inverness), A85 (Tyndrum–Oban) and A96 (Aberdeen–Inverness), a low total reflecting the scattered, relatively sparse population.

Some roads, especially those in the more far-flung corners of the Highlands, must have been in a poor state immediately after the First World War, certainly poor enough for Robert Morrison, the operator of the mail contract in north-west Sutherland, to insert the following in newspapers:

> Owing to the extremely dangerous condition of the roads, I am reluctantly compelled to inform the public that from this date [17 January 1920] all PASSENGERS TRAVEL on the DURNESS LAXFORD MOTOR MAIL AT THEIR OWN RISK, also all Goods will be carried at Senders' Risk.[2]

For all that, motoring was rapidly becoming popular and was boosted by reports such as the one in the *Inverness Courier* in 1921 describing how none other than the prime minister himself, David Lloyd George, had driven from Blair Atholl to the town one sunny August afternoon, stayed overnight in the Station Hotel and had walked out the following morning to the delight of onlookers to buy fishing tackle before heading off for Gairloch.[3]

After the trauma of the First World War, concerned citizens gave much thought to what was termed 'regeneration'. The resettlement of ex-servicemen and employment were major topics in these considerations of the future but transport was also to the fore and, in one document, 'Resettlement in the Highlands', issued by the Highlands Local Employment Committee, it was designated 'the key to all schemes for development'. The conclusions listed in this attempt to cover every aspect of its subject included mention of no fewer than 16 branch rail lines, as well as steamer services, road and canal developments, and telephones.[4] At more or less the same time, the Rural Transport (Scotland) Committee, formed by the Secretary of State, published its ideas on how transport could boost agriculture, forestry and other rural industries, again with an emphasis on rail lines. It was recognised that these services would never be made to pay for themselves and would have to be subsidised: 'Taking the railways as a whole, we are satisfied that the capital cost will have to be met from public funds, and that in most cases not more than a return sufficient to cover working expenses can be looked for.'[5]

Little more was heard about the railway plans and government attention switched to the transport solution offered by the internal-combustion engine. In 1924 the Ministry of Transport decided to rebuild the two main roads to the north: the A9 from Perth to Inverness, and the A82 from Glasgow to Inverness, and assume the full burden of the costs, which came out at about £2 million.[6] For the A9, the estimated cost was set at £8,000 per mile. The needs of the motor car would be met by the design, with the standard width of the carriageway being set at 18 feet, although this stricture would have to be relaxed where the road passed under certain railway bridges, and no gradient was to be more than 5 per cent (1 in 20). The volume of traffic had been steadily increasing and in the summer months 'a steady stream of private cars and charabancs' was making road-mending 'an almost constant task'.[7] About half of the A9 was given a new alignment, and the remainder was left on the old route pioneered by the men working under Wade and then under Telford. The old problem associated with the landscape – the inconvenient occurrence of peat bogs – was dealt with by floating the road on a raft of reinforced concrete, eight inches thick and 21 feet wide. Four large concrete bridges were built at Dalnamein, Newtonmore, Tomatin and Carrbridge, and some 60 other bridges were either replaced or widened. A *Scotsman* reporter ended his story of the road-making with a piece of scene-setting:

> The huts in which the workmen lived . . . have been taken to pieces and the sections are lying in ordered piles, ready to be transported. At some parts of the road broken engines of various kinds can be seen awaiting the advent of the old-iron merchant. Here is an old lorry which has lost its front wheel; there a steam engine toppled into a ditch; and beside a forsaken camp a worn-out cement machine never to be used again.

During the early stages of the reconstruction, some motoring magazines warned drivers to choose other routes to go north, a threat to the economy that outraged the provost and councillors of Inverness, who immediately sought an audience with Sir Henry Maybury, director-general of roads. Sir Henry was very reassuring: he said he had travelled the whole road from Pitlochry to Inverness 'that morning by car' and there had been no point at which 'there was either the slightest danger or discomfort experienced' and he had 'maintained an average speed of 25 miles per hour throughout the whole journey'. The complaints in the press had no foundation, he continued, although the public should bear in mind that an omelette was impossible without breaking a few eggs and some slight inconvenience might be necessarily experienced. Bear in mind what condition the road would have been in today without the reconstruction scheme, he cautioned; it would have been practically impassable.

The newspaper report continued: 'He also advised the deputation not to be unduly apprehensive, as he was confident that the whole excavation and grading work would be completed before the commencement of the tourist season, and that quite a good road would be available for traffic.'[8]

The work on the A82 took longer than that on the A9, and in July 1929 Inverness County Council made a strong appeal to the government to get a move on.[9] Originally there had been no intention to improve the section north of Fort Augustus but, protested the council, its improvement was a matter of extreme urgency. Traffic on the narrow road had increased enormously and was likely to go on growing as tourist numbers swelled and steamer services on Loch Ness were withdrawn. At last the road was tackled and the work hailed in *The Scotsman* as 'one of the greatest achievements in road engineering in Scotland or for that matter Britain', a tribute ensured by work that had involved great cuttings through solid rock, especially along Loch Ness side, where parking places had been 'ingeniously worked into the route-way and attractive rockery walls erected'.[10] The cost per mile had come out at £13,000, held to be a low figure, as it included bridges and compensation to landowners. In June 1933, the road was being surfaced at the rate of one and a half miles a week and completion was expected by September.

The transport minister, Leslie Hore-Belisha, officially opened the new A82 on Thursday, 27 September 1934, taking time out to drive to the venue of the ceremony at Abriachan beside Loch Ness. The *Inverness Courier* hailed it as 'Britain's finest motoring highway' and proudly reeled off the impressive statistics, how the total cost of the 80 miles from North Ballachulish to

Inverness had come to around £1 million, the workforce had numbered 1,200 men at one point, over 55 bridges had been reconstructed, and the parking places for tourists made it all the easier to spot Nessie, who was making a considerable stir at the time.[11] Nessie's discovery was fortuitous – perhaps the road-works had disturbed the beast from her lair, some suggested – but it did wonders for tourism, and during one summer week 10,500 cars had been counted passing one point on the road.[12]

Accepting a silver *sgian dubh* as a gift from Major Robert Bruce, the transport minister said that the road was a symbol of Britain's recovering strength, just like the Cunard liner *Queen Mary* that had been launched the day before. 'I have the honour to name this road Glenalbyn,' declared Hore-Belisha, before he used the *sgian dubh* to cut a ribbon of Cameron tartan stretched across the highway between poles decorated in Fraser and Mackintosh tartan (thus were the main clans of the Great Glen recognised). The guests of honour went off to enjoy a lunch in the Station Hotel; the contractor A.M. Carmichael of Edinburgh threw a dinner for the workmen in their camp at Lochend. After the lunch, the minister and representatives from the five main-land counties in the Highlands held a private meeting to discuss the 'very great financial stress imposed on Highland counties by the ever-increasing burden of road maintenance'; only the state assuming responsibility for all classified roads could meet the demands of modern traffic, argued the councillors, to which plea the minister promised to devote special consideration.

The engineer in overall charge of the venture, an endeavour standing in the mould of Wade's ambitious projects, was Major Robert Bruce, originally from Dundee. A group of prominent Highland citizens feted him and his achievement at a dinner in Inverness on 21 December 1934, at which Sir Murdoch Macdonald MP called the new Glasgow–Inverness highway 'one of the finest roads in the world' and well fitted into the land-scape. Another guest at the dinner struck a more sober note by reminding his colleagues that maintenance of the new roads, which after all formed part of a national road scheme, would need government support.[13] The completion of the new road through Glencoe was also celebrated with a banquet in Ballachulish, where the guest of honour was the engineer in charge of that section, Major W.H. Hunt, who had cut his engineering teeth with the Canadian railways. Less than ten years before, declared Major J.A. Struthers, a mere mountain track, made in 1752, had linked Ballachulish to Tyndrum, and now there was a fine road that would bring in more tourists. There had been determined opposition to building a carriageway through Glencoe, led by the Society for the Preservation of Rural Scotland, but that had been withdrawn after several meetings in Edinburgh and in Glencoe itself, and those who had feared the intrusive newcomer were now said to be loud in its praises.

More than any other form of transport, the private car makes demands on public space. In the Highlands this became a problem to be addressed in the 1920s. Parking fines – of £1 each – were first issued in Inverness in August 1923 to drivers who had left their vehicles unattended and had carelessly impeded traffic flow.[14] Ferries had to adapt to accommodate the new form of transport, and vessels on short crossings such as at Ballachulish had turntables fitted. On its first day of operation in June 1926, one such ferry from Dornie to Totaig, across Loch Duich, carried 17 cars.[15]

Traffic signals flashed for the first time in the early 1930s – for several years, newspapers carried letters and editorials attacking the 'grave menace' of drivers wilfully ignoring red lights[16] – and talk of one-way streets began to be heard.[17] One-way traffic flow was introduced on an experimental basis in Inverness in 1939 to a predictably mixed reaction,[18] but it continued during the war years. It was a sign of the times in the autumn of 1934 when Inverness banned the herding of livestock along the main streets between 10 a.m. and 6 p.m. in the summer months.[19] It did not prove so easy to ameliorate that particular problem, as in 1960 there were still complaints about the congestion of traffic in the town centre on the day of a big sale of cattle or sheep.[20]

The practice of binding the metalled road surface with tar to provide a smoother skin for tyres appeared in the early 1920s, although it was to be several decades before side roads were customarily to receive this treatment. Speed limits of 30 miles per hour and pedestrian crossings with flashing Belisha beacons were introduced from 1934. It was discovered to some dismay in the late 1930s that the Ness Bridge, opened in 1855, was showing grave signs of not being able to cope with the stresses of motor traffic. In January 1939 a speed limit of 15 miles per hour and a weight limit were imposed until a replacement could be completed; the outbreak of the Second World War put a stop to the work and the temporary wooden bridge, strung along-side the old one, continued in use until a new bridge was finally built and opened to traffic in August 1961.

The motor revolution also saw of course the introduction of the bus. MacBrayne began to operate a bus between North Ballachulish and Fort William at the end of 1906, and arguably this may have been the pioneer in the north.[21] Another early service was provided by the Glenurquhart Motor Car Company from about 1910. Bus services expanded rapidly during the 1920s, with many small family firms springing up to provide transport links between every district and village and the nearest town in a way that had hardly existed before, such was the convenience of the short journey times. The country bus became an institution in its own right, the drivers familiar with every road end and happy to do errands for country folk. The ad hoc arrangements did not please all; the reader can feel the sigh of relief in the words written in 1951 in the Third Statistical Account about buses on Lewis: 'The bad old days are now over ... when passengers had to stand because the seats were occupied by bales of tweed or bags of flour, or even a live calf.'[22] As the inter-war years wore on, some of the small firms were taken over and there was a pattern of amalgamation that resulted in the growth of the Highland Transport Company.[23] Long-distance coaches also made their appearance. Macrae & Dick started a coach service between Inverness and Fort William in 1926; the journey took 3 hours 45 minutes and the single fare was 10s, a substantial sum in those days. Inverness & District Motor Services Ltd inaugurated a coach service to Kyle that same summer: 'The coach was a beautiful Albion, nicely upholstered, and the engine was in perfect order,' purred the *Highland News* reporter reassuringly, after going along for the ride. 'Although the road was narrow at parts, and other motor vehicles had to pass with only a few inches of space between the conveyances, the members of the company had no fear about their safety ... The driver ... kept a cool head and steady hand throughout the long journey.'[24]

CHAPTER 24

Changing transport

'It is quicker by rail . . .'

The railways emerged from the years of the First World War in battered shape, after the demands of the nation at war had put a tremendous strain on the rolling stock and the track, much more than the system had been designed to stand. The Royal Navy's Grand Fleet at Scapa Flow and the supporting naval base in the Cromarty Firth ensured trainloads of men – the Jellicoe Specials, so nicknamed after the commander of the Grand Fleet – and material trundling northward continually to Thurso, for trans-shipment across the Pentland Firth. A plaque in Dingwall station survives from those days to tell the curious passer-by that the Ross and Cromarty branch of the Red Cross served 134,864 cups of tea to servicemen in transit between 20 September 1915 and 12 April 1919.[1] The line from Kyle was taken over by the Admiralty in 1918 to carry equipment to US Navy bases at Inverness and Invergordon, and large loads of timber felled by Canadian and Newfoundland forestry units were also transported south. At the outbreak of hostilities all the railway companies were taken under the wing of the so-called Railway Executive Committee, in effect nationalised, and remained so until August 1921. Highland Railway held its 103rd general meeting in February 1920 and revealed that it had earned a net profit of over £256,000 in the previous year[2]

– still a worthwhile business but now, in the 1920s, it had to compete with the burgeoning road transport network for passengers and freight. Almost immediately after they were released from committee control, the rail companies went through a process of amalgamation that brought to an end the independent existence of the Highland Railway and most of the other small concerns. Highland Railway was swallowed up by London, Midland & Scottish (LMS) in November 1922, and the West Highland, which had already been taken over by the North British Railway in 1908, became part of the London & North-Eastern. The Lochgorm railway workshops in Inverness, where all the maintenance of the Highland Railway rolling stock had been done, suffered a reduction in status, with some job losses, and by the end of the 1930s had become a depot for running repairs. The North British had already taken over the Fort Augustus line from Highland in May 1907. The branch struggled to stay open in the face of the competition from cars and buses on the new road through the Great Glen until in December 1933 it closed to all movement except for one weekly coal train. The Fort Augustus branch line was to close altogether on Hogmanay 1946.

Perhaps it was a case of familiarity bringing contempt in its wake, or simply that the new motor vehicles outshone all that had gone before, but the railway had fallen from its position as a glamorous mode of travel and was coming in for a good deal of criticism. At the bash celebrating the opening of the splendid new road through the Great Glen, Lochiel, chief of clan Cameron and a man whose voice was listened to, had a go at it. He related how a friend had told him that he had driven thirty-four and a half miles on the Glencoe road in 35 minutes. 'That was as fast as any train in Scotland,' said Lochiel. 'The railways had a slogan – "It is quicker by rail" ... It might be quicker by rail in England, but not in Scotland.' He wondered what the railway companies made their comparison with – 'Did they refer to a tortoise, a flock of sheep, or a man kicking his hat along the road?' Naturally, concluded the chief, people would prefer to go quicker by road than to dawdle in a railway train.[3]

There was criticism, too, of the seaborne transport system on which life depended in the Hebrides. The cargo vessels linking the western islands with the mainland in the 1920s were of a lower tonnage than in the pre-war period, and there were fewer ports of call. The accommodation for steerage passengers needed to be improved, and charges had risen by between 100 and 300 per cent.[4] At times the movement of cattle was held up, leaving the animals crammed aboard a boat without food. One such incident was a cause of complaint in 1920: the *Hebrides* en route from St Kilda called at Lochmaddy on North Uist in early June to pick up 114 cattle for Oban but, when the cattle owners discovered that their animals would be on board for three days with little or no water while the steamer followed its own agenda and failed to persuade the shipowners to change their schedule, they took the beasts home again and missed the June sale.[5] The *Hebrides* was the only vessel owned by John MacCallum at this time and it specialised in sailing to St Kilda; she later became part of the MacBrayne fleet and ironically finished her days in the 1950s shipping only cargo and livestock out of Glasgow.

The developments in road transport also had, of course, a considerable negative impact on the coastal shipping services, especially on the east coast and in the Great Glen. The regular steamers plying Loch Ness ceased to operate in early 1929, the last one mooring on 28 February to be replaced by motor buses taking over the mail run from Foyers and Fort Augustus on 1 March. The owners may have been resigned to give up, as they had been making a loss for some time, but the crofters along the Great Glen lost a handy way to ship livestock to the mart in Inverness. The steamers of Coast Lines Ltd, a company formed in 1917 that absorbed several other firms in the same business, continued to sail between Manchester and Liverpool, and the east coast ports in Scotland, calling at Leith, Dundee, Aberdeen,

Inverness and Cromarty among others. Advertisements for their sailings appeared regularly, such as in the *Inverness Courier* on 22 February 1929, where readers were told that the *Gloucester Coast* would leave Manchester on 4 March, and Liverpool on the 7th for Inverness; and the *Elgin Coast* would sail from Leith on 25 February for Aberdeen, and then on the 26th continue to Buckie, Lossiemouth, Inverness, Invergordon and Cromarty.[6] Coast Line vessels continued to run on these routes until the Second World War broke out in 1939. The company itself survived with a considerable fleet until it was taken over by P&O Ferries in 1971. During the 1950s, it offered cruises in the Hebrides. The North of Scotland steamers ceased their Wick–Aberdeen–Leith service at the outbreak of the Second World War and did not take it up again after 1945, although cargo vessels continued on the route into the 1950s.[7]

The Caledonian and Crinan Canals were taken under the wing of the Ministry of Transport in 1920 (ownership was transferred to the new body British Waterways in 1962 and then to Scottish Waterways in 2012). This is an appropriate place at which to bring in the Clyde puffer, whose tall smoke-stack and stubby hull represented for many years lifeline services in the south-west and the Hebrides. The first puffer is recognised to have been the *Thomas*, born in 1856 when an engineer put a steam engine into a Union Canal scow. As a canal vessel with a plentiful supply of fresh water under the keel, the *Thomas* had no need for a condenser in its engine to conserve the vital fluid and the regular discharge of steam gave the puffer the name that came to be applied also to later, larger seagoing vessels and even to diesel-engined ones. About 400 puffers are reckoned to have worked over the years, carrying tons of cargo, able to penetrate sea lochs and, in the absence of a pier or harbour, beach to unload vital supplies.[8]

In 1953, Mary Campbell-Preston, writing about life in Ardchattan in the early years of the century, recalled how puffers used to bring goods from Glasgow:

On to the piers and into the rowing boats would be unloaded paraffin, oatmeal, flour, sugar and other necessities. The arrival of Lochnell fortnightly from Glasgow was the high-light of life on Loch Etive. For the bi-annual arrival of the coal boats all carts were commandeered. Social gatherings took place on the little piers, with cups of tea brought down by the maids from the "big house" and at the end of the day a dram from the laird's flask.[9]

These comments sound romantic – they are certainly nostal-gic – but it is nevertheless true that old attitudes lingered in the north long after they had disappeared in urban parts of the country. Throughout much of the Highlands until very recently – and in a few places it still lingers – there was a reverence for the Sabbath, the seventh day of the week when people should rest from quotidian labour, except for acts of necessity or mercy, and spend the time in contemplation and worship. The north-ward creep of secular attitudes inevitably resulted in conflict. In Strome in July 1882 there were riots over the transporting of fish on the railway on the Sabbath.[10] Travellers from outside Scotland were warned what to expect on Sundays – or rather not to expect anything much to happen – and told to enjoy a day's rest themselves. The *Blue Guide to Scotland*, first published in 1927 and re-issued in 1947, makes clear that 'Sunday in Scotland, though no longer so austere an occasion as it used to be, is still a quiet day . . . Transport services are much restricted; on many railway lines there are no Sunday trains at all. Places of entertainment, shops and restaurants, even in the towns, are closed . . . Many of the motor-bus services and excursions, however, ply on Sundays, and the picture galleries in the towns are open on Sunday afternoons.'[11]

CHAPTER 25

Early air travel

'None of the passengers suffered from air sickness . . .'

News about newfangled heavier-than-air machines had appeared in northern newspapers from the first days of flight, even before advertisements for motor cars became widespread. The Wright brothers made their first powered flight at Kitty Hawk on 5 October 1905; J.W. Dunne tested swept-wing glider aircraft at Blair Atholl in 1907, a year before the first powered flight in the UK; Louis Blériot flew across the English Channel on 25 July 1909: the reporting of these developments made exciting reading. At that time no one could have foreseen that some 20 years ahead the Highlands would be home to some of the first civil air services in the country, although some reflection and foresight may have suggested that the north was ideally suited to such a form of transport. The English aviator Sir Alan Cobham visited Inverness in February 1929 and suggested two sites on the edge of the town as being very suitable for airfields; not long after, one of these, the Longman, became the aerodrome, as it was called at the time.

After the First World War, several men who had learned how to handle aircraft in the Royal Flying Corps turned their attention to how they could deploy their skills for peacetime uses. One such was Joseph Cardosi from Thurso, who had a war-surplus aircraft crated and sent north by rail, only to have it and his ambition blown to pieces by a gale after he left the assembled aircraft tied in a field.[1] Another was Ernest Edmund 'Ted' Fresson, a Sussex-born engineer who, after the war, flew for a time in China until the outbreak of revolutionary turmoil led him to break off his Biggles-like adventures and return to Britain in 1927. He took up giving aerial displays and barnstorming, visiting local fetes and fairs to give customers joyrides, nicknamed five-bob flips, in his aircraft, and in the summer of 1930 found his way to the Moray Firth coast, where he landed in a field near Fort George in a single-engine biplane, an Avro 504K.

The public were becoming air-minded and, in the Highlands, this interest was deepened when two aircraft from Imperial Airways spent what was dubbed Aero Week in Inverness in July 1931 and offered brief excursions to all willing to stump up the cost of the fare, between 5s and 10s 6d. The chief pilot was Captain E.B. Fielden and, being good at public relations, the company offered some members and officials from the town council a free spin over their patch. 'To appreciate the real natural charm of Inverness, one has to see the town from the air,' one of the passengers was later quoted as saying. From the published itinerary, it was not a long flight. 'None of the passengers suffered from air sickness,' reported the local newspaper, 'or the slightest unpleasantness. The plane, skilfully handled, was remarkably steady in its flight ...'[2] Rough handling could hardly have been expected, as the object of the exercise, freely described as a propaganda tour, was to demonstrate the safety and comfort of air travel. For the more adventurous passenger, the smaller Avro aircraft offered stunting or aerobatics, and there was also a demonstration parachute descent. Despite the relatively costly tickets and the short flights on offer, more than a thousand locals took advantage of the opportunity.

In contrast to Imperial Airways, whose stay lasted just a fortnight, Ted Fresson liked the north and realised that the northern islands might be fertile territory on which to launch scheduled air services. He flew his first fare-paying passenger from Wick to Kirkwall on 22 August 1931, though it was some time later, not in fact until May 1933, that he was able to secure the financial backing to begin a regular service. Elaborate ground facilities were not required – a firm, level stretch of grass sufficed for a runway, and a shed would do as an airport – and during the early years that was what Fresson used. The inaugural flight of Highland Airways Ltd took place on 9 May 1933 from the Longman aerodrome on the edge of Inverness. The provost's wife christened the aircraft, a twin-engined ST-4 Mk 2 Monospar, by smashing a bottle of whisky on a strategically placed stone on the nose (the stone was then taken away to have a place of honour in a local lady's rockery). The sun was shining and a brisk easterly breeze was blowing in from the Moray Firth as the assembled notables listened to the speeches, then Captain Fresson climbed aboard for the take-off. There were three passengers: the owner of *The Scotsman* and two businessmen, representing the Anglo-American Oil Company and the makers of White Horse whisky. The flight on the first leg from Inverness to Wick took 1 hour 15 minutes, though mist kept their altitude down to 200 feet and must have afforded the travellers an exciting view of the Caithness sea cliffs. In the following year, Fresson made trial flights to Stornoway and in 1934 won the contract to carry mail to Orkney.

The honour for the first scheduled civil air service flight in Britain should go to Midland and Scottish Air Ferries, a company founded by John Sword as an offshoot of the Scottish Motor Transport bus company and based in Renfrew. On 18 April 1933, an M & SAF aircraft carried newspapers from Glasgow to Campbeltown in time for readers to enjoy the pages along with their breakfast. The service was soon extended to include Islay. In November 1934, Northern & Scottish Airways took over the route. An air ambulance service was launched by Inverness County Council in September 1935 to connect the Inverness hospitals with the Hebrides, but for some time before that the newspapers had been carrying dramatic stories of rescue flights.

In May 1933, an aircraft from the Midland and Scottish Airway Ferries service brought a fisherman in urgent need of medical attention from Islay to the Western Infirmary in Glasgow, the nurse 'pluckily' accompanying him.[3] One month later and another fisherman with acute peritonitis had to be flown from Port Askaig.[4] The May rescue flight led to the birth of the Scottish Air Ambulance Service.

Almost contemporary with Fresson, and a rival in the provision of civilian air flights in the north, was Eric Gandar Dower. Cambridge-educated and a trained actor, Gandar Dower based his air operations at Dyce and called his company Allied Airways. His northward route, inaugurated in May 1935, connected Aberdeen to Thurso and Stromness, and beat Fresson to Shetland in June 1936. In 1937 he opened flights between Newcastle and Stavanger.

Barra was brought into the expanding air network in July 1935 when Captain I. Glyn-Roberts of West of Scotland Air Services in Renfrew flew over the island in a twin-engined Scion and landed on Traigh Mhor, the great beach of firm sand at the north end of the island that has ever since been Barra's airfield, although operative only at low tide. A regular weekly or twice-weekly schedule was in prospect. Captain Glyn-Roberts brought two passengers back south with him, and they noted how the flight had taken just 90 minutes, not the 16 hours that the journey normally took.[5] A native of Carnarvon, Glyn-Roberts also experimented with seaplane flights from Greenock.

After Northern and Scottish Airways began scheduled flights in the south-western Hebrides at the end of 1934, the managing director George Nicholson said that they were looking for suitable landing places for seaplanes at Mallaig, Kyle of Lochalsh, Portree and Stornoway. He had in mind Oban and Inveraray as bases where passengers could transfer from seaplane to land aircraft, but it was all in the nature of an experiment, as they had no idea of the amount of passenger traffic that could be expected. The islanders, though, were naturally keen to see the plans go ahead: Islay councillors had had a foretaste of the advantages of air travel in April, when some of them, prevented from sailing by stormy weather, had been able to fly to Campbeltown for a committee meeting.[6]

Details of a proposed service to Skye were made available in November 1935. Northern and Scottish intended to start a twice-weekly service with a twin-engined De Havilland Dragon air liner, reassuringly 'fitted with wireless telephone apparatus'. The plan was to extend the route to the Uists and the fares would range from 25s (Uist to Skye) to £4 10s (Uist to Renfrew). As an example of technologies not keeping pace with each other, airline officials in Uist had to use carrier pigeons to communicate with their colleagues on Skye.

'It is now possible to leave Glasgow after a not too early breakfast, land in Skye and be back in Glasgow for lunch,' declared *The Scotsman*, describing the inaugural flight on 5 December.[7] Take-off from Renfrew was at 9.30 a.m. and the invited guests were back on the ground there at 2 p.m., having in the meantime had a thrilling ride and a detour over Portree just for a look. Luckily, it was a morning of brilliant wintry sunshine: 'glittering white peaks in the north were like the gateway to an enchanted land', wrote the journalist in full lyrical mode, as they flew at 1,500 feet, only rising to 3,000 feet occasionally to avoid cloud or fog. The speed of 100 mph produced less sensation in the eight-seat Dragon than one felt on an Edinburgh tram. When they reached Skye, 'the hills divided and in the cleft appeared a considerable stretch of green flat land, with a collection of tiny motor cars at one point' – this was the airfield in Glen Brittle, in the lee of the Cuillin.

A dramatic first occurred in April 1937 when Captain J.A. Henkins of Northern and Scottish Airways diverted from his now usual flight path between Renfrew and North Uist to land on a 230-yard stretch of sandy shoreland on the islet of Hermish to pick up two sick teenage girls and the mother of one of them from the Monach Islands lighthouse. Henkins flew his passengers south for treatment in Glasgow's Western Infirmary. 'The flight illustrates the usefulness of 'planes in the transportation of ill persons from such lonely islands,' observed *The Scotsman*, 'and also the safety of such a venture.'[8] One year on, and further drama occurred, this time with a tragic outcome: in May 1938, a woman from South Uist was being flown to Glasgow in the air ambulance when she went into labour and gave birth in the air to still-born twins.[9] The air ambulance had become a welcome feature of Hebridean life; in its first five years it dealt with more than a hundred medical incidents.

The Second World War inadvertently boosted air travel in the north by leaving a large number of airfields, more than 35, throughout the region. The Royal Air Force and the Fleet Air Arm built four airfields in Orkney alone, one of which is now Kirkwall airport, and more in Caithness, as part of the defences of the naval base at Scapa Flow. RAF Dalcross is now Inverness airport. Wick airport – recently renamed Wick John o' Groats in a bid to attract tourist name recognition – began as Fresson's landing place; it was taken over by the RAF in 1939.

Many other wartime airfields were left to moulder, becoming industrial estates or being used as stores for livestock and fodder. As to the various pioneering air companies, those that were still around after the Second World War were absorbed into British European Airways when nationalisation took place in 1947.

At a farewell dinner to honour Ted Fresson in Inverness in November 1948, the novelist Eric Linklater paid him an appropriate accolade by comparing him to General Wade.[10]

CHAPTER 26

Threats to the lines

'the life of Scotland is being strangled . . .'

The railway services in the Highlands came close to almost complete shut-down in 1963. This was the era of the now notorious 'Beeching's Axe'. Dr Richard Beeching was serving on a government advisory body on transport when he was appointed chairman of the newly formed British Railways Board in June 1961. The nationalised railway industry was incurring huge losses at the time. Given the task of turning this deficit around, Dr Beeching's solution was draconian, swingeing cutbacks in every aspect of the rail operation. Rumours of the drastic future that this augured for railways in the Highlands began to circulate in 1962; J.M. Rollo, chairman of the grant-awarding Highland Fund, warned that the closure of the lines to Kyle, Caithness, Oban and Fort William/Mallaig was being discussed in London.[1] The tourist industry responded predictably by pointing out how disastrous this would be, and Inverness Presbytery of the Church of Scotland agreed, expressing 'grave concerns' over this being done before roads were improved. 'The life of Scotland is being strangled,' pronounced the Revd A.J.R. Shearer in Auldearn.[2] When the Beeching report was published, with the title 'The Reshaping of British Railways', in March 1963 at a press conference in the Central Hotel in Glasgow, the rumours were proved true. The reaction from all sides was unsurprising – indignation and anger.

In order to make the railways pay – they were operating at an annual loss of £145 million – the good doctor called for the closure of over 40 per cent of the rail lines in Scotland and around 60 per cent of the stations; the cuts in the other parts of the UK were equally severe. This meant the closure of all passenger services north and west of Inverness, the complete closure of the line from Aviemore to Forres, and the shutting of all stations between Inverness, Aberdeen and Perth. The Glasgow–Oban–Mallaig lines were reprieved, but the branch to Ballachulish was marked for the axe. In a long piece in the *Inverness Courier*, its editor Evan Barron conceded that Beeching was right from a purely economic viewpoint but argued that railways could not be regarded solely from that perspective, as they were a vital social service. Farming was losing twice as much in a year, but there was no question over its future. Barron argued:

> Even our better roads are often too difficult for heavily loaded lorries and we have only to recall the number of stoppages, blockages and accidents at Berriedale Brae . . . to shudder at the prospect of all freight going that way once the line north of Inverness is wiped out. As it is, the State does nothing or precious little to improve the roads in the Highlands and all we have to comfort ourselves with, now that our railway lines are under threat of extinction, is a vague promise that some time, Heaven alone knows when, we will get 'adequate roads' – probably far too late and far too few to save the Highlands from being turned from a development into a desolate area.[3]

In June 1959, the government had launched a major enquiry into transport in the Highlands. Chaired jointly by law lords James Shaw (Lord Kilbrandon) and Lord John Cameron, it looked into every aspect of its subject and issued first a report on bus services and then more general conclusions early in 1963. Its major recommendation was the creation of a public body with oversight of public transport and a sound knowledge of the economy and circumstances in the Highlands. The report concluded that, although the rail services were being challenged by increasing road transport, essential rail lines should be kept open or at least not closed until an adequate substitute was provided on the road. It also noted that the main road system should be improved; that sea services were likely to remain the principal means of conveyance for passengers and freight in the islands but that vehicle ferries were likely to bring about changes in the pattern of transport and trade; and that air services were increasing and now an essential part of the system. The need for subsidies was clear and they should be 'openly paid in accordance with decisions about the need for services'.[4]

One line of opposition to the rail cuts was fought by the so-called Scottish Vigilante Association, based in Invergordon and led by Frank Thomson, the managing director of the local distillery. It adopted as its logo a cartoon figure called MacPuff. When the government eventually declined to go along with all of Beeching's recommendations, the *Highland News* headline read 'MacPUFF wins the day'.[5] Engaging though MacPuff was, and although Frank Thomson stated that his vigilante group was considering a takeover of the north lines to run them as a private business, it was probably political pragmatism that saved the north lines. Campaigners from the Northern Transport Executive Committee lobbied the prime minister, Alec Douglas-Home, and made it clear that there was united opposition in the Highlands. On 16 April, in reply to a question in the House of Commons, the minister of transport, Ernest Marples, said that he had refused consent for line closure north of Inverness in view of a report from the Transport Users Consultative Committee that had argued closure would mean 'extreme and widespread hardship'. Marples added that a decision on the closing of intermediate stations on the lines was still to be taken and, indeed, in August and September the public learned that several small stations – at, for example, Invershin, Dunrobin, Kildonan, Forsinard and Glencarron – were to shut up shop. [6] But the lines themselves had been saved, although, as rail officials pointed out, they would incur an annual loss of £350,000.

In the atmosphere at the time, it was no wonder that transport was a key issue in the general election in October 1964. An op-ed piece in the *Highland News* on the topic focused on road transport and the many choke points that slowed lorries[7] but the narrow escape of the railway lines could hardly have been far from voters' minds. The Conservative government was brought down to be replaced by the Labour administration of Harold Wilson. In the north, the Liberal Party captured Inverness-shire and Ross and Cromarty from the Conservatives, and in his maiden speech in Westminster the new MP for Inverness, Russell Johnston, wearing his kilt, spoke of the problems of the transport system exacerbating the 'alleged remoteness' of his constituency. [8]

Some rail lines were taken out of use in the years after the Second World War. The last train to Dornoch ran in June 1960, and the line between Callander and Crianlarich was closed in September 1965. The coast line in Moray ceased to run trains in May 1968. This period also saw the introduction of the diesel engine and the end of steam locomotives. The Dingwall–Kyle line came under threat of closure again in 1973, but British Rail announced that this decision was not irrevocable and was dependent on new factors arising to justify its existence. A campaign started to keep it open and the editor of the *Inverness Courier* again took on the challenge: 'The new factor which we hope to see – vainly, it is to be feared – is a realization by the Government that a public service such as a railway system, publicly owned, exists to serve the public, not to make a profit.'[9] This was an idealistic statement that was likely to cut more ice by the Ness than by the Thames. In June 1973 British Rail made it known that their plans for the next ten years did not include any line closures, a coy statement that was nevertheless a cause for hope.

Attempts to replace the train between Dingwall and Kyle with a bus service were less than successful, as the bus took 45 minutes longer to complete the distance on the winding Highland roads. Then a new factor arose: there was a prospect of oil-related construction work at Drumbuie near Loch Carron and, as the obvious way to transport heavy materials to the site, the Kyle line was reprieved for at least another year. The discovery of oil in the North Sea brought many changes to the north, not the least of which was the need to re-think the transport infrastructure and challenge the very idea of remoteness.

CHAPTER 27

Upgrading the A9

'once the horror of the Highlands . . .'

At the start of the 1960s the roads in the northern Highlands remained relatively quiet arteries of communication. Caithness did not acquire its first set of traffic lights until around 1965, and roundabouts and pedestrian crossings came later – though even then many questioned the need for such a burden on the public purse. A few comic stories circulated about local responses to this unfamiliar system of regulation and lost nothing in the retelling.[1]

That the old A9 had charm could not be denied. In 1967, as students on vacation, two of us cycled from Caithness to Edinburgh, taking five days to cover the distance and staying in youth hostels en route. The thrills of free-wheeling south over the Slochd and down from Drumochter into the forested glens of Blair Atholl made up for the long pushes uphill in other parts of the journey. It was also very noticeable that it was not until we arrived south of Perth that the density of cars and lorries became a problem for the cyclist. On the return journey, pedalling through Wester Ross, single-track highways, sometimes with grass growing through the tarmac in the centre, were common. None of these indicators of sparse traffic lasted much longer.

Improvements were being gradually made but in much of the north and west the single-track carriageway with passing places was the norm. To maintain even these, the local authorities had to struggle. For example, Argyllshire had 1,450 miles to look after but it was not easy to raise the necessary taxes in the form of rates from a population of only some 64,000 spread over a large area of mainland and several islands. Things were arguably worse in Sutherland, where, although around 23 per cent of rates were earmarked for the roads department, some roads remained untarred in the 1950s. Under these conditions, extensive new road-building did not happen, although it was never far from the agenda. Eight times between 1929 and 1954 Inverness County Council considered a new road, 15 miles long, through Glen Feshie, thus connecting Strathspey to Deeside, but nothing was realised on the ground. The main road through the Pass of Brander (A85) had been reconstructed in 1938–39, and in the early 1950s a new road was built between Kilmorich and Lochgoilhead, easing the gradients over the Rest and Be Thankful. During the 1950s many local roads acquired their first coatings of tar, consigning stoor, loose gravel and puddles to history. The steep gradients and hairpin bend at Berriedale, described as 'once the horror of the Highlands', were reconstructed.[2] A government programme launched in 1959 allowed the construction of a road-bridge scheme in Shetland to link the islands of Tronda and Burra with the mainland, remove the road gap between Tighnabruaich and Ormidale in Argyll (A8003), link Shieldaig with Torridon through the Balgy river gap (A896), and lay a new road from Inverailort to Kinlochmoidart.

The Highlands and Islands Development Board was established in 1965 to promote economic development in the northern counties and once and for all settle the age-old 'Highland question'. In its headquarters in Inverness, its general aims were to reduce the economic disparity between the Highlands and islands and the rest of the UK, stabilise the population, improve the economic and social conditions of the inhabitants, and keep a close eye on the impact of developments on the environment.

Transport was a natural part of its remit. One of its roles was to advise the Secretary of State for Scotland on transport questions in its geographical jurisdiction and, in 1975, it published a major review of the subject. In the near-decade since the previous study of similar scope had been done in 1967 by the Highland Transport Board, an event of tremendous and unforeseen significance had altered the economic environment – oil had been discovered in the North Sea.

Now there was an urgent need to revise all the recommendations relating to transport that had been made by earlier studies: for example, it was no longer the case that, as had been thought in 1967, the A9 was adequate to accommodate the road traffic it had to bear. Vociferous complaints were being made about the build-up of cars behind slow-moving articulated lorries, and when the Scottish Development Department proposed in 1971 to dual the A9 only as far as Luncarty some in Perthshire County Council dismissed the idea as 'suicidal'.[3] Priority was afforded to its reconstruction. This was predicted to prove 'by far the most costly single road project ever undertaken' in the Highlands, at an estimated cost of around £110 million for the 127 miles between Perth and Ardullie, above the northern shore of the Cromarty Firth. It included new bridges over the Beauly and Cromarty firths, and sections of dual carriageway; to make dual carriageway along the entire route would cost too much. The minimum width throughout would be set at 7.3 metres (approximately 24 feet)to allow traffic to move at a steady 60 miles per hour. It would take until 1978–79 to complete this project, but there could be delays if problems should arise in acquiring rights of way and bridging. With yards for the construction of oil rigs opening in the inner Moray Firth and economic activity ramping up to unheard-of stir, the traffic burden on the A9 was growing impossible.

In the summer of 1971, Gordon Campbell, MP for Moray and Nairn, and Secretary of State for Scotland in Edward Heath's Conservative administration, announced a scheme to

spend some £8 million on Highland roads in the current financial year, including the A9, the A830 and the A96.⁴ The draft
proposals for the upgrading of the A9 were made public in the
following February. Some welcomed them, others thought they
were not enough. Russell Johnston MP considered them 'patchwork treatment' in comparison with the larger sums being spent
on roads in England.

In August 1973, more investment was put into roads, and
Gordon Campbell declared that he had given 'the highest priority to the A9 between Perth and Inverness, and I announced last
year a substantial acceleration of expenditure on modernising
this route.' Comprehensive preparation was under way, he said,
for rebuilding the whole 117 miles and the cost would be not
less than £60 million.⁵ The detailed plan was published the
following month and tenders were already coming in for some
sections. Draft orders had been issued for the Dunkeld bypass
and some stretches further north, while feasibility studies would
go ahead on other sections. There would be problems between
Dunkeld and Blair Atholl, where the new road had to be
squeezed somehow into the narrow gullet of the Pass of
Killiecrankie. Sections would be built as dual carriageway from
the start and allowance would be made for the later dualling of
the intermittent miles of single carriageway. 'The important and
rapid industrial development in Easter Ross' would mean priority being given to the road between Inverness and Invergordon,
and construction would start before the end of the year.⁶ This
massive project to lay a new road through the heart of the
Highlands was still not enough for a few, who had called for a
motorway; the editor of the *Inverness Courier* scornfully
advised these few to have a good look at the Highway Code to
see how many modes of transport would be banned from such.
Russell Johnston accused the Secretary of State of being too
optimistic, if he thought a new Great North Road could be
completed within five years, with so far – in September 1973 –
fewer than four miles out to tender: 'If General Wade had

proceeded with the same timidity,' cried Johnston, 'we should still be thinking in terms of pony trekking rather than motoring.'[7] The Scottish Association for Public Transport decried the A9 improvements and claimed that they amounted to a £3 subsidy of each vehicle using the Perth–Inverness route; rail was carrying half the present freight traffic over Drumochter and could carry more at low marginal cost.[8]

At the end of June 1976, Lord Kirkhill, minister of state at the Scottish Office, cut the ribbon at Drumochter in front of a hundred onlookers to formally open the completed section of the new road. The planned route was designed to bypass several villages – Dalwhinnie, Newtonmore, Kingussie, Aviemore, Carrbridge – a scheme that led to objections from the locals, not only because some feared the local shops would lose trade but also because the proposed alignment cut across arable ground along the Spey, and arable ground was a scarce enough commodity in the mountains without sacrificing some of it to tarmac. In December 1974 the delays led the Scottish Office to establish a special project team to speed up the reconstruction, now estimated to cost £130 million.[9] Forty-six objections to the section of road bypassing Kingussie led to a public inquiry being held in Newtonmore village hall in September 1975. Two estates, Balavil and Pitmain, who had objected to loss of arable ground, withdrew their disapproval after the plans had been modified to their 'reasonable satisfaction'.[10]

Controversy arose over the construction of the bridge over the narrows between the Beauly and Inverness firths, then served by the Kessock ferry. Inverness-shire County Council put the job out to tender in 1974, when estimates of the cost stood at around £12 million. Test borings of the seabed revealed that there would be problems – the substrate was described as 'a skin of rock floating on mud' – and the estimated costs rose to £18 million and then to £30 million as the inflation of the 1970s took hold of the economy.

The government dithered. Secretary of State Willie Ross came in for a deal of criticism for his indecision, as he wrestled to find a cheaper way to build the bridge and comply with the Labour government's need to cut public spending. Ian Miller, chief executive for Inverness District Council, part of Highland Regional Council, the new local authority that took over from the county councils in 1975, said that to cancel the Kessock Bridge would be to waste the whole A9 reconstruction from Perth northwards. The Ross and Cromarty MP, Hamish Gray, said, 'the whole future of development in the Highland region depends on this one half-mile link in the A9'.[11]

As the waiting dragged on, the ferry *Eilean Dubh* struggled to cope with the increasing commuter flow and the existing A9, running west from Inverness through Beauly, took a battering from traffic it had never been designed for. The Cleveland Bridge and Engineering Company had put in the £30 million bid and naturally pointed out that delays would inevitably raise the cost.

In August 1975 the government confirmed that the Kessock Bridge would be built, although it had not accepted the Cleveland offer and was considering a pre-stressed concrete design that would cost only £20 million. Meanwhile the contract for building the 4.5-mile stretch of dual carriageway to bring the A9 to the south end of the unbuilt bridge was awarded and work started. Christmas and Hogmanay came and went, and in February the government had still not decided how to proceed, although it was argued that every month of delay was adding a quarter of a million to the final cost. Work started on the new bridge across the Cromarty Firth, and the Cleveland company completed a new bridge at Ballachulish. Then it transpired that holding out for a cheaper bridge was not a viable course of action, as the central span of any new structure would have to be high enough to allow the passage of tall-masted sailing vessels to and from the Caledonian Canal, lying upstream in the Firth. Nearly one year after this revelation, Secretary of State Bruce Millan – who had succeeded Willie Ross not long before

– announced that he was considering six tenders shortlisted for the work, and in June 1977 it was at last made public that the Kessock Bridge contract had been awarded to a consortium of Cleveland Bridge Company and Redpath Dorman Long, whose track record included the Forth, Severn and Humber bridges. It was to be a suspension bridge, with two towers and web cabling, with a 240-metre (787 foot) central span; the cost was estimated to be £17.25 million. The Scottish Office had got their cheaper option, thanks to a falling rate of inflation and less competition for welders from oil platform construction yards. Work would start in the spring of 1978.

During the 1970s, transport in the Highlands went through significant changes. To describe each aspect in detail would turn this narrative into a catalogue, but it is necessary to mention some of the developments to bring the story up to date. There was, for example, the introduction of roll-on, roll-off (ro-ro for short) ferries, with their faster turnaround times and greater capacity at a time when vehicle numbers were increasing, replacing the older system whereby vehicles and general cargo were lifted on and off by derrick. On many short inter-island routes the ferries became, in effect, floating bridges.[12] In 1971, there was a dramatic increase in the number of cars crossing between Kyle and Skye when the new ro-ro ferries *Kyleakin* and *Kyle of Lochalsh*, each able to take 28 cars, began to operate; in the summer, at the peak of the tourist season, these boats were shifting 11,000 to 12,000 cars a week.[13] The inter-island services in Orkney and Shetland are now done mostly with ro-ro vessels, although there are one or two destinations, such as Fair Isle and Foula, where substantial open-sea crossings and the need to lift boats from the water to escape the ravages of heavy seas, still require more conventional craft. Caledonian MacBrayne continues to run most of the ferries in the Firth of Clyde and the Hebrides. The North of Scotland, Orkney & Shetland Shipping Company was taken over by Coast Lines in 1961 and then by P&O in 1975, when it was renamed P&O (Orkney and Shetland

Services) and later P&O Scottish Ferries. The Northlink company, a joint concern of Caledonian MacBrayne and the Royal Bank of Scotland, took over the northern isles service in 2002, and since 2012 the company has been owned by Serco Ltd. Two other ferry companies run on the Pentland Firth crossing between Caithness and Orkney – the pedestrian-only *Pentland Venture* in the summer months between John o' Groats and Burwick, and the large ro-ro catamaran *Pentalina* between Gills Bay and St Margaret's Hope. For a few years, from the summer of 1976, the Faroese ferry *Smyril* operated a service between Scrabster and Thorshavn, with onward connections to Iceland and Denmark. A larger vessel, *Norrona*, took over the North Atlantic sailings, this time connecting Lerwick to Bergen, but this experiment in reshaping the old sea routes of the Norse traders sadly came to an end in 2008 and today the Smyril Line's *Norrona* steams between Iceland, the Faroes and Denmark. Many of the domestic ferry routes are defined by the government as lifeline services, vital to the well-being and economy of the islands, and, as such, are supported by public subsidy.

Similarly, the 11 airports in Highlands and Islands Airports Ltd are deemed essential to the localities they serve and also receive government subsidies. Air transport has grown over the last few decades. There was considerable investment in the runway, apron and terminal at Dalcross (Inverness), the hub of the air network in the Highlands, in the early 1970s to accommodate the BAC 1-11 aircraft that began daily jet flights to London Heathrow in 1975. Since then, the pattern of routes and the roll-call of airlines have often changed, but there has been a trend towards increasing activity, with the welcome addition since 2011 of direct international connections to Amsterdam Schiphol, Dublin and, seasonally, Swiss ski resorts. One home-grown airline continues to fly: Loganair, founded by the contractor Willie Logan in 1963. Among its regular routes is the world's shortest scheduled commercial flight, between Westray and Papa Westray in Orkney. The official time is two minutes, but it has been done in less than one, presumably with a strong tail wind. The Islander aircraft used by Loganair became a much-loved sight in the northern skies and were fondly nicknamed the 'paraffin budgies'. Argyll and Bute Council operates airfields at Oban, Coll and Colonsay, with scheduled flights to the islands, under the name of Hebridean Air Services, with support from the Scottish government.

The railway services, too, have undergone something of a rebirth, encouraged in part by a growing awareness of environmental issues, a desire to get heavy transport off the roads and climate change. Saved from closure partly by the growth of the North Sea oil industry, recent years have seen growing passenger numbers, the re-opening of some small stations to form a commuter area around Inverness, and plans to build new ones such as at Dalcross to serve Inverness Airport. The present franchise, for all services apart from the cross-border trains to England, is held by Abellio Scotrail. And the Highlands has seen the return of steam, in the form of the trains operated by the Strathspey Railway Company, founded in 1972, on the restored line between Aviemore and Grantown-on-Spey, and the *Jacobite* steam train that runs between Fort William and Mallaig in the summer and enjoys worldwide fame since its appearance as the Hogwarts Express in the Harry Potter movies.

No account of travel and transport in the Highlands would be complete without mention of the tractor, particularly the Fergie, more properly the Ferguson TE20, which brought a quiet but widespread revolution to the area in the post-Second World War years. Designed by the engineer Harry Ferguson from County Down, the Fergie went through various phases of development before the TE20 emerged in 1946 and quickly became the dependable workhorse on small farms and crofts. More than half a million had been driven off the Coventry production lines by 1956 and many a crofter learned to drive one without taking the wheel of any other motor vehicle. Apart from carting, ploughing and other agricultural work, the Fergie could be pressed into service for a leisurely drive to town for the week's shopping, break through snowdrifts or haul errant southern motorists from roadside ditches. Other tractors were available and widely used, but the Fergie retains a special place in Highland hearts to this day.

Another innovation of the 1970s that brought needed transport links to many small, relatively isolated communities was the postbus. The first one ran in East Lothian, and then the idea was taken up by Trevor Carpenter, chairman of the Scottish Postal Board, as he dealt with postal services in Lewis.[14] Combination post vans and minibuses were already in use in a few places in the UK, but now an enhanced postbus service, taking goods as well as passengers and the mail, was launched in Skye in April 1972, the first linking Broadford and Elgol. The postbuses proliferated – there were 29 services by 1974 – and for a while they were promoted as almost a tourist attraction in their own right. In March 1975 newspapers were recording the start of the 48th service in Scotland – a Land Rover running between Dava and Grantown-on-Spey – and noting that they were covering 667,000 miles and carrying over 50,000 passengers a year.[15] The system did not survive the economic troubles of recent years, when falling passenger numbers and volumes of mail, and a failure to agree levels of subsidy between Highland Council and Royal Mail, took almost all the postbuses off the road.[16] At the time of writing (early 2016), one postbus continues to run in north-west Sutherland between Lairg and Talmine.

*

And then there is the story of Calum's road, rightly celebrated as one man's answer to the intransigence of the establishment. Calum Macleod lived at Arnish on the north end of Raasay. After lobbying fruitlessly for many years to have Inverness-shire County Council provide the community with a proper road to replace the footpath that connected it to the outside world, Calum decided to build a road himself. For ten years he worked with hand tools and a wheelbarrow – Wade's highwaymen would have been proud of him – and completed 1.75 miles of single-track road, obtaining a little bit of help with blasting from engineers from the Department of Agriculture. Once the road had been carved from the rugged landscape, it was finally adopted and surfaced by Highland Regional Council.[17]

CHAPTER 28

Connectivity

'Be ye also ready . . .'

The Kessock Bridge took shape and was finally opened on a very wet August day in 1982 by the late Queen Elizabeth the Queen Mother. The upgrading of the A9 between Perth and Inverness reached completion the following year. The causeway across the Cromarty Firth had been completed in 1979 and the last of the three firths on the east coast, Dornoch, was bridged at last in 1992. The narrow mouth of Loch Leven on the A82 was bridged in 1975 at Ballachulish, and another fine new bridge was constructed at Kylesku in north-west Sutherland in 1984. In the Hebrides, causeways were built to link the islands of Vatersay, Berneray and Eriskay to their larger neighbours. The major bridge linking Kyle of Lochalsh to Skye was opened by Michael Forsyth, Secretary of State, on 16 October 1995; unlike the other bridging projects, this one was wrapped in a cloud of controversy after being built under a Private Finance Initiative (PFI) scheme necessitating the imposition of road tolls by the contractor, an international consortium called Miller-DYWIDAG Systems, to recoup the cost. The tolls turned out to be the most expensive in Europe, eventually reaching £11.40 return, and there was much protesting until in 2004 the new Scottish Executive in Holyrood bought the bridge for £27 million and put an end to the charges.

These dramatic improvements in infrastructure, boosted by considerable development funds from the European Union, brought about some wide-reaching social changes.[1] For example, it suddenly became relatively easy for people living in the north and west to spend a day shopping in Inverness, to the detriment of local outlets in the smaller towns and villages, where shops began to close their doors as retailers retired or gave up an unequal struggle to compete. In the late 1950s, it could take nearly five hours to drive from Wick to the Highland capital, a daunting journey time that was reduced to a little over two hours by the end of the century. New, regular long-distance bus services have also contributed to this centralising tendency.

Among the other casualties of what has amounted almost to a revolution in public transport have been some of the old ferries, for example at Ballachulish, Kessock and Kyle of Lochalsh. Their passing has been an occasion for nostalgia and even tears, despite the fact that during their active lives they had often acquired a chequered reputation that, perhaps unfairly, had overshadowed the faith they had kept with the travelling public. Long queues on approach roads became common in their last years, as increasing numbers of motorists were finding their way around the country. And then there had been breakdowns, strikes, accidents; when it was reported in Inverness Town House in September 1971 that the Kessock ferry had made a profit in the previous year the provost had joked that it had to be the first time on record.[2]

A conflict arose at times between those who favoured a more traditional way of life and the supporters of improved travel facilities. This was exemplified by the rows over ferries on the Sabbath in the Western Isles, where the more conservative Presbyterians opposed unnecessary travel on the seventh day; there were scuffles and arrests, for example, at Kyleakin and Kyle in June 1965, and in 1988 Caledonian MacBrayne opted to back down rather than insist on a service to Harris, although in the following year a Sunday service to North Uist began without difficulty. Only as recently as July 2009 did Caledonian MacBrayne begin a regular Sunday service between Stornoway and Ullapool. And most recently, in October 2011, Tarbert on Harris, the last harbour not to have such a service, timetabled a ferry to Lochmaddy on North Uist and to Uig on Skye on the Sabbath.

In its annual report for 2005–06, Highlands and Islands Enterprise (HIE), the successor to the Highlands and Islands Development Board, observed, 'Transport is an ever-present challenge for any rural area and we know we need to raise our game continually to meet the expectations of today's businesses, residents and visitors.' The environment, of course, continues to throw down challenges. Although winters have been turning milder over the last few years, episodes of heavy rainfall and flooding recur. In February 1989, the central span of the railway viaduct across the Ness, originally built in 1861–62 under Joseph Mitchell's guidance, was torn away by floods. There were fears among a few that it would be left a ruin and the opportunity would be taken to close the lines north of the Great Glen, but Scotrail moved quickly to reassure the public and a new viaduct opened in May 1990.[3] Long-term trends in climate may result in more intense bouts of rainfall and this will probably increase the occurrence of landslips, already a regular mishap on some roads. The government announced in 2013 that the A82 along Loch Ness was closed 97 times between 2010 and 2012, occasionally by accidents but by far most often by falls of rock and soil, and the A83 at the Rest and Be Thankful 43 times in the same period.[4] The Stromeferry road, the A890 between Lochcarron and Kyle, is another landslip blackspot.

Drumochter, the Slochd, the Ord and other high passes are regularly blocked by blizzards and now several of these danger spots have snow gates that are closed when heavy snowfall is imminent. This came about after what was the worst storm for many years, at the end of January 1978. Rail coaches were derailed at Carrbridge, trees were blown down, a train became stuck in the snow at Forsinard, and a married couple and another single motorist were found dead in their vehicles buried in snowdrifts at Ousdale; one man survived an entombment of three days. At the height of the storm it was estimated that as many as 200 people were trapped in trains, buses and cars.[5]

The motor vehicle is of vital importance in the economy and the way of life of the Highlands and Islands. On the one hand there is the simple fact of employment in the many outlets, retail and wholesale, providing tyres, fuel, spares and garage services, as well as a large number of car dealerships, both new and second-hand; on the other hand, there is an endless downstream role in the movements of goods, people and tourism, in practically every aspect of day-to-day activity. The cost of replacing the economic and social edifice built around the internal-combustion engine is almost beyond imagining. The state of the roads is therefore a matter of continual concern.

Maintenance of all the trunk roads is now in the care of the private company Bear Scotland, the holder of the government franchise. Other public roads, by far the bulk of the network, remain in the hands of the relevant local authorities. Lapsing for a moment into the language of the bureaucrat, the Scottish government body Transport Scotland has created a series of transport partnerships, one of which has the statutory authority to oversee the Highlands and Islands (but not Shetland, which has its own body). This is the Highlands and Islands Transport Partnership, or HITRANS, based in Inverness and run by a board comprising councillors from each local authority and other officials. This body has published a strategy for the development of regional transport, covering everything from cycling to aviation, from traffic congestion to investment in ports and ferries, to support a sustainable economic future.[6]

The A9, the spine of the transport network, is seldom out of the news for reasons good and bad. It has been dubbed 'the killer highway' due to the number of fatal crashes. In a parliamentary reply in Holyrood in 2012, the transport minister Keith

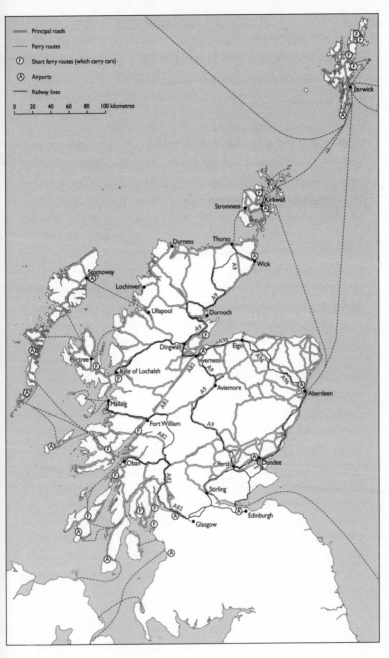

Map 8. The principal features of the transport infrastructure of northern Scotland.

Brown confirmed that the A9 had had the highest, or joint highest, fatality rate of all Scottish roads in 2006, 2007, 2008 and 2010, and that there were on average more than 200 accidents per year. Sixty-seven people were killed in the five years between 2006 and 2010. The reasons for this shocking statistic are vigorously debated – one argument is that speeding or careless overtaking are to blame – but there is a consensus of sorts that the switching between stretches of single and dual carriageway between Perth and Inverness contributes to the accident toll. The government has made the commitment to dual the entire length of the road by 2025, a project estimated to cost £3 billion.[7] In a bid to improve safety, a system of average-speed cameras was installed in 2014. This was only the second time this had been done in Scotland – the first installation on the A77 in Ayrshire was observed to have resulted in a significant drop in speeding and accidents. Many motorists see the speed cameras – or 'yellow vultures' – as an unnecessary imposition, and some have argued that their existence has increased journey times, an illogical conclusion unless previously drivers had been routinely breaking the speed limits.

The long section of the A9 that runs north from Inverness to the final milestone at Scrabster has been modernised only in parts. Apart from seven miles on the Black Isle, it is single carriageway, some of it as it was the 1950s. The crossing of the Ord of Caithness is relatively quick now on a sweeping tarmac ribbon cutting across the Vale of Navidale, but there is still the tricky, acute hairpin bend on the north slope of the Berriedale valley. Plans are in place to ease the gradient, but the work has not yet been done.[8]

The English travel writer H.V. Morton drove this way in 1932, writing of his journey:

Beyond Helmsdale, the road became serious. It left low, green country and shot up into the hills. It twisted and turned into a brown solitude of smooth moors and windy heights, running on and upward over the bleak face of hills . . . in winter-time the Ord of Caithness must be one of the most terrifying roads in Scotland.[9]

He did not spot the stone where the vagrant perished in 1878. The Ord is not the obstacle it once was, but it is as well to remember the message inscribed on William Welch's memorial: 'Be ye also ready.'

Appendices

1: *Bills to account for Frances Cochrane from Drummond to Edinburgh*

Bills to account for Frances Cochrane from Drummond (probably Drummin Skiach, near Evanton) to Edinburgh in 1770 (HA, D538/A/2/7/i)

Date	Item	Cost
25	To the ferry of Scuddel 3d Bealie 4½	7½d
	To a pair of Gloves to the boyie	6d
	To a handkirchieff to Do 1/7d a half pd soap 3½	1s 10½d
	To the boyies eating & drink at Inverness	11d
26	To Hay & corn at Do 5s 9d Bridge 3d hoassler 6d	6s 6d
	To the boie Bill Dalmagerrie for corn & hay	1s 7½d
27	Bill agiemore To corn, hay & the boyie	6s 5d
	Bill petmain " "	2s 3d
	Bill Dalwhinie " "	1s 8d
28	At Dalnacardich for corn & hay	6s
	To the boyie at Do 11d & horsler 6d	1s 5d
	Bill at Blair To corn & hay with beans 2s	2s 6d
	The boyie 6d	
	To the smith at Do for a new shau 8d & removing 4d	1s
	Bill at Inver To corn & hay 1/10d for the boyie 8d	
	Horsler 2d with boat Freight 4½	3s ½d
29	Bill at Pearth corn & hay with beans	5s 7d
	At Do to the boyie 5d½ to the horslar 6d	11½d
	Bill Kinross for corn, hay & beans 1/8½d boyie 6d	2s 2½d
	Bridge of Earn 4½d Queens Farry corn, hay & beans	
	1s 5d of Tolls from Kinross to the Ferrie 6d	2s 3½d
	To Freight 2/6d boathouse toll 2½	2s 8½d
	To one bottle oyle for the coach & harness	9d
	To a servants board wages for five days at 1/6d per day	7s 6d
	To toll going in to Edinburgh	8d
	To two pair shoes bought for the boyie at 1/6d pr pair	3s
		£3 2s 6d

Cochrane names several places en route: Scuddel (Conon Bridge), Bealie (Beauly), Inverness, Dalmagerrie (at Moy), Agiemore (Aviemore), Petmain (Pitmain), Dalwhinnie, Dalnacardich (Dalnacardoch), Blair (Blair Atholl), Inver (near Dunkeld), Pearth (Perth) and Kinross. The payments include sums for horse feed, the services of an ostler, and ferry and toll fees.

2: Road tolls in the Highland counties, 1846–47

Road tolls in the Highland counties, as listed in the *Rental Book of Tolls* for the year running from 25 November 1846 to 25 November 1847

Name of toll bar	Location (as given in the *Rental Book*)	Tenant	Income remitted
Tain	Invergordon road	Margaret Cameron	£106
Novar	Fearn road	Alex Macdonald	£259
Strathpeffer	Contin road	John Macdonald	£139
Conon Bridge		George Tuach	£315 14s 6d
Avoch		John Falconer	£90
Kessock	Kessock branch road	Alex Macdonald	£111
Beauly Bridge	Beauly, Strathglass road	Colin Macdonald	£347
Muirtown	Beauly road	John Macfarlane	£323
Drakies	Moy road	Finlay Matheson	£150
Craggie	Moy road	Duncan Rose	£80
Tomatin	Badenoch road	Kenneth Finlayson	£76
Bridge of Carr	Badenoch road	Donald Dickson	£55
Aviemore	Badenoch road	Lachlan Wilson	£61
Belleville	Badenoch road	Lachlan Wilson	£68
Newtonmore	Badenoch road	John Macpherson	£95
Dalwhinnie	Badenoch road	Alex Macpherson	£132
Tomnahurich	Invermoriston road	Donald Bain	£149
Drumnadrochit	Invermoriston road	Alex Macgregor	£110
Lochy Ferry	Fort William road	William Gray	£159
Raigmore	Fort George road	David Rennie	£242
Milltown of Connage	Fort George road	John White	£36
Mid Coul	Nairn road	Angus Johnstone	£79
Drummond	North Boleskine road	Donald Sinclair	£30 7s 10d
Scaniport	North Boleskine road	James Ross	£23
Thurso	Thurso road	William Swanson	£69 10s
Wick (North)	Thurso road	William Allan	£155
Wick (South)	Dunbeath road	James Angus	£117

The remitted income, the amount a reflection of the amount of traffic through the toll, was sent to the Edinburgh lawyer W. Nacneill, as agent for the Commission for Roads and Bridges (Ref: HCA D1242/1).

3: Foreign and coastal shipping movements in 1893

	Coastal Entered	Cleared	Foreign Entered	Cleared
Aberdeen	2635	2779	339	148
Banff	420	412	26	42
Campbeltown	1163	1158	12	0
Inverness	3343	3373	65	46
Kirkwall	2504	2484	27	33
Lerwick	700	687	125	140
Stornoway	1664	1598	14	19
Wick	1041	1003	32	68

From K.L. Moore 'Maritime Scotland, 1800–1914' in K. Veitch (ed.) *Scottish Life and Society, 8: Transport and Communications* (Edinburgh: Birlinn, 2009)

Notes and References

There are many websites that deal with aspects of the story of transport in the Scottish Highlands. Three notable ones are: oldroadsofscotland.com, www.sabre-roads.org.uk and the timeline sequence on timeline.hie.co.uk, the website of Highlands and Islands Enterprise. Another valuable resource is the National Library of Scotland website, www.nls.uk.

Abbreviations

CS	Commissioners of Supply
HA	Highland Archives, Inverness
HN	*Highland News*
IC	*Inverness Courier*
IJ	*Inverness Journal*
NSA	New Statistical Account of Scotland, 1834–45
OSA	Statistical Account of Scotland, 1791–9
PJ	*People's Journal*
RPCS	Register of the Privy Council of Scotland
SBH	*Strathspey and Badenoch Herald*
SHS	Scottish History Society
TGS	Transactions of the Gaelic Society of Inverness
TSA	Third Statistical Account of Scotland

Introduction

1. The full poem can be found in Miller, James (2002) *Fangan wi Verses: Poems in the Caithness Dialect* (Dingwall: Northwords Folio).
2. James Miller, 2015.

Chapter 1

1. Sage, 1899.
2. Miller, 1854.
3. Dodds, 1887.
4. *The Diary of Alexander Brodie of Brodie* (1863) (Aberdeen: Spalding Club).
5. Donaldson, 1984.
6. Pennant, 1771: see Simmons, 1998.
7. Information from Ullapool Museum.
8. Fleet et al, 2012.
9. Digital versions of the Blaeu map and a large selection of other maps can be viewed on http://maps.nls.uk/counties (accessed April 2016). The Causewaymire road appears as two faint lines on the map.
10. Fleet et al, 2012.
11. Kerr, 1991.
12. Mitchell, J., 1883.
13. Wilson, 2011.
14. Moir, 1947.
15. North of Scotland Archaeological Society: Road through Ross, http://her.highland.gov.uk Ref MHG54956 (accessed March 2016).
16. Ross, A. 'Old Highland roads' TGS XIV, pp. 171–93: 1888.
17. Bain, 1881–88.
18. Mackay, W. 'Three unpublished despatches from General Monck', TGS XVIII, 70–78: 1892. Mackay suggests Browling is Braulen or Brouline in Glenstrathfarrar, and Glenteugh is probably Lon Fhiodla on the way from Kintail to Glenstrathfarrar.
19. RPCS (1908) P. Hume Brown (ed) 2nd Ser, vol. VIII (1544–1660) (Edinburgh). See also http://www.rps.ac.uk A1704/7/37. Overture for an act concerning the justices of the peace and for repairing the highways (accessed October 2015).
20. Ferguson, 1904.
21. Mackay, 1896.
22. OSA X, pp. 113–30: Aberfoyle.

23. The Greene map and the Moll map can be viewed on http://maps.nls. uk/counties (accessed April 2016).
24. Mitchell, A., 1906.
25. Fraser, G.M., 1921.
26. OSA VI, pp. 242–54: Kintail.
27. TSA (1985) XVI, Inverness-shire, pp. 232–43: Urquhart and Glenmoriston.
28. Fraser, 1921.
29. Barrow, 1984.

Chapter 2

1. Haldane, 1952. There is much about droving in the special displays run by the Highland Livestock Heritage Society at Dingwall Mart.
2. Gibson, 2003.
3. Burt's *Letters* were first published in 1754. There have been several editions since then. Burt's first name is given as either Edmund or Edward (the catalogue in the National Library of Scotland has Edward), and there is likewise disagreement over his exact status during his northern sojourn. Although his obituary in the *Scots Magazine* in 1755 states he was a surveyor, this may not be what brought him to the Highlands in the first place. Evidence in Treasury papers shows that in May/June 1725 he was appointed to receive rents on unsold forfeited estates, a task in which he had the assistance of some of Wade's troops. He may have taken on an additional role in support of Wade. Of course he could have turned to surveying at a later time. The information about the licences issued by Wade is quoted in the fifth edition, 1822, Appendix 3.
4. Mitchell, J., 1883.
5. Pallister, 2005.
6. Craven, 1886.
7. Craven, 1886.
8. Alex Gordon's obituary appeared in the *Banffshire Journal* in February 1922. A copy exists in the collection of the Highland Livestock Heritage Society, HA, Inverness, ref HRA D1237/2/1.
9. Burt, 1754.
10. Burt, 1754.
11. Haldane, 1952.
12. Burt, 1754.
13. Calder, 1887. See also Miller, 1994.

Chapter 3

1. Fenton, 1978; also 'Back transport and horse draught before made roads' in Veitch, 2009.
2. OSA, XI, 1792: Watten.
3. OSA, X, 1793: Wick.
4. Miller, J., 2009.
5. MacKenzie, 1921.
6. Knox, 1786.
7. The Carpow boat was on display in Perth Museum and Art Gallery, February 2013.
8. Cunliffe, 2001.
9. Severin, 1978.
10. In Burt, 5th edn, vol. 2, App I. See also Miller, 'Traditional fishing boats' in Coull et al, 2008.
11. McNeill and Nicholson, 1975.
12. *Exchequer Rolls of Scotland*, vol. 4. See also Miller, J., 2004.
13. Miller, J., 2012.
14. Thomas Tucker's report on excise and customs in Scotland, 1656, in *Miscellany of the Scottish Burgh Records Society* (Edinburgh: 1881).
15. Miller, J., 2004.
16. Smith, 1984.
17. Warrand, 1923.
18. Mackay and Laing, 1924.
19. Warrand, 1923.
20. Foden, F. (1996) *Wick of the North* (Wick: NOSN), citing J. Horne (1895) *Ye Towne of Wick in ye Olden Tyme* (Wick: Rae).
22. Adams and Fortune, 1980.
23. Macdonald, 1950.
24. Bain, 1881–88.
25. Martin, 1984.
26. Mitchell, 1906.
27. Paton, 1913.
28. Smout, 1963. See also Martin, C. 'Maritime transport on the Western seaboard from prehistory to the nineteenth century' in Veitch, 2009.

Chapter 4

1. Haldane, 1971.
2. RPCS, 1669; see also Newlands, 1928.

3. OSA, XIX, 1796: Stornoway.

4. OSA, VI: Loth, 1793.

5. Grant, I.F., 1959.

6. Adam, 1960.

7. Dixon, 1886.

8. CS Minutes, Inverness-shire, HA CI/1/1/2.

9. Nairn Burgh Minutes, HA BN/1/1/4.

10. Miller, James (work in progress) *The Dunbars of Hempriggs and Ackergill.*

11. OSA, V, 1792: Inveraray.

12. OSA, XIX, 1796: Stornoway.

13. OSA, XX, 1799: Thurso.

14. OSA, XX, 1796: Kilmorack.

15. OSA, VIII, 1791: Canisbay.

Chapter 5

1. Much has been written about General George Wade. I have made most use of J.B. Salmond's biography (1934) *Wade in Scotland* (Edinburgh: Moray Press). Michael Pollard's *Walking the Scottish Highlands: General Wade's Military Roads* (London: Deutsch, 1984) is also an interesting account of the military roads.

2. Burt, 5th edn, 1822, Appendix II.

3. Allardyce, 1895, has the text of Wade's 1724 Report.

4. Stewart, 1822.

5. Warrand, 1927.

6. Salmond, 1934.

7. Ross, A., 'Old Highland roads' TGS XIV, pp. 171–93: 1888.

8. The exact course followed by Wade's men is now uncertain for several stretches of roadway that they built. Salmond devotes considerable space to this topic and tries to identify the most likely answers.

9. Burt, 1754.

10. Burt, 1754.

11. Murray, 1805.

12. Quoted in Salmond, 1934.

13. Quoted in Salmond, 1934.

14. Quoted in Salmond, 1934.

15. Warrand, 1927.

16. *Scots Magazine*, xvi, pp. 528–30: 1754. The Corrieyairack road passed into the care of the Commissioners for Highland Roads and Bridges in 1814 along with all other military roads, before it was

made obsolete by the construction in 1818 of a new road from Laggan to Spean Bridge. Maintenance continued until 1850 to aid the drovers who brought their herds over the hills from the Great Glen.

17. Burt, 1754.
18. N. Macleod's letter is quoted in Salmond, 1934.
19. Murray, 1805.
21. Wade to the Lord Advocate, in Warrand, 1927.
21. Walker, 2000.
22. Bulloch, 1931.
23. Gray, 1892.
24. OSA, II, 1790: Dunoon.
25. Murray, 1805; also Bulloch, 1931.
26. Boswell, 1786.

Chapter 6

1. Millar, 1909.
2. Millar, 1909
3. Millar, 1909.
4. Millar, 1909.
5. Burt, 1754. Neil Munro incorporated the local attitudes to the new roads into his novel *The New Road* (1914), a romantic adventure set in the Highlands in the early 1730s.
6. Haldane, 1952.
7. Shaw, 1880.
8. Pennant, 1769.
9. OSA, VI, 1792: Kintail.
10. Gray, 1892.
11. Dodds, 1887.
12. Lovat's letter is given in Sir Kenneth Mackenzie's paper 'General Wade and his roads' in the Transactions of the Inverness Field Club, vol V, p.160: 1897.
13. HA, Ref D538/A/2/7/i.
14. Craven, 1886.
15. Simmons, 1998.
16. Murray, 1805.
17. OSA, VIII, 1792: Glenorchy and Inisshail.
18. Quoted in Mackenzie, 'General Wade and his roads' in the Transactions of the Inverness Field Club, vol V, p.160: 1897.
19. CS Minutes Inverness-shire, 1761–74, HA, CI/1/1/1.

20. Wilson, 2011.
21. Ross, A. 'Old Highland roads' TGS XIV, pp. 171–93: 1888.

Chapter 7

1. Bulloch, 1931.
2. Calder, 1887.
3. CS Minutes, Sutherland, HA CS/1/1/1. In the early years the Commissioners were most concerned about 'depredations', by which they meant cattle-stealing.
4. CS Minutes, Inverness-shire, HA CI/1/1/1.
5. Sleishgarve is presumably Slios Garbh in Morar. I have not been able to locate Sleismeen.
6. CS Minutes Nairnshire, HA CN/1/1/1.
7. Nairn Burgh Council Minutes 1784–1816, HA BN/1/1/4.
8. CS Minutes Inverness-shire HA, CI/1/1/1 (1761–74); CI/1/1/2 (1774–84).

Chapter 8

1. OSA, XVII, 1793: Nesting.
2. OSA, VI, 1792: Edderachilis.
3. OSA, VII, 1791: Craignish.
4. OSA, XIV, 1793: Kilfinan.
5. OSA, III, 1791: Dingwall.
6. OSA, XI, 1792: Watten.
7. OSA, III, 1791: Dores.
8. OSA, III, 1790: Petty.
9. OSA, XV, 1793: Avoch.
10. OSA, VII, 1792: Urray.
11. OSA, VIII, 1791: Dornoch.
12. OSA, XXI, 1793: Golspie.
13. OSA, VI, 1792: Ardchattan and Muckairn.
14. OSA, VIII, 1793: Cromdale.
15. OSA, XI, 1792: Watten.
16. OSA, III, 1792: Rogart.
17. Acts of Parliament in the reign of George III relating to assessment for the upkeep of roads and bridges, HA, D1169/4, D1169/5.
18. OSA, XX, 1796: Urquhart and Glenmoriston.
19. OSA, XV, 1793: Avoch.

20. OSA, XIII, 1793: Glassary.
21. OSA, XII, 1793: Saddel and Skipness.
22. OSA, XIX, 1796: Stornoway.
23. OSA, XIV, 1793: Kilninian.
24. OSA, III, 1791: Tongue.
25. OSA, X, 1793: Lochbroom.
26. OSA, I, 1791: Kiltearn.
27. OSA, XX, 1796: Urquhart and Glenmoriston.
28. OSA, XI, 1792: Kilmore and Kilbride.
29. OSA, VIII, 1792: Glenorchay and Inishail.
30. OSA, X, 1793: Lochbroom.
31. OSA, XX, 1796: Urquhart and Glenmoriston.
32. Mitchell, 1906.
33. Beaton, 1995.
34. Henderson, 1812.
35. OSA, XII, 1793: Saddel and Skipness.
36. OSA, XVI, 1794: Sandwick and Stromness.
37. Fraser, 1905.
38. Ross, A. 'Old Highland roads', TGS XIV, pp. 171–93: 1888.
39. Records of the Parliaments of Scotland to 1707, www.rps.ac.uk.
40. OSA, III, 1791: Dingwall.
41. Simmons, 1998.
42. OSA, IV, 1792: Ardclach.
43. OSA, XI, 1793: Rosemarkie.
44. Ferguson, 1904.

Chapter 9

1. *Commissioners for Highland Roads and Bridges*, First Report, June 1804. Haldane, 1962, gives a detailed account of the work done during the first 20 years of the Commissioners.
2. Wilson, 2011. Alexander Nimmo moved to Ireland in 1811 and became a noted road surveyor there.
3. A memorial stone was later erected in Sutherland to Peter Lawson near what is now the A838 between Durness and Rhiconich. Unfortunately it was inscribed with the wrong date, 1883 instead of 1833, an unfortunate error that misled, for example, H.V. Morton, when he drove this way in the 1930s.
4. Mitchell, J.,1883.
5. *Commissioners for Highland Roads and Bridges*, Report 1807.
6. Millar, 1909.

7. Macrae, 1923.
8. *Commissioners for Highland Roads and Bridges*, Seventh Report, 1815.
9. Dunbar Papers, private collection.
10. *Commissioners for Highland Roads and Bridges*, Seventh Report, 1815.
11. Dunbar Papers, private collection.
12. OSA, VIII, 1791: Creich.
13. *Commissioners for Highland Roads and Bridges*, Sixth Report, as quoted in IJ, 28 May 1813.
14. Mitchell, 1883.
15. Dornoch Meikle Ferry Log Book, HA D77.
16. *Commissioners for Highland Roads and Bridges*, Ninth Report, 1821.

Chapter 10

1. Somers, 1848.
2. CS Ross-shire Minutes 1839–53, HA CRC/1/1/1/5.
3. MacKenzie 1921.
4. *The Scotsman*, 4 Jan. 1851.

Chapter 11

1. IJ, 7 Aug. 1807.
2. Anderson, 1900.
3. Newlands, 1928.
4. The Duchess of Gordon was celebrated as a London hostess and leader of a fast and loose lifestyle. She became estranged from her husband some years before her death in 1812. Her exact role in the launch of the coach service is unknown, but she would have found it a useful way to speed connections with her social circle. She is buried at Kinrara, near Aviemore.
5. IJ, 14 Sept. 1807.
6. IJ, 30 June 1809.
7. IJ, 1 Sept. 1809.
8. Grant, E., 1898.
9. Mitchell, 1883.
10. IJ, 17 May 1819.
11. IC, 1 March 1855.
12. IC, 3 April 1839.

13. Cockburn, 1888.
14. Cockburn, 1888. Cockburn's opinion may be similar to the views of those who have observed the arrival of a modern tourist coach.
15. IJ, 19 June 1829.
16. Mitchell, J., 1883.
17. IJ, 19 June 1829.
18. IJ, 17 July 1829.
19. IC, 25 May 1847.
20. Cockburn, 1888.
21. MacKenzie, 1921.
22. Anderson, 1885.
23. Letter, George Dunbar to Major W. Mackay, Dunbar Papers, private collection.
24. Mitchell, J., 1883.
25. Mitchell, J., 1883.
26. Horne, 1907.
27. IC, 26 May 1841.

Chapter 12

1. IC, 3 April 1823.
2. Sutherlandshire County Road Trustees Minutes, HA CS/2/1/0.
3. IC, 18 and 25 April 1827.
4. IC, 8 Aug 1827.
5. IC, 12 Sept 1827.
6. IC, 26 Sept 1827.
7. Haldane, 1952.
8. IC, 17 Oct 1827.
9. *Commissioners for Highland Roads and Bridges*, 14th Report, 1828.
10. IC, 1 June 1847.
11. Ross-shire Road Trustees, 11th District Draft Report, HA CRC/2/14/2.
12. IC, 1 Oct 1857.
13. IC, 23 July 1868.
14. IC, 16 July 1868; *The Scotsman*, 17 Nov. 1871; A.E. Graham 'The Dunkeld Toll Riots', *Scots Magazine*, July 1989.
15. *Report of the Commissioners for Inquiring into Matters Relating to Public Roads in Scotland*, 1859.
16. Inverness-shire County Road Board Minutes HA CI 2/4/1/1.
17. Inverness-shire County Road Board Minutes HA CI 3/1/1.
18. IC, 21 Jan 1892.
19. IC, 2 Feb 1892.

Chapter 13

1. Knox, 1786.
2. Dunlop, 1978, is a general account of this important body.
3. OSA, X, 1793: Lochbroom.
4. NSA, v.14, 1835: Lochbroom.
5. Graham, E.J., 'Maritime Activity, *c.*1650–1790' in Veitch, 2009.
6. Mackay, 1915.
7. OSA, III, 1790: Durness.
8. Hustwick, 1996.
9. Miller, J., 1994.
10. Ferguson, D.M., 1988; 1991.
11. Nairnshire CS Minutes, 4 Jan. 1827, HA CN/1/1/1.
12. Miller, J., 1994.
13. North Highland Archive. Wick Harbourmaster's Log, WHT/Ga/1, 28 Sept. – 24 Oct. 1861.
14. Mackenzie, 1903.
15. OSA, XVI, 1794: Assynt.
16. Graham, E.J., 'Maritime Activity, *c.*1650–1790' in Veitch, 2009.
17. OSA, XI, 1792: Kilmore and Kilbride.
18. OSA, V, 1792: Inveraray.
19. OSA, XIX: South Knapdale.
20. Simmons, 1998.
21. IC, 26 Nov. 1845.
22. OSA, X: Campbelton.
23. OSA, XX, 1799: Thurso.
24. Goudie, 1889.

Chapter 14

1. Warrand, 1925, p.103, Baillie includes the comment in a letter to Duncan Forbes of Culloden, 21 April 1716.
2. Craven, 1886.
3. OSA, VIII, 1791–92: Kilmartin.
4. NSA, VII, 1840: South Knapdale.
5. Fraser, Ian 'The Crinan Canal', *Scots Magazine*, July 1956.
6. Duff, 1980.
7. *Scots Magazine*, v.68, pp. 659–62: 1806, quoted in Millar, 1909.
8. Cameron, 1983.
9. Mitchell, 1883.

10. IJ, 6 Nov. 1807.
11. The silver chain found at Torvean can be seen at Inverness Museum and Art Gallery. It weighs 2.88 kg and is held to be of Pictish origin.
12. Records of Caledonian Canal Construction, HA BWI 5/3/1 – D655.
13. IC, 29 June 1820.
14. IC, 29 June 1820.
15. IC, 24 Oct. 1822.
16. Macculloch, 1824.
17. IC, 26 June 1820.

Chapter 15

1. The growth of the herring fishery and the development of Wick have been covered in several books, for example, by Dunlop (1978), Iain Sutherland (1984) and James Miller (2012).
2. Information about the harbours can be found in many sources, including Anson (1930) and Gifford (1992).
3. Gunn, 1998.
4. Mitchell, 1883.
5. Hustwick, 1994; see also Miller 'Traditional Fishing Boats' in Coull et al, 2008.
6. Miller, 2004.
7. IC, 23 Oct. 1879.
8. IJ, 7 Aug. 1807.
9. Mitchell, 1883.

Chapter 16

1. Mitchell, J., 1883.
2. Martin, 1984.
3. IC, 22 June 1820.
4. IC, 24 Aug. 1820.
5. IJ, 21 March 1823.
6. IJ, 11 April 1823.
7. IJ, 4 Dec. 1829.
8. Tucker, 2013; see also Mackenzie, 1903.
9. Dixon, 1886. Dixon is uncertain about the year of the tragedy.
10. Robins and Meek (2008) give an extensive, detailed account of shipping on the west coast.
11. IC, 18 Jan. 1855.

12. IC, 14 May 1857.
13. IC, 3 Dec. 1857.
14. IC, 25 Feb. 1858.
15. IC, 24 Nov. 1859.
16. Records of the Caledonian Canal: Minutes, HA, Ref BWI 1/3/1.
17. IC, 11 May 1847.
18. IC, 27 Aug. 1857.
19. There are several versions of this rhyme. This is how it is presented in Robins and Meek.
20. McRobb, 1999.
21. Smith, 1984.
22. IC, 4–6 Jan. 1881.

Chapter 17

1. Lauder, 1830.
2. Mitchell, J., 1883. Lauder says that the flooded Spey was 15 feet above its normal level at Craigellachie and spread over the whole haugh. The bridge survived, in his opinion, because the approach works gave way to relieve the pressure of the water.
3. Cockburn, 1888.
4. There is a vast library of books and many websites covering almost every aspect of railways in Britain. For this chapter I have relied mainly on a few, supplemented by contemporary newspaper reports. My main sources are: Ross (2005), Vallance (1996) and Thomas (1998).
5. IC, 15 May 1844.
6. IC, 29 May 1844.
7. Mitchell, 1883.
8. IC, 9 Oct. 1844. This route is now a long-distance footpath, the Dava Way.
9. IC, 12 June 1844.
10. IC, 26 Feb. 1845.
11. IC, 29 Oct. 1845.
12. IC, 26 Nov. 1845.
13. IC, 20 May 1846.
14. IC, 1 Feb. 1849.
15. Milne, 2008.
16. Fraser, 1905.
17. IC, 13 July 1847.
18. IC, 1 Feb. 1855.

Chapter 18

1. Cockburn, 1888.
2. See https://en.wikipedia.org/wiki/Morayshire_Railway (accessed April 2016).
3. IC, 5 May 1853.
4. IC, 18 Jan. 1855.
5. IC, 8 Feb. 1855.
6. IC, 24 June 1858.
7. Mitchell, 1883.
8. IC, 24 June 1858.
9. Coleman, 1965.
10. IC, 22 April 1858.
11. IC, 3 April 1862.
12. IC, 14 Oct. 1858.
13. IC, 11 June 1857. Ross (2005) has a good section on the people who staffed the company in its early years.
14. IC, 29 Mar. 1855.
15. Quoted in *Inverness Advertiser*, 26 Apr. 1859.
16. IC, 11 June 1857.
17. IC, 25 June 1857.
18. IC, 4 Dec. 1856.
19. IC, 1 Jan. 1857.
20. The Friends of the Far North Line, FOFNL, campaigns for improvements to the railways in the north, including a rail link across the Dornoch Firth. See their website www.fofnl.org.uk.
21. IC, 12 July 1860.
22. IC, 12 Oct. 1847.
23. Mitchell, 1883.
24. IC, 3 Sept. 1863.
25. Cockburn, 1888.

Chapter 19

1. IC, 25 Nov. 1858.
2. Horne, 1907.
3. IJ, 9 July 1830.
4. IJ, 19 Jan. 1827; 23 Mar. 1827.
5. Stevenson, R.L. (1868) 'Night Outside the Wick Mail', originally included in a letter from RLS to a cousin in Edinburgh; in T. Hubbard, D. Glen (eds) (2003) *Stevenson's Scotland* (Edinburgh: Mercat).

6. IC, 26 June 1844.
7. Banks, 1972.
8. Gardiner, L. 'The Last Stage-Coachman', *Scotland's Magazine*, Sept. 1961

Chapter 20

1. *The Scotsman*, 23 Oct. 1865.
2. Anderson, 1885.
3. McConnell, 1990.
4. Paterson, 2010.
5. *The Scotsman*, 4 Aug. 1870.
6. IC, 9 Sep. 1858.
7. IC, 6 Jan. 1870.
8. IC, 2 June 1870.
9. *The Scotsman*, 21 Feb. 1852.
10. The long-distance footpath, the Rob Roy Way, now follows the curve of the Glen Ogle viaduct.
11. IC, 8 July 1880.
12. *The Scotsman*, 12 Feb. 1901.
13. Ullapool Museum, *Minutes of the Railway Committee 1918–19* (Ref 1997/97).
14. Holland and Spaven (2013) has a map showing the distribution of unbuilt lines.

Chapter 21

1. IJ, 11 March 1836.
2. IC, 28 Oct. 1858.
3. *Inverness Advertiser*, 26 April 1859.
4. Highland Livestock Heritage Society, HA, D1237/2/1 to D1237/2/4.
5. IC, 28 Oct. 1890.
6. IC, 2 Oct. 1844.
7. Highland Livestock Heritage Society exhibit, Dingwall Mart.
8. Ross, 2005.
9. IC, 7 April 1870.
10. PJ, 12 Jan. 1901.

Chapter 22

1. Mitchell, 1883; Calder, 1887.
2. https://en.wikipedia.org/wiki/William_Murdoch (accessed June 2016).
3. *Scottish Cars* (1968) Museum of Transport, Glasgow, has a good summary of early cars made in Scotland.
4. Inverness-shire Register of Motor Cars, HA CI/3/19/1.
5. PJ, 6 May 1910.
6. PJ, 11 Feb. 1905.
7. PJ, 20 Jan. 1925.
8. PJ, 8 Feb. 1929.
9. PJ, 20 May 1905.
10. PJ, 7 Oct. 1905.
11. Ruddlesden, J.A. 'Leeds to Scotland by 46hp Napier Motorcar in 1907', unpub TS, Highland Folk Museum Library, Newtonmore.
12. IC, 6 Feb 1906.
13. HN, 24 April 1975.
14. PJ, 14 Oct 1905.

Chapter 23

1. Road Estimates, Mid-Ross District, 1912–13, and the Report by Charles Hogg on Mid-Ross District roads in 1919, Highland Folk Museum Library, Newtonmore.
2. PJ, 17 Jan. 1920.
3. IC, 2 Sept. 1921.
4. IC, 6 June 1919.
5. IC, 22 July 1919.
6. *The Scotsman*, 23 Nov. 1924.
7. *The Scotsman*, 6 Sept. 1928.
8. *The Scotsman*, 23 April 1927.
9. *The Scotsman*, 9 July 1929.
10. *The Scotsman,* 3 June 1933.
11. IC, 15 Sept. 1933. This date was a significant one – it was when workmen on the new road reported the sighting of a strange creature in Loch Ness.
12. IC, 25 Sept. 1934.
13. *The Scotsman*, 22 Dec. 1934.
14. IC, 7 Aug. 1923.

15. IC, 29 June 1926.
16. IC, 7 Aug. 1934.
17. IC, 7 March 1933.
18. IC, 18 Aug. 1939.
19. IC, 8 Oct. 1934.
20. IC, 1 Jan. 1960.
21. HN, 25 March 1960.
22. TSA, XIII, Stornoway, p. 450 (1987).
23. Milne, 2008.
24. HN, 7 Aug. 1926.

Chapter 24

1. Ross, 2005.
2. PJ, 21 Feb. 1920.
3. IC, 28 Sept. 1934.
4. IC, 30 Jan. 1925.
5. IC, 12 June 1920.
6. IC, 22 Feb. 1929.
7. TSA (1988) XIXA Caithness.
8. Meek, D.E. 'Puffers', *Scots Magazine*, April 1969. Mention of puffers brings immediately to mind Para Handy, skipper of the *Vital Spark*, the much loved fictional puffer captain created by Neil Munro (1863–1930) who made his debut in print in 1906.
9. TSA, (1961) Argyll.
10. IC, 3 July 1882; 2–3 June 1883; Ross, 2005.
11. Muirhead, L.R. (1932) *Scotland* (London: Benn, Blue Guide).

Chapter 25

1. Peter V. Clegg has written extensively about the early days of aviation in the north of Scotland. See, for example, *Rivals in the North* (1988) and *Wings Over the Glens* (1995).
2. IC, 10 July 1931.
3. *The Scotsman*, 15 May 1933.
4. *The Scotsman*, 12 June 1933.
5. *The Scotsman*, 31 July 1935.
6. *The Scotsman*, 9 July 1935.
7. *The Scotsman*, 6 Dec. 1935.
8. *The Scotsman*, 27 Apr. 1937

9. *The Scotsman*, 10 May 1938.
10. IC, 12 Nov. 1948.

Chapter 26

1. HN, 8 May 1962.
2. HN, 5 Oct. 1962.
3. IC, 29 March 1963.
4. A lengthy article on the Kilbrandon Report appeared in IC, 5 Feb. 1963.
5. HN, 17 April 1964.
6. HN, 14 Aug. 1964; 25 Sept. 1964.
7. HN, 2 Oct. 1964.
8. HN, 27 Nov. 1964.
9. IC, 16 Feb. 1973.

Chapter 27

1. For example, one yarn told how, when he was challenged by the police about not stopping at a red light, an old-timer replied that he was only going around the corner.
2. HN, 2 Oct. 1964.
3. Inverness-shire County Council Minutes, HA CI/3/1/122, p. 952.
4. IC, 16 July 1971.
5. IC, 28 Aug. 1973.
6. IC, 7 Sept. 1973.
7. IC, 11 Sept. 1973.
8. IC, 4 Dec. 1973.
9. SBH, 13 Dec. 1974.
10. SBH, 5 Sept. 1975.
11. HN, 31 July 1975.
12. Detailed critical accounts of the modern administration of ferries in the Highlands can be found in Roy Pedersen's books listed in the bibliography.
13. IC, 3 Sept. 1971.
14. Mackintosh, D. 'The postbus story', *Scottish Field*, July 1974. The Scottish Post Office Board publication *The Post Office in Scotland* (1990) says that the inaugural postbus service began on 4 June 1968, between Dunbar and Innerwick in East Lothian.
15. SBH, 7 March 1975.

16. News item on http://www.bbc.co.uk, 14 March 2009.
17. Hutchinson, 2006.

Chapter 28

1. Miller (2014) has some material on how the Highlands and Islands have fared in the European Union. An article in the *Inverness Courier* on 13 November 1987 claimed that the European Regional Development Fund (ERDF) had awarded over £100 million to projects in the north of Scotland, while the HIDB's annual report for 1990, for example, states that the four years of assistance from the ERDF that was due to end in 1991 had contributed about £18 million per year towards improvements in infrastructure. Many of the piers, harbours and roads in the north of Scotland still sport notices with the blue flag and the twelve gold stars in acknowledgement of this aid. Considerable amounts also came into the region indirectly or under other programmes and schemes. 'Total EC funding for the Highlands and Islands in the last ten years has run to many millions of pounds,' noted the HIDB annual report in 1989.
2. IC, 24 Sept. 1971. The North Kessock and District Local History Society published a booklet in 2007 with a brief history of the ferry, *A Celebration of the Kessock Ferries*.
3. The collapse of the Inverness viaduct in February 1989 is well described on http://www.elginmodelrailwayclub.co.uk (accessed March 2016).
4. *Aberdeen Press and Journal*, 14 Nov. 2013.
5. HN, 2 Feb 1978. After the incident in 1978, when the train was stuck in snow at Forsinard, the railway authorities provided each service with a survival hamper. Months after the original incident, when I was a northbound passenger during a spell of bad weather, the conductor joked that the hamper had only a tube of sweeties in it. One hopes it was a joke!
6. The HITRANS website has comprehensive information on the transport infrastructure: http://www.hitrans.co.uk.
7. Government transport policies can be found on www.transport.gov.scot, which has links to ongoing projects, including the dualling of the A9.
8. *John o'Groat Journal*, 4 April 2014.
9. Morton, 1933.

Bibliography

Bibliography

Adam, R.J. ed. (1960) *John Home's Survey of Assynt* (Edinburgh: SHS, 3rd series, 52)

Adams, I.H. and G. Fortune eds (1980) *Alexander Lindsay: A Rutter of the Scottish Seas* (Greenwich: National Maritime Museum)

Allardyce, J. ed. (1895) *Historical Papers Relating to the Jacobite Period 1699–1750*, vol.1 (Aberdeen: Spalding Club)

Anderson, I.H. (1885) *Inverness Before Railways* (Inverness: Mackenzie, fac. edn, Leakey, 1984)

—(1900) *An Inverness Lawyer and His Sons* (Aberdeen UP)

Anson, Peter (1930) *Fishing Boats and Fisher Folk on the East Coast of Scotland* (London: Dent)

Bain, J. ed (1881–88) *Calendar of Documents Relating to Scotland Preserved in Her Majesty's Public Record Office* (Edinburgh)

Banks, J.S. (1972) *The Heather Blooms at John o' Groats* (John o' Groats, Caithness)

Barrow, G.W.S. (1984) 'Land routes: the medieval evidence' in A. Fenton & G. Stells (eds) *Loads and Roads in Scotland and Beyond* (Edinburgh: John Donald)

Beaton, E. (1995) *Sutherland: An Illustrated Architectural Guide* (Edinburgh: Rutland)

Boswell, James (1786) *The Journal of a Tour to the Hebrides with Samuel Johnson LLD* (London: Dent Everyman edn, 1931)

Bulloch, J.M. (1931) *Old Highland Highways* (Inverness: Carruthers, Highland Handbooks 3)

Burt, E. (1754) *Letters from a Gentleman in the North of Scotland to His Friend in London, Containing the Description of a Capital Town in That Northern Country* (London)

Calder, J. (1887) *Sketch of the Civil and Traditional History of Caithness* (Wick: Rae, 2nd edn)

Cameron, A.D. (1983) *The Caledonian Canal* (Perth: Melven)

Clegg, P.V. (1988) *Rivals in the North* (Godalming)

—(1990) *Sword in the Sky* (City of Glasgow Museum of Transport)

—(1995) *Wings Over the Glens* (Peterborough: GMS Enterprises)

Cockburn, Lord (1888) *Circuit Journeys* (Hawick: Byway Books, 1983 edn)

Coleman, T. (1965) *The Railway Navvies* (London: Hutchinson, new edn Head of Zeus, 2015)

Coull, J.R., A. Fenton and K. Veitch (eds) (2008) *Scottish Life and Society: 4, Boats, Fishing and the Sea* (Edinburgh: John Donald)

Craven, J.B. (ed) (1886) *Journals of the Episcopal Visitations of the Right Rev Robert Forbes MA* (London: Skeffington)

Cunliffe, B. (2001) *Facing the Ocean: The Atlantic and Its Peoples* (Oxford)

The Diary of Alexander Brodie of Brodie (1863) (Aberdeen: Spalding Club)

Dixon, J.H. (1886) *Gairloch and Guide to Loch Maree* (Edinburgh)

Dodds, J. ed. (1887) *The Diary and General Expenditure Book of William Cunningham of Craigends* (Edinburgh, SHS 2)

Donaldson, J.E. ed. (1984) *The Mey Letters* (Sydney, Australia: Donaldson)

Duff, D. ed. (1980) *Queen Victoria's Highland Journals* (Exeter: Webb & Bower)

Dunlop, J. (1978) *The British Fisheries Society 1786–1893* (Edinburgh: John Donald)

Fenton, A. (1978) *The Northern Isles: Orkney and Shetland* (Edinburgh: John Donald)

Ferguson, D.M. (1988) *Shipwrecks of Orkney, Shetland and Pentland Firth* (Newton Abbot: David & Charles)

—(1991) *Shipwrecks of North-East Scotland 1444–1990* (Edinburgh: Mercat)

Ferguson, J. (1904) *The Law of Roads, Streets and Rights of Way, Bridges and Ferries in Scotland* (Edinburgh: Green & Sons)

Fleet, C., C.W.J. Withers and M. Wilkes (2012) *Scotland: Mapping the Nation* (Edinburgh: Birlinn)

Fraser, G.M. (1921) *The Old Deeside Road* (Aberdeen Natural History & Antiquarian Society, reissued 1983)

Fraser, James (1905) *Chronicles of the Frasers: The Wardlaw Manuscript* (Edinburgh: SHS 47, W. Mackay (ed.))

Fraser, John (1905) *Reminiscences of Inverness* (fac. edn, Inverness: Leakey, 1983)

Gibson, R. (2003) *Plaids and Bandanas: From Highland Drover to Wild West Cowboy* (Edinburgh: Luath)

Gifford, J. (1992) *Highlands and Islands* (Penguin Buildings of Scotland series)

Goudie, G. ed. (1889) *The Diary of the Reverend John Mill* (Edinburgh: SHS 5)

Grant, E. (1898) *Memoirs of a Highland Lady* (London: John Murray, edn 1972)

Grant, I.F. (1959) *The Macleods: The History of a Clan* (London: Faber)

Gray, J.M. ed. (1892) *Memoirs of the Life of Sir John Clerk of Penicuik* (Edinburgh: SHS 13)

Gunn, R.P. (1998) *Inventors and Engineers of Caithness* (Latheronwheel, Caithness: Whittles)

Haldane, A.R.B. (1952) *The Drove Roads of Scotland* (London: Nelson; reissued Edinburgh: Birlinn, 1997)

—(1962) *New Ways through the Glens* (Newton Abbot: David & Charles)

—(1971) *Three Centuries of Scottish Posts: An Historical Survey to 1836* (Edinburgh UP)

Henderson, J. (1812) *General View of the Agriculture of the County of Caithness* (London)

The Highland Railway Company and Its Constituents and Successors 1855–1955 (1955) (London: Stephenson Locomotive Society)

Holland, J. and D. Spaven (2013) *Mapping the Railways* (Glasgow: Collins)

Horne, J. ed. (1907) *The County of Caithness* (Wick: Rae)

Hustwick, I. (1994) *Moray Firth Ships and Trade* (Aberdeen: Scottish Cultural Press)

—(1996) *The Peggy and Isabella: The story of an eighteenth-century Orkney sloop* (Kirkwall: Altmachar Press)

Hutchinson, R. (2006) *Calum's Road* (Edinburgh: Birlinn)

Kerr, J. (1991) *Highland Highways: Old Roads in Atholl* (Edinburgh: John Donald)

Knox, John (1786) *A Tour through the Highlands of Scotland and the Hebrides Isles* (London)

Lauder, Sir Thomas Dick (1830) *The Great Moray Floods of 1829* (fac. edn, Forres: Moray Books, 1998)

McConnell, D. (1990) *Rails to Wick and Thurso* (Dornoch Press)

Macculloch, J. (1824) *The Highlands and Western Isles of Scotland* (London)

Macdonald, C.A. (1950) *The History of Argyll* (Glasgow: Holmes)

Mackay, W. ed. (1896) *Inverness and Dingwall Presbytery Records 1643–88* (SHS 24)

—ed. (1915) *The Letter-Book of Bailie John Steuart of Inverness 1715–52* (SHS, 2nd series, vol. 9)

Mackay, W. and G.S. Laing eds (1924) *Records of Inverness* (Aberdeen: Spalding Club)

MacKenzie, Osgood H. (1921) *A Hundred Years in the Highlands* (Edinburgh: Birlinn, new edn, 1995)

Mackenzie, W.C. (1903) *History of the Outer Hebrides* (Paisley: Gardner)

McNeill, P. and R. Nicholson (1975) *An Historical Atlas of Scotland* (Conference of Scottish Medievalists)

Macrae, N. (1923) *Dingwall's Thousand Years* (Dingwall)

McRobb, A.W. (1999) *The North Boats* (Narbeth, Pembrokeshire: Ferry Publications)

Martin, Angus (1984) *Kintyre: The Hidden Past* (Edinburgh: John Donald)

Millar, A.H. ed. (1909) *A Selection of Scottish Forfeited Estates Papers 1715, 1745* (Edinburgh: SHS 57)

Miller, Hugh (1854) *My Schools and Schoolmasters* (Edinburgh: Morton, 1905 edn)

Miller, James (1994) *A Wild and Open Sea* (Kirkwall: Orkney Press)

—(2004) *Inverness* (Edinburgh: Birlinn)

—(2009) *The Foresters* (Edinburgh: Birlinn)

—(2012) *The Gathering Stream: The Story of the Moray Firth* (Edinburgh, Birlinn)

—(2014) *Europe, the Highlands and Me* (Amazon Kindle)

—(2015) *Scotland, England and Me: A Referendum Diary* (Amazon Kindle)

Milne, W.J. (2008) *Highland* (Glossop: Venture)

Mitchell, A. ed. (1906) *Geographical Collections Relating to Scotland Made by Walter Macfarlane* (Edinburgh: SHS 51, 52, 53)

Mitchell, J. (1883) *Reminiscences of My Life in the Highlands* (Newton Abbot: David & Charles, 1971 edn)

Moir, D.G. (1947) *Scottish Hill Tracks 2: Northern Scotland* (Edinburgh: Albyn Press)

Morton, H.V. (1933) *In Scotland Again* (London: Methuen, 8th edn, 1942)

Murray, Sarah (1805) *A Companion and Useful Guide to the Beauties of Scotland* (Hawick: Byway Books, 1982 edn, W.F. Laughlan, ed.)

Newlands, A. (1928) *Travelling in Moray and the North of Scotland Over a Century Ago*, (booklet reprinted from *Elgin Courant & Courier*)

Pallister, Marian (2005) *Lost Argyll* (Edinburgh: Birlinn)

Paterson, A.M. (2010) *Pioneers of the Highland Tracks: William and Murdoch Paterson* (Highland Railway Society)

Paton, H. ed. (1913) *The Clan Campbell* (Edinburgh: Schulze)

Pedersen, Roy (2010) *Pentland Hero: The Saga of the Orkney Short Sea Crossing* (Edinburgh)

Pedersen, Roy (2013) *Who Pays the Ferryman? The Great Scottish Ferries Swindle* (Edinburgh: Birlinn)

—(2015) *Western Ferries: Taking on Giants* (Edinburgh: Birlinn)

Pennant, Thomas (1769) *A Tour in Scotland*, facsimile edition (Melven Press, Perth)

Pollard, M. (1984) *Walking the Scottish Highlands: General Wade's Military Roads* (London: Deutsch)

Robins, N.S. and D.E. Meek (2008) *The Kingdom of MacBrayne* (Edinburgh: Birlinn)

Ross, David (2005) *The Highland Railway* (Stroud: Tempus)

Sage, Donald F. ed. (1899) *Memorabilia Domestica, or Parish Life in the North of Scotland* (Wick: Rae, 2nd edn)

Salmond, J.B. (1934) *Wade in Scotland* (Edinburgh: Moray Press)

Severin, Tim (1978) *The Brendan Voyage* (London: Hutchinson)

Shaw, A.M. (1880) *Historical Memoirs of the House and Clan of Makintosh and of the Clan Chattan* (London: Clay & Taylor)

Simmons, A. ed. (1998) *Thomas Pennant: A Tour in Scotland, and Voyage to the Hebrides, 1772* (Edinburgh: Birlinn). The original editions of Pennant's travels in Scotland were published in 1771 and 1774; there have been many editions since then.

Sinclair, J. (2013) *Highland Buses* (Stroud: Amberley)

Smith, H.D. (1984) *Shetland Life and Trade 1550–1914* (Edinburgh: John Donald)

Smout, T.C. (1963) *Scottish Trade on the Eve of Union 1660–1707* (Edinburgh: Oliver & Boyd)

Somers, Robert (1848) *Letters from the Highlands* (Inverness: Melven, fac. edn, 1977)

Stewart, D. (1822) *Sketches of the Character, Manners and Present State of the Highlanders of Scotland* (Edinburgh: Constable; fac. edn John Donald, 1977)

Sutherland, Iain (1984) *Wick Harbour and the Herring Fishing* (Wick)

Thomas, J. (1998) *The West Highland Railway* ((Colonsay: Lochar, ext. edn of a work first published in 1965)

Tucker, C. (2013) *Steamers to Stornoway: Ships and Shipping Services to Lewis Since 1750* (Lewis: Islands Book Trust)

Vallance, H.A. (1996) *The Highland Railway* (Colonsay: Lochar, ext. edn of a work first published in 1938)

Veitch, K. ed. (2009) *Scottish Life and Society, 8: Transport and Communications* (Edinburgh: Birlinn)

Walker, F.A. (2000) *Argyll and Bute* (Penguin Buildings of Scotland)

Warrand, D. ed. (1923) *More Culloden Papers* (Inverness)

—ed. (1925) *More Culloden Papers, Vol. II 1704 to 1725* (Inverness: Carruthers)

—ed. (1927) *More Culloden Papers, Vol. III, 1725 to 1745* (Inverness: Carruthers)

Wilson, N.P. ed. (2011) *Alexander Nimmo's Inverness Survey & Journal 1806* (Dublin: Royal Irish Academy)

Index